CHINA VERSUS THE US

Who Will Prevail?

CHINA

VERSUS THE

US

Who Will Prevail?

Alfredo Toro Hardy
Venezuelan Scholar and Diplomat

World Scientific

NEW JERSEY • LONDON • SINGAPORE • BEIJING • SHANGHAI • HONG KONG • TAIPEI • CHENNAI • TOKYO

Published by

World Scientific Publishing Co. Pte. Ltd.
5 Toh Tuck Link, Singapore 596224
USA office: 27 Warren Street, Suite 401-402, Hackensack, NJ 07601
UK office: 57 Shelton Street, Covent Garden, London WC2H 9HE

British Library Cataloguing-in-Publication Data
A catalogue record for this book is available from the British Library.

CHINA VERSUS THE US
Who Will Prevail?

ISBN 978-981-121-851-4 (hardcover)
ISBN 978-981-121-852-1 (ebook for institutions)
ISBN 978-981-121-853-8 (ebook for individuals)

For any available supplementary material, please visit
https://www.worldscientific.com/worldscibooks/10.1142/11776#t=suppl

Desk Editor: Sandhya Venkatesh

Typeset by Stallion Press
Email: enquiries@stallionpress.com

To my sister in law María Cristina, with life-long shared memories.

To my grandson Alfredo, who captured my heart.

ACKNOWLEDGMENTS

I would like to express my utmost gratitude to the distinguished group of scholars and authors that have sponsored this book, and honored me, with their foreword and back cover comments.

Dr. Gloria Carnevali-Hawthorn, a Cambridge-based philosopher and author, read the manuscript of this book and corrected my English deficiencies, while suggesting several enriching ideas that were subsequently incorporated into the text. My gratitude for her continuous intellectual support is priceless.

My very special thanks go to World Scientific as well for harboring for a fourth time a work of mine under their prestigious editorial label, and very particularly to Ms. Venkatesh Sandhya for supporting and editing this book.

ABOUT THE AUTHOR

Alfredo Toro Hardy is a retired Venezuelan diplomat, scholar and author. He received a PhD from the Geneva School of Diplomacy and International Relations; masters degrees from the University of Pennsylvania and the Central University of Venezuela; postgraduate degrees from the Ecole Nationale d'Administration, ENA, and the University of Paris II; a Harvard University's attestation for a course on International Negotiations; and a Bachelor of Law degree from the Central University of Venezuela.

Before resigning from the Venezuelan Foreign Service in protest due to the events occurring in his country, he was one of Venezuela's most senior career diplomats, having served as Ambassador to the United States, the United Kingdom, Spain, Brazil, Singapore, Chile and Ireland.

A scholar, he was also the Director of the Diplomatic Academy of the Venezuelan Ministry of Foreign Affairs and Associate Professor of the Simón Bolívar University in Caracas, where he was Director of the Center for North American Studies and Co-ordinator of the Institute for Higher Latin American Studies. He was elected as "Simon Bolivar Chair Professor for Latin American Studies" by the Council of Faculties of the University of Cambridge, but had to decline due to diplomatic constraints. A Visiting Professor at Princeton University, he also taught at the universities of Brasilia and Barcelona, while lecturing extensively at universities and think tanks in the Americas, Europe, and Asia. He has been a member of the Advising Committee of the Diplomatic Academy of London, a Fulbright Scholar, and a two-time Rockefeller Foundation Bellagio Center Resident Scholar. He has also been a member of the Bellagio Center Nominations Committee.

He is the author of 20 books and co-author of 13 more on topics of international affairs and history. He has received the "Latino Book Award" (best book by an author whose original language is in Spanish or Portuguese) twice at the ExpoBook America fairs that took place in Chicago and Los Angeles in 2003 and 2008, respectively. His three previous books were also published by World Scientific: *The World Turned Upside Down: The Complex Partnership Between China and Latin America* (2013), *Understanding Latin America: A Decoding Guide* (2017) and *The Crossroads of Globalization: A Latin American View* (2018). The online cataloguing LibraryThing selected the first of these titles as one of the nine basic readings on South America.

He has published 30 peer-reviewed papers on international affairs and is a regular columnist for several publications, including the "Observatory on Chinese Policies".

He is also a member of the Iberian-American Network of Sinologists, Global Labour Organization, Chatham House, Canning House, the Windsor Energy Group, and several other similar institutions.

FOREWORD

Ours is an era fraught with paradigm shifts that have put paid to ideas of balance and harmony. Technology is re-writing the fundamental functioning of our world at every level. The global order is rearranging itself as international law, trade, and political leadership move away from relationships and agreements that defined the short century of Pax Americana. Climate change looms inchoate and unimaginable.

Add this mix of dangers emerging from the shifting sands and a titanic clash slowly takes shape as history and destiny reanimate the global military stage. This is conflict writ large between the oldest and youngest of the globe's powers, China and the United States (US). It is the story Alfredo Toro-Hardy engages with here in a nuanced diplomatic history of a deeply complex encounter. Weaving together into a seamless narrative the many strands of past and present changes, this is soft-power writing that reveals the hard-power implications that lie in wait.

While every empire has been led by an unusual civilisation and state structure — the Persian, the Roman, the Ottoman, the British, to name just a few of the bigger and longer-lived ones across the eras, the legacy, mission, and modern experience of the US and China mark them out as behemoths even in such historic company. Toro-Hardy provides an arresting anecdote in the Introduction to focus the reader's mind on just how old, and centrally organised,

China has been as a power, keeping records, evolving a culture, strategising war, and most importantly, acting as the master of its universe. Where the United States measures history in hundreds of years, the Chinese measure it in thousands.

But, what may seem by that accounting to be an unequal balancing is recalibrated by the effect of the temporal — the childhood of America provided it lessons and capacities that the Chinese are only now beginning to engage with. The US grew up in a world of multipolarity. Though shockingly ambitious, the Monroe Doctrine, as Toro-Hardy points out, was a declaration by a nation with cities and an army only a fraction of the size of those in Europe. And yet, Monroe put the world on notice that the young US was a player to be reckoned with, ready to lay claim to geostrategic territory because of its 'conviction of moral superiority, of providential entitlement of leadership, projected itself by way of a precocious assertiveness' (p. 34). Steeped in the schooling of both World Wars, the US is a creature of modern multilateral power politics.

The hegemonic leadership of both China and the US is defined by a zealous worldview, which, crucially, they understand in terms of others seeking, and wishing to adopt. Leadership for each is thus destiny, and therefore, for both, it is existential. In neither case does this mean their image of self as practitioners of the ideal is promoted similarly at home and abroad. Their missions, simultaneously protective and projective, are processes of exerting control beyond their wider borders in order to maintain their civilisations untrammelled at home. In this, the world seems little changed from Thucydides' day, 'when the strong do as they can and the weak suffer what they must'. International relations throughout the American era was a translation of US national interest to expand the security of American borders through alliance and trade. But in fact, the world has moved on from Thucydides, binding all states together in the United Nations (UN), and tying them to agreed laws through treaties. When the Soviet Union fell, and American unipolarity girdled the globe, it was a small step for US national interest to assert itself as coincident with international order.

Toro-Hardy focuses on the period of dormancy and retrenchment of China during this time, in the wake of its crushing loss of territory and prestige in the 19th and 20th centuries as significant in creating the nation it is today. Having gone from having the world's largest GDP in the 18th century to one of the smallest during World War I, China, with its many millions of people far over-shadowing the population of the US, had shrunk. It had become a periphery player seemingly without global ambitions. Initially, it was not even recognised by the UN as representative of the Chinese people, although its acquisition of the nuclear bomb led to a rapid reassessment and an invitation to take its place on the Security Council in 1978.

The fascinating section on the relationship between China and the US, which began prior to the Communist takeover in 1949, and then rekindled with Nixon's visit to Beijing, provides a critical backdrop to the events as they have unfolded since. Toro-Hardy describes their nascent friendship as one of teacher-apprentice, with the young, street-smart US leading the wizened leaders of China into a new economic and political order. 'The US,' writes Toro-Hardy, 'thus envisaged its relation with China as that of a mentor, whose duty was to translate into that society the blessings of its own values.' This view prevailed when China reopened with the ascent of Deng Xiaoping, who 'put in motion a process of economic opening. From that moment onwards, the United States convinced itself that the final result of such process could be none other than the conversion of China into the values of liberal democracy and the free market' (p. 40). Washington facilitated China's membership into the World Trade Organization, and supported economic and technological integration spurred on by the opportunities represented by China's significant market. It was, for both parties, a period of pragmatic engagement as, in Deng's words, China bided its time, and exploited its almost unrestricted access to US knowledge exchange, including military know-how.

The break came in 2008, when the US financial crisis, China's thunderous economic growth, its acquisition of a large quantity of

US debt, and its success in holding the Beijing Olympics set the two powers on divergent paths. Seeing 2008 as a turning point that initiated the foreclosure of their pragmatic engagement. Toro-Hardy draws on the Chinese concept of shi, 'an alignment of forces', a 'momentum, strategic advantage, or strategic configuration of power' that if used skilfully, can result in favourable outcomes (p. 80) to explain the dynamics behind the resurgence of China as a contender for supremacy. It was, he notes, a bruising experience for both powers, as China felt belittled, and the US felt betrayed (p. 45).

This is a history filled with unexpected twists and turns, startling tales of leadership, and resilience that defies easy prognostications about the future. Toro-Hardy offers striking statistics to illustrate the speed and dimensions of China's recent resurgence, drawing on a wealth of academic and government sources to bolster his argument. 'Since 2014, China has launched more submarines, warships and other vessels than the total number of ships currently serving in the combined navies of Germany, India, Spain, Taiwan and the United Kingdom. At the same time, China went from 50 fourth-generation aircrafts in 2000 to 500, while it is engaged in the most active land-based ballistic and cruise missile program in the world' (p. 100). Similar achievements took place in manufacturing output, energy source acquisition, and in launching the China brand globally, including the massive Belt and Road Initiative, and the Made in China 2025 programme. Equally, China developed the idea of soft power alternatives as what Toro-Hardy describes as the shock-therapies of the Washington Consensus, establishing a brand of economic growth for emergent economies which came to be known as the Chinese Consensus. Scale, as is pointed out repeatedly, is something that China can achieve with a rapidity that no other international contender comes close to — as the building of a complete hospital in just two weeks during the Corona Virus outbreak in early 2020 amply illustrated.

Yet, China's moves to counter US leadership elicited a counter-reaction on Washington's part that likewise was quick and significant, including Obama's pivot to Asia strategy, and Trump's trade war and encirclement of allies around China, leading Toro-Hardy to question Beijing's timing and wisdom. Seeing in China's current Chairman a straightforwardness and defiance uncharacteristic of the country's legacy of subtle cleverness, Toro-Hardy quotes from the Stratagems of the Warring States, still considered a key manual for statecraft in China, which notes the biggest mistake that a rising leader can commit is to provoke a confrontation with his most powerful rival before the point of maximum opportunity had been attained.

Yet, as Toro-Hardy also observes, if the Stratagems of the Warring States' maxim has been followed, then China's strategy may as such reflect the assessment that the point of maximum opportunity has indeed been attained — a conclusion with significant consequences (discussed later in the volume). Thus Toro-Hardy asks: 'Did China challenge the United States too hard and too soon and, by doing so, seriously hamper its chance of attaining its objectives?' and 'Can the United States still contain China's ascendancy and retain its current leading status?'

These questions, and their evocative answers, structure the second part of the book. Toro-Hardy breaks his analysis into six 'aptitude' categories to test the balance of power capacity in what he sees as an emergent Cold War between China and America, establishing measures by which to assess each power's preparedness and resilience for the ultimate competition that lies ahead. He grounds his assessment of China in the character of its culture, which 'naturally includes the complementarity of opposites ... [as] exemplified by the duality of yin and yang' (p. 135). Thus, for example, China's 'grabbing with two hands' policy can be understood in terms of the complementarity of nationalism and globalisation (the two hands), a perspective quite at odds with that of Europe and the United States, where they are seen as antithetical forces. 'China First', for example, would, if so phrased, be understood as both an inward-facing and outward-facing project, as both aspects, he argues, are seen as 'interdependent expressions of State policy, which converge in the aim of legitimizing the regime in the eyes of its citizens' (p. 134).

In chapters four through nine, Toro-Hardy takes the opportunity to investigate in greater depth the aptitude shown by each party in processes of convergence, mistake-avoidance, universalist power, military strategy, economics, and finally, technological development. These six areas, involving very different capacities, resources, and positions within the established system, together form a mosaic of capabilities and strengths in which supremacy over the modern world will be established and maintained. They provide focused histories of how both the US and China have managed structures internally; relationships with neighbours, allies, and enemies; international institution-building and geostrategic expansion; and economic and technological dominance. What Toro-Hardy develops is a thick analysis of the character of both China and the United States as seen through these various prisms in which their habits were formed, their outlooks challenged, and their views and responses to modernity tested.

A diplomat skilled in the art of balance, Toro-Hardy's assessments, examples, and anecdotes offer depth while remaining starkly realist. Neither power escapes his sharp eye unscathed. Their unvarnished ambition, colossal errors of judgement, and enormous challenges as they face not only the multiple modernities of our current age, but the internal stressors placed on their societies and identities by the vagaries of technology, produce a fascinating if deeply worrying picture of power with insufficient principle, capable of extraordinary destruction.

This is an important modern history of two powers, deeply ingrained in every layer of global activity, and yet located in their own worlds. The timing is critical — as captured in Toro-Hardy's simple, yet fundamental, questions: Is it too early for China? Is it too late for the US? It offers a considered view of both: China as newly resurgent, still awkward, playing catch-up economically, its modern identity hardening, and with staggering potential to change the course of history. And of the US, at a key juncture but at a different point on the spectrum — war-weary, politically and economically divided domestically, its international credibility prone to accusations of both bullying and isolationism, and yet still, beyond all other nations, mighty. It is a tricky field in which to stay even-handed, a feat Toro-Hardy handles deftly. Pointing out that neither China nor the US are powers that will accept the number two position easily, he offers several options of possible outcomes in the years ahead.

And yet, although designed to reveal the articulations of power which both China and the United States are building as they move toward confrontation, what emerges is a devastating picture of US leadership, all the more disturbing because of the skill Washington exercised in constructing a hegemonic system of global political and economic governance based on international consensus that reflected its ideology as well as its needs, that it then systematically unravelled through hubris. This is the opening, Toro-Hardy argues, that has enabled China to move in with such force — though, possibly, with less preparation than needed — as opportunities have presented themselves to 'scale the back fence' (as in South America), or re-stake old claims, as in the South China Sea. What is clear is that this will be a thoroughly new form of global conflict fought at every level of modernity. Toro-Hardy has produced a detailed, accessible, and insightful text to understand the coming fury.

Roxane Farmanfarmaian
Director of Global Politics and International Studies
Institute of Continuing Education, University of Cambridge
Academic Director, Master of Studies Programme
Department of Politics and International Studies
University of Cambridge
Former Editor-in-Chief
Cambridge Review of International Affairs

CONTENTS

INTRODUCTION

In 476 AD, the Western Roman Empire came to an end and a millennium of European Dark Ages followed in its wake. Let us imagine for a moment that this had not happened — that since its mythical foundation in 753 BC, the civilizing strength of Ancient Rome had continued uninterrupted to date and that its cultural and institutional contribution to humanity had not ceased. Even in that case, the age of Rome and its continuity as an organized society would have been amply surpassed by China.

As Henry Kissinger wrote: "Chinese civilization originates in an antiquity so remote that we vainly endeavor to discover its commencement".[1] However, a sophisticated and clearly identifiable Chinese civilization can be traced back to 1500 BC, representing the oldest continuous civilization of the world, one that still presents itself with vibrancy and full of future outlook.[2]

The Chinese word for China, *zhongguo*, can be translated into English as "Middle Kingdom" or "Central Kingdom". The Zhou Dynasty first articulated the notion during the first millennium BC. At that time, China had already consolidated its administrative

---

[1] Henry Kissinger, *On China* [Kindle version], New York: Penguin Books, 2012, retrieved from Amazon.com, p. 5.

[2] Paul S. Ropp, *China in World History*, Oxford: Oxford University Press, 2010.

power in the Yangtze River valley.[3] The term "Middle Kingdom" would thus precede the first unified Chinese empire, established by the Qin Dynasty in 221 BC.

The "Middle Kingdom" was considered to be the geographical center of the world, and the center of the world power, while maintaining a middle position between the heavens and other inferior civilizations. The epitome of this centrality was the emperor. The principle of world order was based on *Tianxia*, "all-under-heaven", the center of which was the emperor, whose "rule would recognize no boundaries or limits".[4]

According to John K. Fairbank, this order was based on a set of ideas and practices developed and perpetuated by the rulers of China over many centuries. The imperial Chinese order was built on a hierarchy. According to this view, the world could be roughly divided into two broad categories: civilization and non-civilization. The first was represented by those people who accepted the supremacy of the emperor, the Son of Heaven, and the second by those who did not. Within the former group, the imperial system involved a series of vassal states, organized according to their proximity to Chinese power in a graded and concentric hierarchy. This was a world order that rested upon the principle of "superordination–subordination". China's system and its approach to the world was thus marked, as Fairbank writes, by a "concept of Sinocentrism and an assumption of Chinese superiority".[5]

In Howard W. French's opinion: "Functioning in this way, Chinese power came to underpin one of the most remarkable international systems that human civilization has ever seen — a unique form of what has sometimes been described as an extremely lose and distant brand of indirect rule by China over a very considerable

---

[3] Parag Khanna, *The Future is Asian: Global Order In The Twenty-First Century* [Kindle Version], London: Weidenfeld & Nicolson, 2019, retrieved from Amazon.com, location 444/6214.

[4] Mark Leonard, *What Does China Think?*, New York: HarperCollins, 2008, p. 131.

[5] Jonathan D.T. Ward, *China's Vision of Victory and Why America Must Win* [Kindle version], Washington, D.C.: The Atlas Publishing and Media Company, 2019, retrieved from Amazon.com, locations 3192/6589, 3198/6598, 3205/6589, 3238/6589.

slice of humanity (...) But at the foundation of this remarkable and resilient Pax Sinica lay a basic proposition that was reasonably consistent: Accept our superiority and we will confer upon you political legitimacy, develop a trade partnership and provide a range of what are known in the language of modern international affairs as public goods".[6]

It was a tributary system in which peoples in China's imperial orbit regularly dispatched "embassies" to perform ritual submissions before the Chinese emperor. Within this system, rulers of compliant states whose dynasties may have gone back for many centuries "owed" their very titles to the grant of recognition, via patents of appointment, bestowed by the Chinese emperor.

Approaching the apogee of its global power in the late 1700s, the United Kingdom sent a mission to China to try and establish relations with the Qing dynasty on an equal footing. This was the Macartney Mission. After the many protocol differences and incomprehension of their respective cultures, British request for trade and the concession for a trading spot were denied. As he left, Lord Macartney was given a letter from Emperor Qianlong to King George III, the initial paragraph of which read as follows: "You, O King, from afar have yearned after the blessings of our civilization, and in your eagerness to come in touch with our converting influence have sent an Embassy across the sea bearing a memorial [memorandum]. I have already taken note of your respectful spirit of submission, have treated your mission with extreme favor and loaded it with gifts, besides issuing a mandate to you, O King, and honoring you at the bestowal of valuable presents. Thus has my indulgence been manifested".[7]

Having been one of the cradles of human civilization, and a continuous and commanding one all along recorded history, China

[6] Howard W. French, *Everything Under Heaven: How the Past Helps Shape China's Push for Global Power* [Kindle version], New York: Alfred A. Knopf, 2017, retrieved from Amazon.com, p. 9.

[7] Ch'ien Lung, (Qianlong) Letter to George III (1792), http://academics.wellesley.edu/Polisci/wj/China/208/READINGS/qianlong.html. Accessed October 27, 2019.

enjoyed the benefits of a leading presence among the great powers of the world. Between 1600 and the beginning of the 19th century, China accounted for between a quarter and a third of the global GDP. According to Adam Smith, in 1776 China was richer than all of Europe put together; even as recently as 1820, China accounted for 30% of the the world's GDP.[8]

However, while parts of Europe, with Britain at the head, immersed themselves in the industrial revolution, experiencing a tremendous economic boost as a result, China remained tied to its traditional economy. This was accompanied by a European military modernization, which again was not followed by China. Moreover, as Parag Khanna explains: "The Qing, meanwhile, could not sustain their grandeur, with rapid population growth, fiscal pressures, and corruption bringing the dynasty to the brink of disintegration. As Asia's large imperial and bureaucratic powers resisted change, smaller European nations outmaneuvered them to achieve global domination".[9]

The result of this was none other than so-called "Century of Humiliation", which brought this great and proud civilization to its knees. In 1900, China and India together accounted for just 7% of the global output.[10] The itinerary of this dramatic downturn began with the opium wars with Britain between 1840–1842 and 1856–1858. They brought with them opprobious military defeats, the imposition of the opium consumption with all its social degrading burden and the acceptance by China of multiple consessions that included the loss of Hong Kong.

Taking advantage of China's frailty, Moscow imposed on Peking the 1858 and 1860 treaties. These deprived China of all the lands on the left bank of the Amur River as well as those between the Ussury

---

[8] Angus Maddison, *The World Economy: Historical Statistics*, Paris: OECD, 2003; Andre Gunder Frank, The World Economic System in Asia before European Hegemony, *The Historian*, 56(2), December 1994, pp. 259–276; Mark Leonard, *op. cit.*, p. 83.

[9] Parag Khanna, *op. cit.*, location 664/6214.

[10] Philip S. Golub, Quand la Chine et L'Inde dominaent le monde, *Maniere de Voir*, París, Janvier–March, 2006.

River and the Pacific Ocean. In total, this represented for China the loss of 2.6 million square kilometers. In 1860 came the Franco-British ocupation of Peking, which in turn led to the impossition of new and significant concessions. On that ocassion, the Summer Palace — a building that had taken 150 years to build — was burned by the invaders as a lesson to China, which thus played "a defining role in the Chinese psyche".[11] In 1879, Japan, which was in the process of moderizing itself according to Western patterns, annexed China's Ryukyus islands. A few years later, in 1894, Japan dealt it a resounding miltary defeat. This was particularly humilliating to China since Japan was an offspring of its own civilization. This defeat entailed the loss of Taiwan and of its formal control over Korea.

In 1898, Russia annexed its strategic ports of Dalian and Lüshum. The 1885 Treaty with France forced China to give away to that country its formal control over Vietnam, in the same manner in which the 1894 Treaty with Britain had forced it to relinquished Burma. In 1900 came the occupation of Peking by ten Western countries plus Japan. All of these just foreshadowed what was to become China's worst nightmare: The Japanese occupation, with its 20 million deaths, between 1937 and 1945.

China is now back. In former Australian Prime Minister Kevin Rudd's words, what has happened in China is the equivalent to "the English Industrial Revolution and the global information revolution combusting simultaneously and compressed into not 300 years, but 30". Rudd finds himself asking how China will exercise this new-found power in the future international order: "Will it accept the culture, norms and structure of the postwar order? Or will China seek to change it? I believe this is the single core question for the first half of the 21st century, not just for Asia, but for the world".[12]

Jonathan D.T. Ward has no doubts about this: "China's rise, in the mind of its leaders and many of its people, is not a rise, but a

[11] Mark Leonard, *op. cit.*, p. 10.

[12] Kevin Rudd, The West Isn't Ready for the Rise of China, *New Statesman*, July 11, 2012, https://www.newstatesman.com/politics/international-politics/2012/07/kevin-rudd-west-isnt-ready-rise-china. Accessed October 25, 2019.

restoration. It is a restoration, simply put, of the power and prosperity enjoyed by the Chinese Empire (…) All of this was broken apart in the 'Century of Humiliation'. Since that fateful time. China's leaders have worked to restore Chinese power on the world stage".[13]

Xi Jinping's "China Dream of National Rejuvenation" seems very much in tune with the idea of restoration. During the expanse of several millennia of continuous civilization, the century of humiliation was but a blink of the eye. Now, with its strengths renewed, China seems ready to retake the central role that, in its eyes, it always held. The crucial question is: What would this entail?

Amid the several characteristics that Martin Jacques foresees in a China back in control of its historical preponderance, three appear particularly worrying. First, China considers itself to be a civilization-state, which means that its traits as a civilization precede its conscience as a nation-state. Seeing itself as much more than a nation-State also means that it is more than a simple member of the international community. This, by implication, makes it a revisionist power. Second, historically, China was the epicenter of a tributary system and, as such, the object of tribute and deference by surrounding nations. This derived from its preponderance and cultural superiority. Its emergence onto the world's center stage will be accompanied by this hierarchical and stratified vision. However, this will go beyond its neighbors in order to acquire a global projection in which countries dependent or indebted to China will be seen under this optic. Third, China perceives itself as the expression of a special race, the Han, which again entitles it to deferential treatment. Once more, this translates into a hierarchical perception of the world.[14]

According to Martin Jacques: "The Chinese are enormously proud of their historical achievements. They believe that theirs is the greatest civilization there has ever been. They have a strong sense of their own superiority in history. They have long had a

---

[13] Jonathan D.T. Ward, *op. cit.*, locations 3173/6589, 3181/6589.

[14] *When China Rules the World*, London: Allen Lane, 2009.

hierarchical view of the world, with China at the top. And he rise of China is likely to accentuate these views".[15]

Jonathan D.T. Ward also concurs with this self-perceived hierarchical vision with China at the top. In his words: "While history does not repeat itself, its realities are a guide. In a world where China is supreme, we may ultimately see the erosion of the Westphalian world order, one maintained by the US and its allies since the end of the Second World War, and its replacement with a system built on Chinese supremacy. China as the arbiter of 'order and peace' for all 'under heaven'".[16]

China's reemergence on top of the world's stage, thus, seems accompanied by three frames of mind. First, a fixation with its past. China cannot look into the future without the lenses of its glorious past. In that sense, moving forward implies moving backward. Second, a grievance burden, a historical debt yet to be paid. China's past humiliations still reverberate strongly within its population and leadership, feeding a strong nationalist sentiment. Third, a revisionist approach to the prevailing international order and, in particular the regional *status quo*. This originates not only from its aversion towards a system molded when China was weak but also because it does not fit within its hierarchical vision of the world.

As Lee Kuan Yew asserted, China's return cannot be treated lightly. In his words: "It is not possible to pretend that this is just another big player. *This is the biggest player in the history of the world*".[17] The implications of China's being back will certainly shake the world, as Napoleon once predicted.

In counterbalance, facing the Middle Kingdom, we find the "exceptional nation" as Alexis de Tocqueville called the United States, giving traction to the notion of America's exceptionalism. If

[15] Martin Jacques, A Point of View: What kind of superpower could China be?, *BBC News Magazine*, October 19, 2012, https://www.bbc.com/news/magazine-19995218. Accessed December 9, 2019.

[16] Jonathan D.T. Ward, *op. cit.*, location 3272/6589.

[17] Graham Allison, Robert D. Blackwill, and Ali Wyne, *Lee Kuan Yew: The Grand Master's Insights on China, the United States and the World*, Cambridge, MA: MIT Press, 2013, p. 42.

the century of humiliation was no more than the blink of an eye within China's grandiose multi-millenary trajectory, the United States' history should in principle represent no more for that country than a couple of blinks. However, things are not so simple.

Americans have always acted as if entrusted by providence to fulfil a special purpose on earth. Theirs, indeed, is not a nation like any other, certainly not one that any other can look down on. As Herman Melville wrote in the 19th century: "We Americans are the chosen people, the Israel of our time. We are the bearers of the Arch of Liberty of the world".[18] The U.S.' most famous 19th century philosopher Ralph Waldo Emerson also expressed that being American represented "a religious experience".[19]

In Lawrence E. Harrison words: "In his 1835 book for the ages *Democracy in America*, Alexis de Tocqueville argues that you can't have democracy without democrats. He explains the successful US experiment as importantly the consequence of a 'form of Christianity which I cannot better describe than … a democratic and republican religion. This contributed powerfully to the establishment of a republic and a democracy … from the beginning, politics and religion contracted an alliance which has never been dissolved'".[20]

Its national mythology, thus, makes the U.S. perceive itself as a society with a special purpose on Earth. This gives support to a sort of secular religion, which is assumed with the same intensity as its fervent Christianity. This secular religion expresses itself through the conviction of possessing a superior societal model and being the expression of an exceptional history within the annals of humanity. Their society is the "City upon a Hill", preconized by Massachusetts' founding father John Winthrop. Not surprisingly, Thomas Jefferson believed that U.S.' foreign policy was called to rest on moral values rooted in the country's civil religion: Democracy. Their society had

---

[18] Niall Ferguson, *Colossus: The Rise and Fall of the American Empire*, New York, Penguin Books, 2004, p. 60.

[19] Alfredo Toro Hardy, *Hegemonía e Imperio*, Bogotá: Villegas Editores, 2007, p. 165.

[20] Lawrence E. Harrison, *Jews, Confucians and Protestants: Cultural Capital and the End of Multiculturalism*, Plymouth: Rowman & Littlefield Publisher, Inc., 2013, p. 127.

the mission to serve as an example for humanity, which by extension brought with it the impulse of spreading this model around the world.

This attitude could be roughly attributed to two facts. On the one hand, that the cradle of American society was formed by dissident protestants. As Andre Maurois wrote: "Spain did not allow its religious heterodox to go to the colonies as it feared that they could contaminate them. England, more realistically, thought that the heterodox was the perfect exportation product".[21] On the other hand, as Samuel P. Huntington asserts, the U.S. never ceased to be what its puritan colonists wanted it to become. In his words: "The main culture of the United States was and remains that of the colonists of the seventeenth and eighteenth centuries who founded the American society (...) Given not only its origin but also its continuity in time, it can be said that the United States remains a colonial society".[22]

Not surprisingly, their leaders have so frequently expressed themselves as Colonial puritan preachers. In Thomas Jefferson's words, the United States represented "a light unto the nations", in the same manner in which Abraham Lincoln presented his country as "the last best hope to Earth", or Ronald Reagan, paraphrasing Winthrop, referred to it as a "Shinning City upon a Hill".

It comes at no surprise, then, that being such a young country, the United States presents itself clothed in tradition and in old conceptions. There seems to be more than a grain of truth, indeed, in the following assertion by Jeremy Rifkin: "The American Spirit is tired and languishing in the past".[23] America's is a culture settled in the immanent values defined by their founding fathers, where God and divined protection represent daily references. A culture fixated

---

[21] Andre Maurois, *Historia de los Estados Unidos*, Barcelona: Círculo de Lectores, 1972, p. 33.

[22] Samuel P. Huntington, *¿Quiénes Somos? Los Desafíos de la Identidad Nacional Estadounidense*, Barcelona: Paidós, 2004, p. 65.

[23] Ross Schroeder, *The European Union: Blessing or Modern Tower of Babel?*, *Beyond Today*, May 27, 2007, https://www.ucg.org/the-good-news/the-european-union-blessing-or-modern-tower-of-babel. Accessed October 30, 2019.

on its roots and its sense of mission. This makes the United States a paradoxical society — one that can be at the forefront of the modern world, while at the same time clinging to its past in an inexorable way.

With the notable exception of Theodore Roosevelt, a political realist for whom American foreign policy should pursue national interest, U.S. leaders always insisted that the country's foreign policy was to serve as a "beacon" for the rest of mankind. In Henry Kissinger words: "Roosevelt commands a unique position in America's approach to international relations. No other president defined America's world role so completely in terms of national interest, or identified the national interests so comprehensively with the balance of power".[24]

However, it was to be Woodrow Wilson a few years later who, in line with Thomas Jefferson's vision, provided guidance to the U.S. foreign policy for years to come. Again, as Kissinger explains: "Woodrow Wilson was the embodiment of the tradition of American exceptionalism, and originated what would become the dominant intellectual school of American foreign policy".[25] According to Kissinger: "Wilson restated what had become the American wisdom since Jefferson, but put it in the service of a crusading ideology:

— America's special mission transcends day-to-day diplomacy and obliges it to serve as a beacon of liberty for the rest of mankind.
— The foreign policies of democracies are morally superior because the people are inherently peace-loving.
— Foreign policy should reflect the same moral standards as personal ethics.
— The state has no right to claim a separate morality for itself".[26]

Little matters if reality and myth have seldom followed the same road, within U.S. foreign policy. What it is significant is that, in the Americans' eyes, their country is called to fulfil a "special mission", serving as "a beacon of liberty for the rest of mankind".

[24] Henry Kissinger, *Diplomacy*, New York: Simon & Shuster, 1994, p. 39.
[25] *Ibid.*, p. 44.
[26] *Ibid.*, p. 46.

A recent example of this line of thought is represented by an important 2016 presidential campaign speech by Hillary Clinton: "The United States is an exceptional nation ... And part of what makes America an exceptional nation, is that we are also an indispensable nation. I fact, we are the indispensable nation. People all over the world look at us and follow our lead ... When we say America is exceptional ... it means that we recognize America's unique and unparalleled ability to be a force for peace and progress, a champion for freedom and opportunity. Our power comes with a responsibility to lead ... So no matter how hard it gets, no matter how great the challenge, America must lead".[27]

Even George W. Bush's raw national interest was covered by the mantle of a special mission: Transforming Iraq into a democratic showcase, susceptible of spreading this system across the region and, in the process, draining the swamp of autocracy. Not surprisingly, Neoconservatives called themselves "democratic imperialists" and proclaimed themselves as devout Wilsonians.

This conviction of moral superiority, of providential entitlement for leadership, projected itself by way of a precocious assertiveness: One that would not stop growing until it became all encompassing. The future Latin American countries were still mere colonies, when two of the founding fathers of the United States were already envisaging them as the natural expansion ground for their country. According to Brian Loveman: "Thomas Jefferson worried (in 1786) that Spain might be too weak to hold onto to its colonies 'till our population was sufficiently advanced to gain it from them piece by piece' (...) Six years later Alexander Hamilton advised: 'Beside eventual security against invasions, we ought certainly to look to the possession of the Floridas and Louisiana, and we ought to squint at South America'".[28]

---

[27] Victor Bulmer-Thomas, *Empire in Retreat: The Past, Present, and Future of the United States* [Kindle version], New Haven: Yale University Press, 2018, retrieved from Amazon.com, pp. 7–8.

[28] Brian Loveman, U.S. Foreign Policy towards Latin America in the 19th Century, *Oxford Research Encyclopaedia of Latin American History*, July 2016, http://oxfordindex.oup.com/view/10.1093/acrefore/9780199366439.013.41. Accessed September 21, 2017.

These assertions undoubtedly required an utter conviction on the part of the U.S. on its own destiny as, at that point in time, the Iberian empires in the Americas showed great strength. Not only were their universities one or two centuries older than those in the United States, but their cities were much larger and more magnificent too. In 1790, New York had 33,000 inhabitants; Philadelphia, 28,000 and Boston, 18,000. Meanwhile in 1800, Mexico City was a city with a population of 137,000 people. Fortunes in Hispanic or Portuguese America were also much larger than those in the North. It was extremely difficult to foresee that the correlation of power between these two spheres would be reverted in the way it eventually did.

And then, there was the Monroe Doctrine. In order to avoid the European monarchies from again reclaiming the recently independent Iberian American countries, James Monroe, fifth President of the country, delivered a in 1823 a message to Congress stating: "The American continents by the free and independent condition which they have assumed and maintain, are henceforth not to be considered as subjects of future colonization by any European powers (...) We could not view any interposition for the purpose of oppressing them [the Iberian Americans], or controlling in any other manner their destiny, by any European power in any other light than as a manifestation of an unfriendly disposition to the United States (...) It is impossible that the allied powers should extend their political system to any portion of either continent without endangering our peace and happiness; nor can anyone believe that our southern brethren, if left to themselves, would adopt it of their own accord. It is equally impossible, therefore, that we should behold such interposition in any form with indifference".[29]

The American President, thus, was clearly stating that any attempts to reconquer the recently independent Spanish American states or to impose upon them a monarchical form of government against their will were inadmissible and tantamount to an act of war

---

[29] The Avalon Project, Monroe Doctrine December 2, 1823, Yale Law School, http://avalon.law.yale.edu/19th_century/monroe.asp.

to the United States. Needless to say that in 1823 this ambitious proposition was entirely impossible to enforce. Moreover, it required much self-assurance for a still weak, rural country to speak in those terms to the coalition of conservative monarchies in Europe, which were in fact discussing the possibility of reconquering the Spanish American countries. These monarchies included Spain, France, Russia, Austria and Prussia.

A similar sort of attitude holds for China. Kissinger has asserted that the sense of time in China beats at a completely different rhythm than that of the United States. When an American is asked about a certain historical event, he immediately thinks in terms of a concrete date in the calendar. On the contrary, when a Chinese describes a historical event, he places it within a dynasty. As it happens, China has had 14 imperial dynasties, of which 10 did have a larger duration than the whole of American history.[30]

Almost 100 years before Columbus' three tiny caravels left Spain, in the momentous trip in which he came in contact with what was to be called the American continent, China possessed a fleet of 1,681 ships, of which 250 had nine masts and were 145 meters long by 54 meters wide. Moreover, in 1776, when 13 rural colonies from Eastern North America declared themselves an independent State under the name of the United States of America, Adam Smith wrote that China was richer than all Europe put together.

Common sense would have dictated that the United States approached China with a sense of deference towards its history and identity. However, both countries' relations were always marked by the United States' desire to transform China into a projection of itself and of its own superior ideals. When the U.S. barely bordered its first 100 years, it was already making manifest its intention to make of China a subsidiary of its own culture and values.

Formal diplomatic relations between the two began in 1844. The same year a Treaty of Peace, Amity and Commerce between the U.S. and the Chinese Empire was signed — the so-called Treaty of

---

[30] Henry Kissinger, *Does America Need a Foreign Policy?*, New York, Simon & Schuster, 2001, p. 137.

Wangxia. However, this was a decade later that Christian American missionaries had began to arrive in China. From then on, a relationship that was established in continuity took on a very special form. In Hugh White's terms: "The fate of China became the first issue of world politics outside the Western Hemisphere in which America took the part of a great power".[31]

Trade was a fundamental reason for the U.S.' interest in China. However, there was more. Again, according to Hugh White: "But America's motives were not purely commercial. Its ideas about China had been shaped by the Christian missionaries who had flocked there. Back home they promoted an image of the Chinese as a people eagerly receptive to American ideas — not just religious ideas, but political and economic ones too. With that image grew the conviction that America had a unique mission to raise China up and bring it to the modern world. China was the place where America could play its part as a 'civilised' country ... in a uniquely American way (...) It wanted China to be preserved intact, open to all comers for economic opportunities, and encouraged towards reform and modernization along American lines".[32]

The U.S. thus envisaged its relation with China as that of a mentor whose duty was to translate into that society the blessings of its own values. That perception endured until the moment in which the triumphant communist revolution of 1949 closed China's doors to Western influence. However, three decades later, the arrival of Deng Xiaoping to power put in motion a process of economic opening. From that moment onwards, the United States convinced itself that the final result of such process could be none other than the conversion of China into the values of liberal democracy and free market, i.e., a society forged of its own image and likeness. By virtue of such conviction, the U.S. gave its unrestricted economic, technological and military support to China's expansion And, subsequently,

[31] Hugh White, *The China Choice: Why We Should Share Power* [Kindle version], Oxford: Oxford University Press, 2012, retrieved from Amazon.com, p. 14.
[32] *Ibid.*, p. 15.

felt utterly deceived when it found out that China had its own ideas and projects.

So, while many talk about China's audacity in pretending to rival and even overcome the United States, few refer to the gigantic audacity always shown by the United States *vis-à-vis* the weight of China's history and identity.

The Middle Kingdom and the exceptional nation find themselves now at cross-purposes. Three elements will make this a difficult point in history. The first is because both China and the United States are prisoners of their history and their national myths. Neither of them can objectively look at the future without distorting their analyses by the subjective lenses of their perceived sense of superiority and mission. While as a Civilization-State with millennia of glorious past China feels entitled to a leading role, Americans feel challenged in their self-perceived providential entitlement to be a beacon for humanity.

The second element is because China's restoration comes hand in hand with the impulse to revise both the regional *status quo* and the international order, while the United States, as the sole superpower in the last three decades, serves to be their main custodian. Moreover, having emerged victorious from its competition with the Soviet Union, the U.S. feels validated in its own vision of the world and on its commanding role within it.

The third element is because while China sees itself as the epitome of human civilization, with no lessons to be given, the U.S.'s "we know best" attitude led Americans to believe that by helping China's economic success they were promoting at the same time a freer society and economy in tune with their own values. As a result, while the Chinese feel belittled, the Americans feel betrayed, thus generating mutual resentment.

A very difficult time lies ahead, indeed.

Chapter One

THE GOOD YEARS

On February 21, 1972, President Richard Nixon arrived in Beijing. This ended the more than two decades of acute hostility between the People's Republic of China (PRC) and the United States — a hostility that had included almost two years of bloody confrontation during the Korean War.

NIXON GOES TO CHINA

President Nixon's historic trip had been preceded by a complex succession of opening attempts between the two parties, in which even the so-called ping–pong diplomacy played an important role. However, National Security Adviser Henry Kissinger's two trips to Beijing in 1971 had been fundamental in paving the way.

Both Nixon and PRC's Chairman Mao Zedong had been publicly advocating for a rapprochement between their two countries. The former did so quite explicitly in a well-known article published in *Foreign Affairs* in October 1967 and again, in a subtler way, in his inaugural address on January 20, 1969. Mao's interview with American journalist Edgar Snow in October 1970 walked the road from the opposite end. In the interview, he stated that he would soon start inviting Americans of all political persuasions to visit China, while President Nixon would be welcome to do so as a dialogue with him would be the best way to solve the problems between their two countries.

Nixon had single-handedly visualized the need for such an opening. Mao had reached the same conclusion through the advice of three Marshalls of the People's Liberation Army, whom he had recalled from internal exile to provide strategic insights into the international situation. For different reasons, both sides converged on the need of a high-level dialogue.

Nixon wanted to disentangle his country from the Vietnam nightmare, without giving an opening for China to exploit the situation. Preserving America's credibility in the region was a fundamental part of this process. Moreover, he needed the Chinese to put pressure on the Vietnamese for them to engage in serious negotiations. And, of course, that would be conducive in making the Soviets more receptive to détente with the U.S. and, by natural extension, to increase the linkage between strategic arms limitations and outstanding issues such as the Middle East, Berlin and, foremost, Vietnam. The key to China's door might, indeed, open many other important doors.

Mao needed reconciliation with the Americans for a simpler reason: To dissuade the Soviets from attacking China. Since the summer of 1969, clashes around the Ussuri River and signals of an impending war between China and the Soviet Union had increased significantly. The number of the latter's troops along the Chinese borders had increased to about 42 divisions: more than a million soldiers. The possibility of a Soviet preemptive attack was very much in the air. In October 1969, Mao, believing that an attack was imminent, had ordered all leaders to disperse across the country, while putting China's small nuclear forces in state of readiness. This rapprochement to the Americans followed the ancient Chinese formula of negotiating with faraway barbarians while confronting those that are near.

To approach each other, after more than two decades of bitter quarrel, was not easy for either side. Only an American President with such impeccable anti-communist credentials as Nixon could have gotten away with it domestically. As for Mao, not even his even more impressive anti-imperialist ones seem to have prevented his heir and second in command, Lin Biao, for rebelling against this move. As Henry Kissinger explains: "The prevalent view at the time was that Lin Biao, the compiler of the Little Red Book of Mao's sayings, seemed to have concluded that China's security would be better assured by returning to the principles of the Cultural Revolution than by maneuvering with America".[1] At the end, though, strategic imperatives prevailed as both sides needed each other.

PRESERVING EACH OTHER'S NATIONAL INTERESTS

However, respective and opposing convictions were very much there. How to find common grounds when their values and views were so utterly divergent? The answer was to be found in sheer pragmatism: preserving each other's national interest and aiming for agreement wherever those interests could converge. Again, in Kissinger words: "How would global coordination between the United States and China be implemented? Mao suggested that each side develop a clear concept of its national interest and cooperate out of its own necessity".[2] This not only provided reliability but was also calculable and reciprocal. Moreover, it provided the basis for a long-term understanding among the parties. Indeed, even if international circumstances were to evolve, so could their national interests and the possibility of convergence between them.

If the structure of the understanding had been dynamic, so was the way in which it was forged. Nixon's trip to China allowed for the big picture to emerge. However, notwithstanding the seminal nature of the trip, subsequent events were needed for the picture to get into more precise focus. These included the meetings held between Mao and Zhou Enlai with Kissinger, in February and November 1973. It is generally considered, nonetheless, that the following

---

[1] Henry Kissinger, *On China* [Kindle version], New York: Penguin Books, 2012, retrieved from Amazon.com, p. 267.

[2] *Ibid.*, p. 284.

trilogy shaped the architecture of the U.S.–China relationship: The Shanghai Communiqué corresponding to Nixon's visit in August 1972, Carter's normalization of diplomatic relations with China in January 1979 and the so-called Third Communiqué of August 1982, during the Reagan Administration.[3]

A SIMPLE BUT TRANSFORMATIVE AGREEMENT

The essence of the agreement was simple. The United States would recognize the Chinese Communist regime as the legitimate government in China, and China would no longer seek to constrain or check the projection of American power in Asia, meaning its leadership.

As an expression of such leadership, China willingly accepted the U.S. alliance with Japan, which would constrain the latter's military resurgence. In other words, this agreement not only greatly strengthened China's position against the Soviets, acting as a deterrence against a possible Russian invasion, but also assured China about its security from Japan.

In Hugh White's words: "In 1972 they reached what was in essence a very simple deal. America would recognise the CCP as the legitimate government of China, and China would accept America's role as the leader of Asia. There was also, implicitly but crucially, a third party to the deal — Asia's other latent power, Japan (…) In return for acceptance of US primacy, America assured China about its security from Japan and the Soviets (…) At the same time, Japan's continued subordination to America provided China with welcome assurances against the risk of a resurgent Japan".[4]

As Kissinger explains it, henceforward the United States could behave as the regional leader: "From then on, Beijing no longer sought to constrain or check the projection of American power … Instead China's avowed goal became to enlist the

---

[3] *Ibid.*, p. 382.

[4] Hugh White, *The China Choice: Why We Should Share Power* [Kindle version], Oxford: Oxford University Press, 2012, retrieved from Amazon.com, pp. 19–20.

United States as a counterweight to the 'polar bear' by means of a strategic design".[5]

By natural extension, this agreement gave China an economic opening to the West. As Hugh White states: "Even more importantly in the long run were the economic dividends. American recognition gave China what it needed: an opening to the non-communist world, which alone could provide the capital, technology and markets that China needed ... It is certain as such things can be that without the opening to America in 1972, China would not be where it is today".[6] The full implications of this would become evident after Deng Xiaoping's arrival to power, thus the evolving nature of this agreement, which explains its longevity.

SURVIVING THE COLLAPSE OF THE SOVIET UNION

The fact that the agreement was able to survive the collapse of the Soviet Union, a tempestuous change of leadership in China, followed by generational shifts in that leadership, as well as the presence of successive American administrations from opposite sides of the aisle says much about its strength and adaptability. Moreover, it was able to withstand subsequent challenges that tested its resilience, and it could have been derailed on several occasions.

Surviving the end of the Soviets was the first testimony of the robustness of the said agreement, as it was the main reason that threw the Chinese into America's arms and, to a lesser but still very important extent, induced the U.S. to approach Beijing. Had it not been for this common threat, their respective national interests would have not met in the way they did. Moreover, neither side would have risked a confrontation between themselves as long as the Soviet Union remained a common strategic threat. It is not implausible to assume that its disintegration might have dissolved the special ties between the United States and China.

[5] Henry Kissinger, *op. cit.*, p. 279.
[6] Hugh White, *op. cit.*, p. 20.

And yet, what happened was very different, as Henry Kissinger explains: "Both the United States and China were edging away from the previous alignment in which they saw themselves as strategic partners facing a common existential threat. Now that the Soviet menace had begun to recede, China and the United States were in effect partners of convenience on selected issues on which their interests aligned".[7]

In 1991, China's economic involvement with the U.S. had sufficient standing for their agreement to survive and thrive. This was the area where their interests aligned more clearly. Deng Xiaoping's accession to power had made it happen. His accession had required not only his return from internal political exile for a second time but also overcoming the challenges represented by the radical Gang of Four and the presence of Mao's designated heir Hua Guofeng in the premiership. According to Thomas P. Bernstein: "Deng Xiaoping rapidly consolidated his power in 1978 ... by the time of the Third Plenum of the Central Committee in December 1978, he emerged as the nation's premier leader".[8] With his consolidation of power, pragmatism took control of China.

DENG XIAOPING AND THE PRIMACY OF ECONOMY

Although Deng forcefully opposed the Soviets and played an important role in support of the Afghan insurgency while sharing intelligence with the U.S., China's modernization was his main goal. Some of Deng's trademark issues speak for themselves, such as the following: The need to emphasize science and technology in the country's economic development, the encouragement of individual initiative and talent, the re-professionalization of the Chinese workforce, the

---

[7] Henry Kissinger, *op. cit.*, p. 394.

[8] Thomas P. Bernstein, Muted Differences: The Negotiations to Normalize U.S.-Chinese Relations, Institute for the Study of Diplomacy, Case Study Program, Edmund A. Walsh School of Foreign Policy, Georgetown University, Case 140, p. 6.

relevance of professional competence over political correctness, the loosening up of ideological constrains and the encouragement of individual creative thinking. Two of his main principles were those of "seeking truth from facts" and "integrating theory with practice".

The example of the Meiji restoration was very much present in his mind, and therefore China's challenge was to do even better than Japan had done. For such an aim to be attained, Deng insisted that China needed to acquire foreign technology, expertise and capital. As a result, in the December 1978 Third Plenum of the Eleventh Central Committee of the Chinese Communist Party, he formulated the slogan that would guide all his subsequent policy endeavors: "Reform and Opening-Up". This, of course meant that a long period of stability in the relations with the United States had to be guaranteed.

Reform and opening-up would become responsible for China's economic growth and social achievements — the most impressive ever attained in recorded history. Abandoning a centuries-old vision of economic self-sufficiency, China opened its doors to foreign direct investments and technology. However, for Deng Xiaoping, this reform and opening up process had to follow an endogenous course of action. He called it "socialism with Chinese characteristics". It could not have been otherwise given the strength of the country's civilization.

This implied a highly pragmatic model that allowed for trial and error. While clearly defining a goal to aim at through strategic planning, the model gave itself ample tactical room for manoeuver, leaving space to react to undesirable effects or changing circumstances. According to Deng, this was tantamount to "crossing the river by feeling the stones".

Such a process took the pathway of progressive stages and periodic adjustments in which transitory policies acted as bridges from one stage into the next one: "The reform process has been gradual and pragmatically introduced in progressive stages that build on, and adjust to, experience in the development of greater market forces in the economy. This incrementalism involves the interaction of initial conditions with transitional policies".[9]

The gradualness of the model was shown through the management of its export and domestic production industries. The former was channelled through special areas that subsequently expanded, while the latter saw a progressive reduction of the levels of protection assigned to them.

Deng Xiaoping also insisted on the model of "one country, two systems", which meant that while the country would be governed by a socialist system, market forces would prevail in open regions and eventually also in Hong Kong. Those open regions were formed by the so-called Special Economic Zones, which began in 1979.

Its initial centers were in South-Eeast China, in the newly created cities of Shenzhen, Zhulai and Shantou in the province of Guangdong, and Xiamen in the province of Fujian. In 1983, eight additional zones were established in the Beijing–Bohai Bay area, the Shanghai Zone, the Wuham Zone and the Pearl River Delta Zone. In 1984, 14 additional coastal cities were opened up for foreign investment (Tianjin, Shanghai, Dalian, Qinhuangdao, Lianyungang, Nantong, Ningbo, Wenzhou, Fuzhou, Guangzhou, Zhanjiang, and Beihai). In 1985, 52 Pearl River Delta and Yangtze River Delta cities were incorporated to the opening process. In 1988 came the East coast open belt, also called gold coast, which comprised 160 million people.[10]

Into all of these areas, foreign investments and technology flew abundantly. All along this process, the U.S. became a vital partner. Moreover, the opening up process implied joining the World Bank and the International Monetary Fund, which Beijing did in 1980. Here, again, support of the United States was of the utmost importance.

In order to concentrate on economic development, Deng negotiated compromise deals on the outstanding land frontiers, while

[9] Inter-American Development Bank, *The Emergence of China: Opportunities and Challenges for Latin America and the Caribbean*, Washington D.C., March 2005, p. 32.
[10] Alfredo T. Hardy, *The World Turned Upside Down: The Complex Partnership between China and Latin America*, New Jersey: World Scientific, 2013, pp. 21–22.

maintaining the approach of "mutual inaction" on China's various maritime sovereignty disputes. The principle behind this last approach was synthetized in the idea that "our generation is not wise enough" to find a solution on these issues, and hence the "next generation will certainly be wiser" and find a solution acceptable to all. With the exception of India, this led to normalization of relations with all of China's neighbors. This included Japan in 1978 and Vietnam in 1991 (after their conflict in 1979). Moreover, in 1992 China agreed on mutual recognition with South Korea, which closed the chapter that had resulted from Beijing's participation in the Korean War.[11]

DENG'S FINAL LEGACY

Deng's final legacy expressed itself in the form of guidance for future generations and took shape through a set of maxims and by the ideas contained in his final speeches during an iconic inspection tour through southern China. Amid the former were notions such as the following: "Observe carefully; secure our position; cope with affairs calmly; hide our capacities and bide our time; be good at maintaining a low profile; and never claim leadership". But also within the maxims were the following: "Enemy troops are outside the walls. They are stronger than we are. We should be mainly on the defensive".

During this southern tour, Deng insisted that what mattered were results and not the doctrine under which they were achieved. He also advocated for the importance of productivity and entrepreneurship, of risk taking and the daring to experiment, of private initiative and of the profit principle. In Shenzhen, which would soon develop into a metropolis of millions of people, he stated that there was no inherent conflict between a market economy and a state-planned one. According to his famous dictum, which he

---

[11]Jude Woodward, *The U.S. vs. China: Asia's New Cold War* [Kindle version], Manchester: Manchester University Press, 2017, Amazon.con, locations 1349/9348, 1356/9348 and 1363/9384.

repeated several times during the tour: "Development is the absolute principle".

In Henry Kissinger words: "In time, Deng's 'Southern Tour' would take on an almost mythical significance, and his speeches would serve as the blueprint for another two decades of Chinese political and economic policy".[12]

This legacy also included the choice of a successor: Jiang Zemin. Already a CCP General Secretary since 1989, he represented the perfect successor to Deng's policies. Between 1993 and 2003, he was President of the People's Republic, while Zhu Rongji was the Prime Minister. They were able to oversee the peaceful return of Hong Kong, maintain China's relations with the U.S. and the West in good track notwithstanding highly difficult challenges, and keep the economic rudder under firm control. The latter included negotiating China's entry into the World Trade Organization (WTO), which materialized in 2001. As a result of this, in 2006 China's tariffs went down to 6%, representing a further, substantial opening of its economy.

JIANG ZEMIN AND HU JINTAO: THE THIRD AND FOURTH GENERATIONS

Well read, highly educated, knowledgeable in foreign languages and Western culture, and socially engaging, Jiang Zemin was the perfect interlocutor for his American counterparts. During this period, the United States would become instrumental in helping China to fully integrate into the international economic order. This was well represented by China's entry into WTO, which was done with the support of the Americans.

Jiang was the first Chinese Communist leader who had no revolutionary or military credentials yet managed to reach the top leadership post through his bureaucratic credentials. From then on, this was to be the norm. His immediate successors, President Hu Jintao and Premier Wen Jiabao (2003–2013), had impressive

[12] Henry Kissinger, *On China, op. cit.*, p. 441.

credentials as well. Moreover, they had benefited from an elite higher education.

They represented a fourth generation within the CCP leadership, which meant that they were the first to attain power without having personally experienced the revolution. Their arrival to the top positions was also marked by the fact that China had already become an economic powerhouse. Indeed, between 1980 and 1990, the country's GDP had doubled, and it doubled again between 1990 and 2000. According to the International Monetary Fund, China's GDP rose from US$309 billion in 1980 to US$1.2 trillion in 2000.[13]

If the main task of Jiang Zemin and Zhu Rongji had been to turn China into a strong and fast-growing economy, firmly entrenched within the international economic order, the fundamental responsibility that fell on the shoulders of Hu and Wen was to maintain stability. That meant promoting, as was officially stated, a harmonious society within a harmonious world. Moreover, "China's peaceful rise" thesis, presented by the government, aimed at symbolizing a country whose emergence did not represent a threat for anyone. Preserving good working relations with the United States was a clear priority when Hu and Wen attained the top leadership positions.

CHIMERICA

During their period in power, which began in 2002 with Hu's accession to the General Secretariat of the CCP, both countries experienced an important fusion of their economies. Although this process had begun in the 1990s, it was after 2002 that it took full shape. Total trade between them increased from almost US$150 billion in 2002 to nearly US$450 in 2008. Before 2002, trade had grown steadily but not exponentially as it did afterwards. China thus showed a clear trade surplus. In 2002, it exported US$125 billion and imported US$22 billion; in 2007, it exported US$320 billion and imported US$65 billion; and in

[13] John Naisbitt and Doris Naisbitt, *China's Megatrends*, New York: Harper Business, 2010, p. 65.

2008, exported US$350 billion and imported nearly US$90 billion. On the other hand, though, as its foreign reserves grew as a result of this surplus, China began to buy U.S. debt. In 2001, it held nearly US$700 billion, in 2007 close to US$1 trillion and in 2009 it surpassed US$2 trillion.[14]

The complementarity between Americans buying Chinese goods and Chinese buying U.S. debt in return gave rise to the term "Chimerica". Coined in 2007 by Niall Ferguson and Moritz Schularick, they explained it as follows: "Their relationship isn't necessarily unbalanced; more like symbiotic. East Chimericans are savers; West Chimercans are spenders. East Chimericans do manufactures; West Chimericans do services. East Chimericans export; West Chimericans import. East Chimericans pile up reserves; West Chimericans obligingly run deficits, producing dollar-denominated bonds that the East Chimericans crave. As in good marriages, the differences between the two halves of Chimerica are complementary".[15] Mark Leonard termed this complementarity as the "*yin* and *yang* of the global economy".[16]

Hence, from Mao to Hu and Wen, i.e., from the first to the fourth generation of CCP leaders, a clearly strategic line was maintained. The evolving imperatives of national interest allowed China to remain committed in a dynamic way to the agreement derived from Nixon's 1972 trip to China. Notwithstanding big changes in the international environment, successive Chinese leaders stuck to the principles of their understanding with the United States.

Conversely, successive American Presidents from both the Republican and Democratic parties, representing changing generations, also remained committed to the aforementioned agreement.

---

[14] Zachary Karabell, *Superfusion: How China and America Became One Economy and Why the World's Economy Depends on It,* New York: Simon & Schuster, 2009, pp. 154 and 163.

[15] *Ibid.*, p. 256.

[16] Mark Leonard, "The US and China Are the Closest of Enemies", *Project Syndicate,* November 27, 2018, https://www.project-syndicate.org/commentary/america-china-closest-of-enemies-by-mark-leonard-2018-11?barrier=accesspaylog. Accessed January 10, 2019.

While the pressure of public opinion was much more compelling from this side of the Ocean during those years, a strategic line was also followed, although in a haphazard manner. National interest was the guiding principle for the United States as well.

FORD AND CARTER: FOLLOWING UP

The switch from Nixon to Ford in 1974, although incomprehensible in its reasons for the Chinese leadership, represented an easy transition. Not only did Henry Kissinger remain as Secretary of State, providing policy continuity, but President Ford had been personally chosen by Nixon. Jolts in Washington and the briefness of this American Administration unfortunately prevented the normalization of diplomatic relations agreed by both countries while the atmosphere remained so friendly.

It would be after a worrisome change of administration and political party in 1977 that the normalization of diplomatic relations came to fruition in January 1979. To Jimmy Carter's tribute — who was the first in succeeding the two Republican administrations directly involved with the agreement — he emphasized continuity. In Thomas P. Bernstein words: "On Carter instructions, Brzezinski told the Chinese ... that the United States had a 'fundamental, enduring interest' in forging a cooperative relationship with China, one that would not merely be tactical in nature. He emphasized that the United States had an interest in a 'strong and secure' China".[17] This was the beginning of Washington's non-partisan strategic policy towards China.

This meant that the American Embassy would move from Taipei to Beijing and that an Ambassador from Beijing would replace Taiwan's diplomatic representative in Washington. By extension, this also meant that the U.S. would recognize that China's seat in the United Nations Security Council corresponded to a representative from Beijing and not from Taipei. Henceforward, the notion of a single China would be identified with the former and Communist

---

[17] Thomas P. Bernstein, *op. cit.*, p. 9.

China would become the legitimate government of the Chinese people.

Moreover, Carter believed that increasing China's technological and military capabilities would be helpful not only for international equilibrium but also to strengthen his country's national security. During this period, not only did scientific exchanges with China multiply but thousands of Chinese students, mainly in the physical sciences, went to American universities.

An immense outpouring of American scientific and technological expertise passed to China during these four years. Presidential Directive 43, signed in 1978, established numerous programs to transfer American scientific and technological developments to China in the fields of education, energy, agriculture, space, geosciences and public health.[18] Moreover, for the first time Washington granted China with the "most-favored nation" status as a U.S. trading partner.

THE REAGAN AND BUSH YEARS

Ronald Reagan's arrival to the White House in 1981 presented Beijing with new challenges. Although firmly committed to policy continuity in relation to Beijing, he strongly supported Taipei as well. This ambivalence led to a compromise: Washington would supply arms to both China and Taiwan. This compromise took shape in an ambiguous text: the so-called Third Communiqué of August 17, 1982.

Notwithstanding the sinuous nature of the bilateral relations during this period, things worked quite well because Washington was ready to support China in many areas. This included the selling of advanced air, ground, naval and missile technology, while simultaneously inaugurating nuclear cooperation to expand China's military and civilian nuclear programs. The United States also helped

---

[18] Michael Pillsbury, *The Hundred Year Marathon: China's Secret Strategy to Replace America as the Global Superpower* [Kindle version], New York: Henry Holt and Company, 2015, Amazon.com, location 1377/7620.

China in the development of several technological areas such as genetic engineering, automation, space technology, manned spaceflight, lasers and biotechnology, among others.[19]

Meanwhile, Washington and Beijing covertly cooperated in opposing the Soviets in Afghanistan and other fronts. Following in the steps of Nixon, Ford and Carter, Reagan believed that a strong, secure and stable China would become a force for peace both in Asia and the world. Thus, helping China's modernization was considered to be in Washington's best interests.

The transition to the administration of George H.W. Bush in 1989 was an easy one, as he had not only been Reagan's Vice President but also Chief of the American Liaison Office in China during the Ford presidency. No other U.S. President knew China and its sensibilities as he did. This proved to be particularly useful for adroitly navigating through some of the most important crises in the bilateral relations that surfaced during this period. Under a different leadership, these could have easily derailed 17 years of fruitful convergence of interests, especially so as the Soviet threat which had gotten them together in the first place was melting away. As an expression of his commitment to the inherited policy towards China, in the middle of this very tense period Bush ordered the Pentagon to complete a promised delivery of important military supplies.

CLINTON AND BUSH: FROM A DIFFICULT TRANSITION TO AMERICA'S UNILATERALISM

Bill Clinton's arrival to the White House in 1993 brought the usual concerns associated with a change in the governing party. At least initially, those concerns proved to be well justified. Two powerful domestic forces exerted their influence upon the President in relation to China. On the one hand was the human rights movement; on the other, the business lobby. While the former projected a hard

---

[19] *Ibid.*, locations 1390/7620 and 1403/7620.

stance against Beijing, the latter wanted to preserve the good business opportunities associated with policy continuity.

Clinton's first year in power was clearly aligned with the human rights movement, which translated into rhetorical overtones and a more conflictive approach towards China. During the remaining seven years in the White House, however, response was more to the interests of the business lobby and to what Clinton himself called "constructive engagement". His decision to separate national interest, which in this case was represented by economic considerations, from human rights issues meant following in the line set by his predecessors.

Nonetheless, despite the good intentions and policy continuity, two events took place during this period that greatly strained bilateral relations. In context, although both governments remained committed to the need for cooperation, the preponderance given to trade and business softened the friction. The fact that trade between both countries increased manifold during those years, and that American corporations viewed China as an essential part of their business strategy, helped significantly.

Then the Republicans and another Bush came into the White House in 2001. Not long after, another important crisis shook the bilateral relations. Moreover, Taiwan was always a stone in the shoe of the said relations. But yet again, the importance given to trade and business allowed for the overcoming of frictions. At this point in time, however, events would push China out of focus even though policy continuity prevailed. From September 11, 2001, America's attention, indeed, turned towards the Middle East.

While Chinese leadership did not go along with America's blatant unilateralism in the management of its affairs there, it undoubtedly felt relief from the fact that while trade and investments kept their course, Washington's political focus had moved elsewhere. Not surprisingly, China's leadership began to speak gleefully of the surprising two-decade-long "period of strategic opportunity".[20] The

---

[20] Nathan Levine, "China Will be the True Winner of a U.S.-Iran War", *The National Interest,* May 29, 2019, https://nationalinterest.org/feature/china-will-be-true-winner-us-iran-war-60052. Accessed June 1, 2019.

U.S., on its side, felt relief in those circumstances as well because of the belief that it could turn its back to the Asia-Pacific region without China's challenging its leadership there. In Washington's eyes, this was the best demonstration that the agreement reached with China was alive and healthy.

As seen before, multiple events shook the good progress of bilateral relations, threatening derailment. The willingness shown by both parties to overcome such crises, and to continue with the basic terms of their agreement, was proof of the importance that they attached to it. The most relevant of those crises were as follows: the Tiananmen massacre of 1989, the controversies surrounding the Chinese dissident Fang Lizhi between 1989 and 1990, the events in the Taiwan Strait in 1996, the U.S. bombardment of the Chinese Embassy in Belgrade in 1999 and the air incident near Hainan Island in 2001.

TIANANMEN AND FANG LIZHI CRISES

In 1989 a younger generation of students and many CCP officials believed that Gorbachev's reforms in the Soviet Union were a possible path for China to follow. The funeral of Hu Yaobang, a reformist former Secretary General of the CCP ostracized by Deng after having been his protégé, triggered demonstrations on behalf of political reforms. These demonstrations eventually progressed into the occupation of Tiananmen Square, which challenged the authority of the government. As Mark Leonard explains: "The incredible display of people power that dominated the streets for six weeks gave the world a glimpse of a democratic China until it was abruptly wiped out by soldiers and tanks on June 4, 1989. The crackdown was more than a human tragedy; it became a defining moment in China's political and economic development".[21] For Deng, this protest no only brought to mind the Chinese fear of chaos but to memory the turmoil of the Cultural Revolution. After a few weeks of hesitation, Deng and the majority of the Party's Politburo decided indeed to strike back with might.

---

[21] Mark Leonard, *op. cit.*, p. 28.

The American Congress and public opinion were deeply stirred by the harsh suppression of the protest. President George H.W. Bush, recently elected, found himself walking on a tight rope, weary of antagonizing the Chinese government yet, at the same time, facing pressure from all sides in his own country. Faced with a barrage of American criticism, the Chinese authorities reacted with outrage. At the same time, they failed to understand why democratic institutions had to enter the equation of their respective national interests. To his domestic constituency, Bush argued that the only way to influence events in China was by not pushing their authorities into a corner. In the end, Deng and Bush proved to be flexible enough to overcome the first significant challenge to the agreement that Nixon's trip had put in motion. This challenge would turn out to be the first of a troublesome list.

Indeed, a parallel crisis had emerged by way of the dissident physicist Fang Lizhi. In the aftermath of the Tiananmen Square crackdown, he and his wife had sought protection at the American Embassy. The Chinese government, seeking their arrest for the instigation of the recent events, not only demanded the U.S. authorities that they be handed back but refused to allow them to leave the country. Washington's unwillingness to turn them over generated a high-profile impasse. As the issue proved resistant to negotiation on both sides, it took over a year for a compromise to be reached, with the couple leaving the country.

TAIWAN AND THE TWO AIRCRAFT CARRIER BATTLE GROUPS

In 1996, after a few years of respite, a new problem came to ligts that hindered the bilateral relations. Taiwan was the bone of contention this time, with Jiang Zemin and Bill Clinton on opposing sides. Since the Taiwanese constitutional amendment of 1994, which laid the ground for the direct election of the President by universal suffrage, the island's political landscape had become much more vocal. Chief among these voices was the mercurial politician Lee Teng-hui, who played a leading role in the Nationalist Party. He was outspoken about Taiwan's distinct institutional and historical identity.

While in the United States, as an invitee of Cornell University, Lee bluntly spoke about his "country" and his "nation", while referring to the imminent demise of communism in Mainland China. This not only led to Beijing's recalling of its Ambassador in Washington but to delaying the approval of the American ambassadorial nominee. Moreover, it led to Beijing firing several rounds of missiles into the Taiwan Strait, allegedly intending to intimidate the Taiwanese electorate from voting for Lee Teng-hui in the 1996 Presidential election. In response, the U.S. sent two aircraft carrier battle groups to the Strait of Taiwan, the largest display of American might since the Vietnam War.

"Approaching the precipice, both Washington and Beijing recoiled, realizing that they had no war aims over which to fight or terms to impose which would alter the overriding reality ...".[22] More significantly, in the wake of the crisis, it became clear to both parties how necessary it was to keep the bilateral relationship in good standing. This was not to be for long though, as a new crisis was already looming in the horizon, and again it fell on Jiang and Clinton to deal with it. This new crisis was as sudden as it was intense. It took place in 1999 during the Kosovo war.

BELGRADE AND HAINAN ISLAND

An American B-2, bombarding targets in Belgrade, hit and damaged the Chinese Embassy. While Washington promptly apologized and claimed it as an inadvertent mistake, China's citizens and authorities felt outraged. How could the world's most sophisticated military make such a gigantic mistake? Suspicion and emotions ran amok in China, especially since the bombardment came on the heels of the so-called Cox Report, which declared that the People's Republic of China had been stealing U.S. nuclear technology through the 1990s.

While a firestorm of protests expanded all over China and Jiang spoke of a deliberate provocation, anti-Chinese sentiments began to take shape in Washington in response to events in China. To almost

[22] Henry Kissinger, *On China, op. cit.*, p. 476.

everyone's surprise, nonetheless, what might have ended 27 years of policy engagement actually did not. Yet again, pragmatism and flexibility had prevailed on both sides. Quietly but quickly, both governments moved to restart negotiations and overcome tensions.

Barely two years later, in 2001, soon after Bush Junior had moved into the White House, relations were shaken yet again by an air incident close to China's Hainan Island. Jiang, still in power, was the one to manage it. An American reconnaissance plane that was flying just outside Chinese territorial waters was tailed by a Chinese military plane. This resulted in a collision in mid-air and the death of the Chinese pilot. The American aircraft was forced to make an emergency landing on Hainan, and its 24 crew members were detained and interrogated. Both the cause of the crash and the assignment of blame were disputed by the parties. The crew was released 10 days after the incident, while the plane was returned once the Chinese had gathered all the intelligence available on board. Yet again, both parties did their best to find a quick solution. Neither Bush nor Jiang allowed the incident to escalate and harm the relationship.

Notwithstanding the several jolts encountered, both partners made a conscious effort to overcome them and continue along the path on which the journey was started in 1972. Their agreement showed not only a high degree of resilience but also the ability to evolve. Through four generations of Chinese leaders and seven American administrations, consistency prevailed. However, 2008 became an inflexion point. From that moment onwards, everything began to unravel, as we shall see next.

Chapter Two
THE UNRAVELING

How then to understand what happened in 2008? What put in jeopardy and began reversing 36 years of entente and constructive relations? The cause seemed to be an alien concept to the West but familiar to the Chinese: the *shi*. Several events converging that year convinced the Chinese leadership that the *shi* was in motion.

SHI

In essence, the *shi* can be considered as an alignment of forces that allows to shape a situation. More widely, it can be understood as momentum, strategic advantage, or strategic configuration of power.[1] The *shi*, as a shaping force, was drawn upon by the different philosophical schools of thought during the Chinese Warring States Period. "At the heart of Chinese strategy is *shi*, which is a difficult concept to explain to a Western audience. It cannot be translated into English, but Chinese linguists describe it as 'the alignment of forces' or 'propensity for things to happen', which only a skilled

[1]Timothy L. Thomas, Geothinking like the Chinese: A Potential Explanation of China's Geostrategy, 2011, https://www.usafa.edu/app/uploads/Thomas-Geothinking-Like-the-Chinese-2011.pdf. Accessed May 18, 2019.

strategist can exploit …”.[2] According to Chinese strategic thinking, indeed, the skilled strategist has to take advantage of *shi* to mold a favorable environment.

In 2008, what was then the alignment of forces which might have shaped a new situation or created a new environment? The answer can be found in the convergence of the following situations: The largest global economic crisis since 1929 resulting from American financial excesses; the fact that by having become the largest creditor to the U.S., China had also become a hostage to its financial hubris and foolishness; the sweeping efficiency with which China overcame its own risk of contagion; the fact that China's economic growth was the fundamental factor in preserving the world from a major economic downturn; and the boost to Chinese self-esteem after the highly successful Beijing Olympic games of that year.

The above convergence was compounded by America's military frailties and the substantial erosion of its hegemonic standing. While the former was made evident by its bogging in two peripheral wars, the latter had resulted from a wide international rejection to the arrogant and abrasive leadership role played by the U.S. in relation to the Iraq invasion. If the “war on terror” had demonstrated the limits of America's military power and hegemonic standing, the financial crisis was now showing the limits of its economic might.

In the eyes of the Chinese administration, they themselves appeared to be much stronger than previously assumed, while the U.S. was proving to be considerably weaker than presumed: “… the year 2009 marks the beginning of a new era of Chinese–US relations after the Global Financial Crisis of 2008 … China emerged relatively stronger and it was relatively unscathed compared to the U.S. and other developed economies, and the Asia-Pacific region became the new global economic powerhouse”.[3]

---

[2] Michael Pillsbury, *op. cit.*, location 810/7620.

[3] Minseon Ki, The motives of China's ‘new model of major country relations” in China–U.S. relations, *Journal of International Relations and Foreign Policy*, 2015, **3**(1), p. 25.

Deng's guidance for future generations of leaders emphasized the need to strategically wait for a position of strength, while preserving a low-profile and a defensive attitude. But didn't the events of 2008 show that the long-awaited moment was finally materializing? Wasn't it clear that the curves of China's emergence and America's decline were crossing each other? Hadn't a turning point been reached? The Chinese leadership seemed convinced that this was the case. The *shi* appeared to be in motion, as the flux of events showed the presence of a new strategic configuration of power. This was a configuration that needed to be exploited in order to advance their own interests and strategic aims.

PEACEFUL RISE

Few countries have made such a systematic and conscious effort to project a constructive international image as China did until 2008. In the spring of 2004, several dozen Chinese scholars and intellectuals had gathered on the island of Hainan, with the purpose of giving form to a China "brand" which could be successfully promoted internationally, which was where they coined the concept of "peaceful rise".[4] This implied a path different from that followed by Germany in World War I and by Japan in World War II, when they tried to overhaul the world's political landscape. China's path relied upon reciprocity and the search for mutual benefit in relation with other countries. It was a brilliant soft power marketing strategy that provided China with huge dividends of good will.

In addition to the above efforts, China adroitly presented its economic model as the natural alternative for emerging economies all around the world as a pragmatic model that differed from the controversial and damaging shock therapies of the Washington Consensus. Instead of the inflexible directives of the former, China's pathway allowed for trial and error, for tactical room of manoeuvre and for progressive stages and periodic adjustments in which transitory policies acted as bridges from one stage to the other. By

[4]Joshua Cooper Ramo, *Brand China*, London: The Foreign Policy Centre, 2007.

branding this model as the "Beijing Consensus", Joshua Cooper Ramo has provided a great service, as it created the obvious contraposition to the discredited Washington Consensus.[5]

This soft power strategy also included cooperative multilateralism as China's route into international affairs. All of this was accompanied by the proliferation of Confucius's institutes around the world and led to the launch of CCTV and Xinhua News Agency. While the former aimed at fostering the knowledge of the Chinese culture, the latter aimed at a worldwide dissemination of China's image and points of views. Few countries, indeed, had associated their foreign policy to soft power in such a deliberate and efficient manner.

The results of the strategy became evident. The European Union regarded China as a congener in the search for a multipolar and peaceful world. Writing in 2008, before the change of attitude materialized, Mark Leonard said the following about China: "Like Europe it has many twenty-first-century qualities. Its leaders preach a doctrine of stability and social harmony. Its military talks more about soft than hard power. Its diplomats call for multilateralism rather than unilateralism. And its strategists rely more on trade than war to forge alliances and conquer new parts of the world".[6]

Meanwhile, developing countries saw China as a benevolent and respectful power that did not wish to impose its own convictions upon others. However, they found in its economic model a credible path to development that clearly differed from the abrasiveness and rigidity of the Washington Consensus.

Not surprisingly, in its edition dated September 20, 2005, *Oxford Analytica* made reference to a world survey on China by the BBC, stating that the majority of the world's public opinion, in five continents, had a favorable view of the country. Even more significant was the fact that even China's neighbors viewed it favorably.

---

[5] *The Beijing Consensus*, London: The Foreign Policy Centre, 2004.

[6] Mark Leonard, *What Does China Think?*, New York: HarperCollins, 2008, p. 109.

However, China's soft power turned into hard power whenever Taiwan, Tibet or Xinjiang entered into the scene. Considered as core interests, they represented non-negotiable issues. In balance, though, that didn't affect its image much as a constructive international actor, whose economic model had many lessons to offer. The prevailing perception was that of a benevolent emerging superpower that China had turned itself into.

A NEW ASSERTIVENESS

From 2008 onward, this rosy-tinged perception changed in tone as a result of a much more assertive foreign policy. This coincided with Obama's election at the end of that year. For the Americans, the first hint that something had changed came from the United Nations Climate Change Conference in Copenhagen in 2009. On that occasion, President Obama was verbally assailed by a medium-rank Chinese representative, which coming from a country so conscious of its hierarchies was clearly an inauspicious sign.

Moreover, although Premier Wen Jibao was present at the conference, he did not participate in the deliberations, which was considered a snub to an actively engaged President Obama. To make matters worse, Wen Jibao refused to have the bilateral encounter requested by the American President. Finally, Obama had to crash a meeting that had been arranged by China without the knowledge of the U.S.[7]

China's new muscular approach to the South China Sea contention became evident as well. The fact that the other contesting countries were far weaker than China didn't play well to its international image or to the nature of its contention. In 2010, Chinese Foreign Minister Yang Jiechi not only stated that Beijing considered the South China Sea as a "core national interest" but also affirmed that "China

[7]Per Meilstrup, The Runaway Summit: The Background Story of the Danish Presidency of COP15, The UN Climate Change Conference, http://www.fao.org/fileadmin/user_upload/rome2007/docs/What%20really%20happen%20in%20COP15.pdf, Accessed May 19, 2019.

is a big country and other small countries are small countries".[8] The former seemed to have elevated the South China Sea controversy to the same level as that of Taiwan, Tibet or Xinjiang. The latter, on its part, was reminiscent of Thucydides' Melian Dialogue, "... while the strong do as they can and the weak suffer what they must", which in this case literally means that the powerful act in their own interest, no matter how it affects the weaker.

SOUTH CHINA SEA

And, indeed, Beijing reclaimed 90% of the South China Sea and the energy supplies and fishery resources beneath it, appealing to rights which they claimed went back to time immemorial. That is the case of its own Nine-Dash Line, which contravenes the United Nations Convention of the Law of the Sea, of which China is a signatory. As Howard W. French explains: "Almost all non-Chinese experts agree that claiming distant waters as one's own 'historic waterway' is not something that international law or conventions governing the sea either contemplate or permit".[9]

Moreover, again in French's words: "In defending China's nine-dash line, academics working in Chinese state think tanks have routinely argued that it was the Chinese who discovered the rich fishing waters that are scattered throughout the South China Sea along with the islands and other formations that do them. It was the Chinese, they say, who first made traditional use of them, and therefore established a continuous historical claim to them. In effect, according to this view, little does it matter that the waters in question come right up to the very shores of modern-day states...".[10] Meanwhile, China

---

[8]Antoaneta Becker, China: Middle Kingdom Syndrome Touches Puts Neighbours on Edge, *Global Issues*, 2010, http://www.globalissues.org/news/2010/10/25/7385. Accessed October 22, 2019.

[9]Howard W. French, *Everything Under Heaven: How the Past Helps Shape China's Push for Global Power* [Kindle version], New York: Alfred A. Knopf, 2017, retrieved from Amazon.com, p. 70.

[10]*Ibid.*, pp. 73–74.

has refused to accept the jurisdiction of the International Court of Justice on the matter. Not surprisingly, an image of Middle Kingdom's arrogance began to take shape.

However, China wanted to play it both ways by obtaining control of 200 miles of exclusive economic zone (EEZ) which, according to the United Nations Convention of the Law of the Sea, the islands confer. In order to claim this, China began building full-fledged islands, by reclaiming land from the sea, in what were previously submerged coral reefs. Hence, by one way or the other, China aimed at obtaining control of these waterways. And although it is almost universally acknowledged that these artificial islands do not possess territorial or maritime rights, by building extensive military structures and installations in many of them, they were attaining *de facto* control of what they reclaimed. Moreover, these outposts generated area denial capability, *vis-à-vis* foreign natives. Even though China was not the first to build artificial islands, it went substantially further and at a much faster pace than all its neighbors put together.

The not-so-hidden ambition of Beijing in transforming the South China Sea into its own Caribbean Sea also became a controversial issue.[11] This implied replicating the same kind of hegemony that the United States had historically exerted over the Caribbean Basin countries, while driving away other powers from the area. Interestingly enough, the so-called Greater Caribbean is roughly the size of the South China Sea.

FIRST ISLAND CHAIN AND BLUE WATER NAVY

China's military strategists became vocal in relation to controlling the geographical space between its shores and the so-called first island chain (principally composed of the Kuril Island, the Japanese Archipelago, Ryukyu Island, Taiwan, the northern Philippines and Borneo). A sensitive area which needs to be off-limits for American bases and aircraft carrier groups. By extension, this implied sealing

---

[11] Robert D. Kaplan, *Asia's Cauldron: The South China Sea and the End of a Stable Pacific*, New York: Random House Trade Paperbacks, 2014; Hugh White, *op. cit.*

off from the American presence not only the South China Sea but also the East China Sea and the Yellow Sea.[12]

Howard W. French compares China's expansionism with that of Japan a century ago. He does recognize, however, that the former is trying to accomplish its aim without going to war, which paradoxically would be attained by arming itself to the teeth. In his words: "What most obviously distinguishes China's expansionism from Japan's one slightly less than a century earlier, is that Beijing is hoping to accomplish its grab without the direct resort to force. Military power, though, is an essential tool for China in this effort; indeed, the overwhelming preponderance of strength it is building toward constitutes the very foundation of its strategy".[13]

Meanwhile, Beijing began its process of building a blue-water navy, able to operate in "distant seas". This was for reasons of prestige and to protect its sea trade routes in the Indian Ocean. This meant becoming a two-ocean power (Pacific and Indian), while transforming its navy from the "sea denial" type, aimed at protecting its coastline, to a more formidable "sea control" type. With that aim in mind, China undertook the construction of deepwater ports in Myanmar, Bangladesh, Pakistan and Sri Lanka. Analysts have insisted that these civil infrastructures, which fall within the so-called "string of pearls" strategy, could be turned into Chinese naval bases in the future. By implication, the Indian Ocean and the Bay of Bengal also became part of a strategic plan to secure China's future.[14] Needless to say, this has placed China in a collision course with India.

---

[12] China's military rise: The dragon's new teeth, *The Economist*, 2012; China's military rise: There are ways to reduce the threat to stability that an emerging superpower poses, *The Economist*, 2012.

[13] Howard W. French, *op. cit.*, p. 66.

[14] Tim Marshal, *Prisoners of Geography: The Maps that Tell You Everything you Need to Know about Global Politics*, London: Elliot and Thompson Limited, 2015; Robert Kaplan, *op. cit.*; Steven Metz, How to know when China is pulling even with the United States, *World Politics Review*, 2018, https://www.worldpoliticsreview.com/articles/24282/how-to-know-when-china-is-pulling-even-with-the-united-states. AccessedSeptember 25, 2018.

COLLISION COURSES

Japan is also in a collision course with China. As if the first island chain strategy was not enough to antagonize that country, the "Air Defense Identification Zone" declared by Beijing over most of the East China Sea in 2013 was added to the equation. This sprang up in 2012 from the heated dispute over the Senkaku (Diaoyu) uninhabited island chain, which in fairness was initiated by Japan and not China. The air identification zone created problems with South Korea as well.

The bigger picture of the problem, though, goes beyond regional actors. It not only involves the other contending parties in the South China Sea (Malaysia, Vietnam, Taiwan, the Philippines and Brunei) as well as India, Japan and South Korea but also includes the United States. Washington unequivocally rejects not only China's first island chain strategy but also Beijing's muscular South China Sea policy. History, international credibility and maritime free passage are the reasons behind its position. The former responds to the fact that since 1854, the United States has uninterruptedly been a Pacific naval power.

It might well be that for a millennia-old nation such as China, an American presence in the area that dates back to 1852 is tantamount to the ephemeral flight for a tree leaf. For the U.S., however, this represents a consistency of purpose held for more than half of its independent history, a purpose for which they were ready to sacrifice countless American lives in four major wars.

International credibility is also involved. Should the U.S. abdicate its leadership in East Asia, a snowball effect would follow, affecting its superpower status all over the world. This is something no world power would willingly accept. Finally, there is the involvement of the argument on maritime free passage. The United States claims for itself and for others such rights in the South China Sea. This free passage would become seriously compromised if China's control of 90% of that sea materializes.

Oil transport has been one of China's major considerations in relation to the South China Sea. However, 80% of China's crude oil imports sail through that sea, as does more than 80% of the crude oil imported by Japan, South Korea and Taiwan.[15]

Hence, if controlling that area becomes an existential need for China, maintaining the guarantee of maritime free passage becomes equally existential for Japan, South Korea and Taiwan. America's leadership is thus committed to preserve the area as "maritime commons" and to avoid the abuse of a dominant position by China. Needless to say, for many countries in that region, America's balancing role is perceived as being fundamental. As a consequence, China is involved in a collision course with the United States as well.

XI JINPING'S VISION

Beijing's post-2008 muscular foreign policy clearly intensified after Xi Jinping's arrival to power. Under his leadership, China has become much more controlling, confident and assertive. Driven by its pride in millennia of glorious history and by its sheer size and huge population, the country seems determined to recover its leading role in Asia and all over the world.

As Chairman Xi explained at a speech delivered at the 19th Communist Party Congress held in October 2017: "Rooted in a land of more than 9.6 million square kilometers, nourished by a nation's culture of more than 5,000 years, and backed by the invincible force of more than 1.3 billion people, we have an infinitely vast stage of our era, a historical heritage of unmatched depth, and incomparable resolve that enable us to forge ahead…".[16]

Xi's vision of China as a superpower has become more unequivocal and blunter, as the challenge to the United States has become more straightforward. Jonathan D.T. Ward explains: "From outer space to the deep sea, from Africa to the Artic, from artificial

---

[15] Office of the Secretary of Defense, "Annual Report to Congress: Military and Security Developments Involving the People's Republic of China 2018", p. 49, https://www.hsdl.org/?abstract&did=814130. Accessed March 15, 2019.

[16] Full text of Xi Jinping's report at the 19th National Congress, Xinhua, November 3, 2017, http://www.xinhuanet.com/english/special/2017-11/03/c_136725942.htm, Accessed July 11, 2019.

intelligence to hypersonic missiles that can 'kill' American aircraft carriers, the Chinese Communist Party has mobilized its country to become the global leaders in virtually every form of economic, military, technological, and diplomatic activity on earth".[17] As a result, not only have the issues mentioned above gotten hotter but numerous additional contending elements have arisen as well.

Deng's maxims of hiding the capacities and biding for time while not claiming leadership have definitely become a matter of the past. Xi has advocated *fenfa youwei* or "striving for achievement". This translates into active calls for greater leadership in world affairs, while asserting China's footprint in its own region. As argued, this can simply mean that according to Xi's calculations it is time to act, as China is now powerful enough, its economy big enough, its neighbors dependent enough and the military resolve of the U.S. uncertain enough.[18]

Not surprisingly, his faith in the country's capacities and the sense of entitlement for China to have a leadership position have been brought to the fore, as can be seen from the following views: "Mr. Xi assumed power when China was still riding high on its so-called economic miracle (and the United States remained mired in the after effects of the 2008–9 recession) … But Mr. Xi has been aggressively hard-liner. Under him, anti-American rhetoric has spread in official media. The Chinese government has been explicit about wanting to challenge the United States' military presence in Asia. It has made aggressive moves toward Taiwan and in the South China Sea. It has sent Chinese battleships through American waters off the coast of Alaska … These efforts have set off alarms … Mr. Xi may have challenged the global leadership of the United States too hard and too soon".[19]

---

[17] Jonathan D.T. Ward, *China's Vision of Victory and Why America Must Win* [Kindle version], Washington, D.C.: The Atlas Publishing and Media Company, 2019, retrieved from Amazon.com , location 266/6589.

[18] Hugh White, Mary Kay Magistad, and Zha Daojiong, It is time for America to consider accommodation with China, *Foreign Policy*, 2015.

[19] Yi-Zheng Lian, Xi Jinping Wanted Global Dominance. He Overshot, *The New York Times*, May 7, 2019.

A WAVE OF NATIONALISM

The current wave of nationalism is indeed forceful. Michael Pillsbury, whose knowledge of China dates back to Kissinger's first trip to Beijing, has assessed the current political climate in that country in the following terms: "I now see the hawks as mainstream. The moderates sometimes seem to defer quietly to the hawks ...".[20]

Earlier in 2017, China published its first-ever white paper on "China's Policies on Asia-Pacific Cooperation", in which it made clear its intention of establishing itself as the dominant power in Asia while dislodging the United States. The maps of the region that the Chinese now print show almost the whole of the South China Sea as theirs. Since 2014, China has "reclaimed" more than 3,000 acres of the sea in its seven Spratly Islands reefs. It has equally deployed in them intermediate-range missiles in massive numbers, as well as other modern military equipment, while it has been building military infrastructure that include an airfield on Fiery Cross Island. It has also deployed huge numbers of missile batteries as well as tactical fighters to the disputed Woody Islands in the Paracel Archipelago. In 2014, it expanded a preexistent air base there. Many of these advanced missiles are designed to attack aircraft carriers and the bases that form the backbone of U.S. military dominance in the region.[21]

In the next few years, the country is expected to have 75 submarines, instruments of sheer aggression by definition, outpacing the United States in that area. Meanwhile, by 2021, they are expected to

---

[20] Michael Pillsbury, *The Hundred Year Marathon: China's Secret Strategy to Replace America as the Global Superpower. New York, NY: Henry Holt and Company*, location 640/7620.

[21] Timothy R. Heath, Trump's national security strategy ratchets UP U.S. competition with China, *World Politics Review*, 2017, https://www.worldpoliticsreview.com/articles/23889/trump-s-national-security-strategy-ratchets-up-u-s-competition-with-china. Accessed November 12, 2018; Robert D. Kaplan, *op. cit.*, p. 34; Michael Fabey, *Crashback: The Power Clash Between the U.S. and China in the Pacific* [Kindle version], New York: Scribner, 2018, retrieved from Amazon.com. pp. 228–229; Michael Martina, China warns of countermeasures if U.S. puts missiles on its 'doorstep', *Reuters*, 2019, https://www.reuters.com/article/us-china-usa-defence/china-warns-of-countermeasures-if-u-s-puts-missiles-on-its-doorstep-idUSKCN1UW044. Accessed August 6, 2019.

have three aircraft carriers that are equipment of national prestige and expressions of a "sea control navy". Since 2014, China has launched more submarines, warships and other vessels that the total number of ships currently serving in the combined navies of Germany, India, Spain, Taiwan and the United Kingdom. At the same time, China went from 50 fourth-generation aircrafts in 2000 to 500, while it is engaged in the most active land-based ballistic and cruise missile program in the world. This includes long-range land attack and anti-ship cruise missiles, with some of them capable of reaching supersonic speeds, operated from ground, air, ship and submarine platforms. China is also working on a bomber with a nuclear mission, which would give Beijing a nuclear triad of land-, air- and sea-based nuclear weapon systems. But in addition to its military buildup, China opened the road to overseas military bases when, in August 2017, the PLA's Djibouty Support Base in the Horn of Africa entered into service. The base includes equipment for the maintenance of four task groups.[22]

Currently, China's military expenditure is the second largest in the world, having increased it in 2018 by 8% compared to 2017 and by 7.5% in 2019 compared to the previous year. Its spending in 2018 reached US$250 billion, which represented 14% of the world's military spending.[23] This is supplemented by technological investments in sectors with clear warfare capacity, such as space-based or oceanic developments,

---

[22] Robert D. Kaplan, *op. cit.*, pp. 35, 36 and 38; Tim Marshall, *op. cit.*, p. 53, 59; James Reini, News.com.au, March 7, 2018, Pentagon Official Warns China is an Even Bigger Threat Than We Thought, https://www.foxnews.com/tech/pentagon-official-warns-china-is-an-even-bigger-threat-than-we-thought. Accessed May 21, 2019; The State Council Information Office of the People's Republic of China, "China's National Defense in the New Era", July 2019, http://www.xinhuanet.com/english/2019-07/24/c_138253389.htm. Accessed August 10, 2019.

[23] Stockholm International Peace Research Institute, World military expenditure grows to $1.8 trillion in 2018, April 29, 2019, https://www.sipri.org/media/press-release/2019/world-military-expenditure-grows-18-trillion-2018. Accessed May 21, 2019; *Clarin,* China aumenta su presupuesto militar: Este este año serán 17.500 millones de dólares, May 3, 2019, https://www.clarin.com/mundo/china-aumenta-presupuesto-militar-ano-175000-millones-dolares_0_rJHRlJsOM.html. Accessed July 15, 2019.

artificial intelligence, robotics or quantum communications. The latter also includes private investments in the aforementioned areas, as according to the recent policy of "Civic Military Fusion", the Chinese Communist Party demands that "new technologies developed by the private sector must be shared by the military".[24]

CHINA'S RESURRECTION

Xi Jinping aims at China's "resurrection", which translates into converging strategies like the "China Dream of National Rejuvenation" or "Made in China 2025". The first pursues a powerful and prosperous China, the expansion of the country's geopolitical footprint, a focus on military power and military technology and the change of China's strategic geography.[25] "Made in China 2025", on its part, aims at turning China into a world leader in science, technology and innovation by the mid-21st century. All these objectives have become a direct challenge to the supremacy of the United States.

At the end of all this process lies the vision of 2049, a date that will mark the 100th anniversary of the founding of the People's Republic of China. In the 19th Party Congress Report, the CCP's most authoritative strategy document, released in 2017, China articulated for the first time, in 2017, its ambition to contend for global leadership. It stated that in 2049, China seeks to have "become a global leader in terms of composite national strength and international influence".[26] What remains unclear, still, is how large a role does China aspire to have within that vision.

Jerry Hendrix frames the situation well when writing: "Does it wish to join the family of nations as a co-equal power in the current globalized order operating under accepted international laws? Does it wish to become a great power with a sphere of influence in Eastern

---

[24] Kathrin H. Richard, Washington unnerved by China's 'military-civil fusion, *Financial Times*, https://www.ft.com/content/8dcb534c-dbaf-11e8-9f04-38d397e6661c. Accessed May 15, 2019.

[25] Graham Allison, *Destined for War: Can America and China Escape Thucydides' Trap* [Kindle version], Boston: Mariner Books, 2018, retrieved from Amazon.com, p. 109.

[26] Timothy R. Heath, *op. cit.*

Asia and in the Western Pacific as the imperial European powers divided up the globe for most of the 19th century? Or, perhaps most ominously, does China wish to reassert itself globally in the manner of its cultural vision of itself as the Middle Kingdom, establishing hegemonic suzerain and supplicant relationships with all nations …?".[27]

The latter would be, indeed, the most worrisome option. That is, China is aiming to reclaim the place it has envisioned for itself during most of the recorded history. In other words, a revival of its Middle Kingdom mentality with the country becoming the geographical and political center of the world. Within this vision, China rises within a stable system of nations, with the final intention of undermining and completely transforming such a system. The possibility of that being China's aim has sufficiently raised the alarm bells for the United States.

Mark Leonard adds to this worrying perception. Referring to the ancient Chinese difference between the "Wang" and the "Ba", he says: "The 'Wang' system was centered around a dominant superpower, but its primacy was based on benign government rather than coercion or territorial expansion. The 'Ba' system, on the other hand, was a classic 'hegemonic' system, where the most powerful nation imposed order in its periphery through force". Inside Chinese Asia, as Leonard explains, the "Wang" prevailed, but when dealing with "barbarians", the "Ba" system was enforced.[28] Back in 1972, as Kissinger reported, Prime Minister Zhou Enlai had referred to the United States as the "Ba", which shows that these ancient concepts are undoubtedly a part of the Chinese contemporary mind-set.

CHINA'S OVERSIZED AMBITIONS

Xi Jinping's projects and words have done little to lessen the fears in relation to these oversized ambitions. As China's strategic aims have

---

[27] Leveraging History: What Britain's Decline and America's Rise Can Tell Us about China's Future, Center for a New American Security, 2017, https://www.cnas.org/publications/reports/leveraging-history. Accessed July 17, 2019.
[28] Mark Leonard, *op. cit.*, p. 112.

evolved into the open, the idea of its emergence as the future geographical and political center of the world has also gained ground. In addition to the countdown toward world economic dominance, three major Chinese strategies are fueling that perception. The first one is the Belt and Road Initiative, which pursues an integrated Asian–Australian–African–European transcontinental superstructure (both physical and digital), that would have China as its epicenter. The second one is "Made in China 2025", which envisages China's global dominance in key strategic sectors, mainly in a broad range of cutting-edge technologies. The third strategy is military modernization, where China's armed forces aim at becoming "second to none". Winning the space strategic competition, which would be a corollary to points two and three, has also been considered within this context.

The nature of China's rise, with its aspiration to achieve the superpower status, is also unclear. Here, the record is mixed. On the one hand, as Martin Jacques outlines, during the 500 years up to the middle of the 19th century, China fought only one war with another country: Vietnam. A war that it lost.[29] Hence, its peaceful tradition seems to speak for itself. China was until that moment arrogant but not bellicose. However, since the arrival of the CCP regime to power, China has fought three wars: with the United States and the U.N. forces in South Korea during the 1950s, with India in the 1960s and with Vietnam in the 1970s. Moreover, during the 1960s and 1970s, it remained at the brink of a major war with the Soviet Union. So, what would China's rise to the center stage entail? Is it the peaceful nature described by Martin Jacques or the military assertiveness that has prevailed since 1949?

Here, as well, Xi Jinping has done little to reduce the fears. His words have at times been overtly ominous, generating the perception that China is ready to fight its way ahead if necessary. This goes from his "Preparing for war and combat" to "The Chinese people

---

[29]What China will be as a great power: Martin Jacques, *China Plus*, 2019, http://chinaplus.cri.cn/opinion/opedblog/23/20190507/285780.html. Accessed August 14, 2019.

have been indomitable and persistent, we have the spirit of fighting the bloody battle against our enemies to the bitter end" and to his equally frightening "All must be done with the ultimate goal of improving battle command capacities measured by the standards of being able to fight and win wars".[30]

Brookings summarizes the situation as follows: "It was likely inevitable as China's economic growth gave it global interests, but the shift in tone under Xi has been marked ... Xi has been aggressive, perhaps reckless. Much of the foundation for this was laid under Hu, but Xi accelerated the timeline and sharpened the edges — and in doing so put paid to residual hopes of China's 'peaceful rise'".[31]

---

[30] Is a USChina war in Asia inevitable?, *AlJazeera*, October 28, 2018, https://www.aljazeera.com/news/2018/10/china-war-asia-inevitable-181029195111603.html. Accessed May 21, 2019; Jonathan D.T. Ward, *op. cit.*, locations 1069/6589 and 1128/6589.

[31] Bruce Jones, Brookings, The era of U.S.–China cooperation is drawing to a close: What comes next?, 2019, https://www.brookings.edu/blog/order-from-chaos/2019/01/07/the-era-of-u-s-china-cooperation-is-drawing-to-a-close-what-comes-next/. Accessed May 22, 2019.

Chapter Three

SAILING AGAINST THE WIND

In James A. Lewis words, "Preoccupied with their misadventures in the Middle East and bemused by optimistic Western views of the direction China's economy and politics would take …", the United States did not pay much attention to China and allowed it ample room for maneuver.[1]

Actually, as Hugh White remarks: "Most people believed that America's place at the head of the global order had become unchallengeable. Under US leadership, the core of the global system had entered a long and perhaps permanent era of stability, and the only threats to global order and US leadership would come from weaker players at the periphery system — such as failing states, rogue states and terrorists".[2] Washington had not even realized that it was in the middle of a contest with China, when it was suddenly taken aback by that country's post-2008 assertiveness.

PIVOT TO ASIA

America's response to China's new developments would take some time in arriving. Its first expression was a landmark article published

[1]James A. Lewis, Technological Competition and China, Center for Strategic & International Studies, CSIS, November 2018, https://www.csis.org/analysis/technological-competition-and-china. Accessed January 10, 2019.
[2] *Op. cit.*, p. 26.

in autumn 2011, by Obama's Secretary of State, Hillary Clinton. The article stated that the U.S. stood at a "pivot point", which critically demanded a fundamental reorientation of its foreign policy. As Asia had become "the key driver of world politics", it was therefore necessary to "sustain our leadership, secure our interests, and advance our values" in that part of the world. To such an end, it became fundamental for the United States to make "similar investments as a Pacific power", like the ones it had made in Europe as a result of its post-World II commitments. That implied building a comprehensive and lasting network of institutions and relationships, engaging with regional multilateral institutions, expanding trade and investments, forging a broad-based military presence and advancing democracy and human rights.[3]

This purpose not only represented a comeback to East Asia as a priority focus of U.S. foreign policy. The policy therein outlined became known as America's "pivot to Asia". According to Jude Woodward: "With this policy shift, the US was declaring that 'the US would not sit aside as China ... established itself as regional leader'".[4] The Obama Administration's pivot took shape through an Asia-Pacific security and prosperity area for the 21st century.

Two broad aims supported this project. The first was to seek sustainable regional security by rebalancing China's emergence. This, would be achieved by the coming together of the United States and its traditional allies in the area and by way of military deployments. The second objective was to promote what President Obama called "our shared prosperity", the aim of which was an increased and improved trans-Pacific trade and economic liberalization agreement. This agreement was the so called Trans-Pacific Partnership (TPP). This double-aimed pivot was described by Hugh White, as "America's most ambitious new strategic doctrine since Truman

[3] Hillary Clinton, America's Pacific Century, *Foreign Policy*, October 11, 2011, https://foreignpolicy.com/2011/10/11/americas-pacific-century/. Accessed May 22, 2019.
[4] Jude Woodward (2017). *The US vs China: Asia's New Cold War. Manchester, UK: Manchester University Press.*, location 218/9348.

committed America to contain the Soviet Union".[5] The merit of this assertion was calling things by their true name. More than a simple "rebalancing", the new policy implied a clear containment of China.

CONTAINING CHINA

On the security side, the majority of U.S. naval resources were shifted from the Atlantic to the Pacific. This implied basing 60% of nuclear and high-tech naval vessels in the Pacific, including at least six aircraft carriers. It also included plans to surround China with stealth planes — B-2 bombers as well as F-22 and F-35 fighter planes. At the same time, its bases in the region expanded in size, particularly in South Korea, while a new base was opened in Darwin, Australia. Finally, its allies, particularly Japan, were encouraged to rearm.[6] On the other hand, the U.S. Navy challenged China's so-called "excessive maritime claims" in the South China Sea, preserving access to waterways "governed by international law", while the U.S. Air Force challenged the "Air Identification Zone" over the East China Sea.

Obama's key economic counter to China was the TPP, a 12-country comprehensive Free Trade Agreement that implicitly excluded China. This, basically through its provision that state-owned companies represented unfair competition. The TPP aimed at including most of China's Pacific neighbors in an economic integration mechanism with the U.S., hence reducing China's economic clout over them. If ever Beijing decided to join the TPP, it would have to be at the price of dismantling its state-run economy, which for all practical purposes represented a veto to its participation. This led some China analysts to describe the TPP as an "economic NATO".[7]

But besides offering an option to China's economic might in the region, the Obama Administration did its best to curtail Beijing's economic projection. That was the case in relation to the Asian

[5] Hugh White, Contain China?, *The Straits Times*, November 26, 2011.

[6] Jude Woodward, *op. cit.*, locations 174/9348, 439/9348 and 446/9348.

[7] Jude Woodward, *Ibid.*, location 407/9348.

Infrastructure Investment Bank (AIIB), a multilateral development bank aimed at supporting the building of infrastructures in the Asia-Pacific region. This initiative was proposed by China in 2013 and its formal launching took place in Beijing in October 2014. Since its inception, the United States opposed the project and tried to prevent its main European and Asian allies from participating in it. The simple fact that China could attain a high degree of financial influence in the fastest growing region of the planet was seen as a threat by Washington.

The boycott's fortune, however, fell together with the first domino piece that did not buckle under the U.S.' pressure: the United Kingdom. As soon as London decided to be a founding member of AIIB, the rest of the domino row followed: Germany, France, Italy, the Netherlands, Switzerland, Spain, Australia, New Zealand, South Korea, etc. Washington's opposition proved to be insufficient against the opportunities offered by China's initiative.

TRUMP'S WITHDRAWAL OF TPP

Donald Trump's arrival to the White House brought some changes to his predecessor's pivot, albeit of a contradictory nature. In real terms, though, his policy essentially represented a continuation of the one launched by Obama's Administration. Indeed, containment then became its main element. Trump began with a symbolic gesture — the acceptance of a congratulatory phone call from Taiwan's President shortly after the election victory. From a protocol point of view, this implied that the U.S. was giving her an equal status with that of the President Elect. This was followed by a series of appointments of hardline anti-China officials in key positions, chiefly that of Peter Navarro as Director of the White House National Trade Council. However, Trump's first act in the White House was to withdraw his country from TPP.

As a result of withdrawal from the TPP, Obama's "shared prosperity" approach suddenly disappeared from the equation. Henceforward, there would be just be the security leg to contain China's emergence. This one leg seemed clearly insufficient to fulfil that role, as many countries of the region would be ready to accept a certain degree of "Finlandization", if China remained as their only available economic option.

As it happened, TPP moved to completion with its 11 remaining members. But instead of becoming a counterbalance to China, as envisaged by President Obama, TPP has become an economic counterbalance to President Trump's protectionism. Indeed: "A trade act originally conceived by the United States to counter China's growing economic might in Asia now has a new target: President Trump's embrace of protectionism".[8]

Both China and TPP members now have, as a common denominator, the rejection of Washington's protectionism. As Professor Jeffrey Wilson, head of the U.S.–Asia Center at the University of Western Australia, expressed: "If you're a trade policy maker in Asia, your number one fear is that Trump is going to take a swing at you … The U.S. is really delivering the region to China at the moment".[9] Meanwhile, Indonesia, South Korea, the Philippines, Taiwan and Thailand have expressed their interest in becoming members of TPP —[10] a TPP that is now beyond the reach of Washington's influence.

TRUMP'S OFFENSIVE

If that had been the end of the story, Trump would have helped China benefit at the expense of its own country's leverage in the region. However, he had more plans in store. On the one hand, the military containment process followed suit. Trump's team announced a major build-up in East Asia, including proposals to base a second aircraft carrier in the South China Sea, deploying additional submarines and destroyers and expanding or adding new bases in Japan

[8] Ernesto Londoño and Motoko Rich, U.S. Allies Sign Sweeping Trade Deal in Challenge to Trump, *The New York Times*, March 8, 2018.

[9] *Ibid.*

[10] Peter Pietri, Michael G. Plummer, Shujiro Urata, and Fan Zhai, Going It alone in the Asia-Pacific: Regional Trade Agreements Without the United States, Peterson Institute for International Economics, October 2017, https://papers.ssrn.com/sol3/papers.cfm?abstract_id=3047895. Accessed March 19, 2018.

and Australia. At the same time, there have been talks of installing long-range air force strike assets in South Korea.[11]

Meanwhile, the U.S. Air Force keeps routinely challenging China's "Air Defense Identification Zone" over the East China Sea, while its Navy follows ahead with "freedom of navigation patrols", in China's claimed areas in the South China Sea. Moreover, on repeated occasions, its warships have navigated also through the Taiwan Strait.[12]

But together with the military process in motion, the Trump Administration has sought to contain China by way of an ambitious trade war and by targeting some of China's high-tech companies, mainly Huawei. Although there may be legitimate security concerns involved in relation to the latter, Washington's intent on coercing China to abandon its industrial policies has no other explanation than economic containment itself. The constraint of China's trade with the U.S. by way of unattainable demands can have no other objective than burdening and slowing its economic growth.

President Trump has, indeed, taken a series of escalating measures against China. Since May 2019, the United States imposed 25% tariffs on US$250 billion worth of Chinese imports, while it later imposed a 10% tariff on the remaining US$300 billion. The result has been that, up to August 2019, 41% of American companies manufacturing in China have moved away or are planning to move away from that country.[13] Even more aggressively, at the end of the same month, Trump threatened to use executive powers to forbid American companies from doing business with China. Arguing that

---

[11] Jude Woodward, *op. cit.*, location 193/9348.

[12] Reuters, The US Navy again sails through Taiwan Strait, angering China, May 22, 2019, https://www.reuters.com/article/us-usa-china-navy/u-s-navy-again-sails-through-taiwan-strait-angering-china-idUSKCN1ST062. Accessed May 24, 2019; Reuters, US warships sails in disputed South China Seas amid trade tensions, May 19, 2019, https://www.reuters.com/article/us-usa-china-military/us-warship-sails-in-disputed-south-china-sea-amid-trade-tensions-idUSKCN1SQ067. Accessed May 24, 2019.

[13] Jodi Xu Klein, Trump tariffs haven't brought jobs back to the US, Inkstone, August 2, 2019, https://www.inkstonenews.com/business/trumps-tariffs-havent-brought-jobs-back-us/article/3021159. Accessed August 2, 2019.

the Emergency Economic Powers Act of 1977 entitled him to do so, he claimed that he had "the absolute right" to "order" U.S. companies to leave China.[14]

Washington's officials have maintained that the tariff issue is entirely disconnected from the national security concerns involved in the escalating measures against Huawei. However, it is difficult not to see them as part of an overall strategy. And this was especially so, as slowing Huawei's lead in the once-in-a-generation 5G technology would hinder China's supremacy in this strategic area. However, it is not only Huawei that has been targeted by Washington. Through different means, the Trump Administration is trying to stall China's innovation process.

PENCE'S REMARKS

Vice President Mike Pence delivered a speech at the Hudson Institute, in October 2018, that outlined the terms under which the Trump administration visualizes its relationship with China. His remarks defined a clear containment policy: "Under our administration, we've taken decisive action to respond to China with American leadership ... In the 'National Security Strategy' that President trump released last December, he described a new era of 'great competition'. Foreign nations have begun to 'reassert their influence regionally and globally', and they are 'contesting [America's] geopolitical advantages and trying to change the international order in their favor' ... Now, through the 'Made in China 2025" plan, the Communist Party has set its sights on controlling 90% of the world's most advanced industries, including robotics, biotechnology, and artificial intelligence ... China now spends as much on its military as the rest of Asia combined, and Beijing has prioritized capabilities to erode America's military advantages — on land, at sea, in the air,

[14]Veronica Stracqualursi, Trump claims he has 'absolute right' to order US companies out of China under 1977 law, CNN, August 24, 2019, https://www.cnn.com/2019/08/24/politics/trump-china-trade-war-emergency-economic-powers-act/index.html. Accessed August 25, 2019.

and in space. China wants nothing less than to push the United States from the Western Pacific and attempt to prevent us from coming to the aid of our allies … We've been making the strongest military in the history of the world, stronger still. Earlier this year, the President signed into law the largest increase in our national defense since the days of Ronald Reagan — $716 billion to extend our military dominance in every domain … And at President Trump's direction, we're also implementing tariffs on $250 billion of Chinese goods, with the highest tariffs specifically targeting the advanced industries that Beijing is trying to capture and control … The President will not back down — and the American people will not be swayed. We will continue to stand strong for our security and our economy … Our administration will continue to act decisively to protect American interests, American jobs, and American security. As we rebuild our military, we will continue to assert American interests across the Indo-Pacific. And to advance our vision of a free and open Indo-Pacific, we're building new and stronger bonds with nations that share our values, across the region … as we gather here, a new consensus is rising across America … China should know that the American people and their elected representatives in both parties are resolved …".[15]

According to Jude Woodward: "The core of the US strategy has been to encircle China with a compelling series of the facto or de jure military alliances with China's neighbours, encouraging and aiding their rearmament and ratcheting up local disputes with China so as to constrain and pressure it. The endgame is a pro-U.S. … noose around China that can be tightened to veto, punish, pressure or threaten China and narrow its options on a range of issues".[16]

The fact is that a consensus not seen since the rivalry with the Soviet Union has taken hold of the United States. As Fareed Zakaria

[15] Mike Pence, Vice President Mike Pence Remarks on the Administration Policy Towards China Hudson Institute, October 4, 2018, https://www.hudson.org/events/1610-vice-president-mike-pence-s-remarks-on-the-administration-s-policy-towards-china102018. Accessed March 1, 2019.

[16] Jude Woodward, *op. cit.*, location 470/9348.

points out: "A new consensus, encompassing both parties, the military establishment, and key elements of the media, hold that China is now a vital threat to the United States both economically and strategically, that U.S. policy toward China has failed, and that Washington needs a new, much tougher strategy to contain it. This consensus has shifted the public's stance towards an almost instinctive hostility".[17]

CHINA'S UNSOLVED PROBLEMS

It would seem that Deng's prescription of hiding capacities and biding for time were abandoned prematurely. On the same note, the *shi* signs may have been misread. Not only is China's dependence on the American market still substantial, but the country is in the midst of a difficult transition towards a consumption-driven growth economy. Many of China's huge domestic challenges still remain unsolved. Among them would be the debt trap, the demographic or aging trap and the middle-income trap. To these problems, additional ones of a chronic problem of misallocation of resources, huge environmental challenges and a looming housing bubble have to be added. Xi Jinping may have inherited a more prosperous economy but, at the same time, he also has on his shoulders a much more complex one.

What worked in the past no longer works under a mature economy, a circumstance that projects a higher degree of uncertainty to the current scenario. Just a few examples can attest to what has been mentioned earlier: China accounted for about half of all new credit created worldwide between 2005 and 2016, thus giving an idea of its gigantic debt; China cannot have high rates of economic growth and

---

[17]Fareed Zakaria, The New China Scare: Why America Shouldn't Panic About Its Latest Challenger, *Foreign Affairs*, December 6, 2019, https://www.foreignaffairs.com/articles/china/2019-12-06/new-china-scare?utm_source=Fareed%27s+Global+Briefing&utm_campaign=cf93a98758-EMAIL_CAMPAIGN_2019_12_06_09_05&utm_medium=email&utm_term=0_6f2e93382a-cf93a98758-101619633. Accessed December 7, 2019.

simultaneously reduce the risk of financial instability, which places it in a Catch-22 situation; the old-age dependency ratio is predicted to rise from 13%, today, to 25% in 2030 and to 47% by 2050, which shows the financial burden that a rapidly aging population will entail; by 2050, China will have nearly three times more senior citizens than children, giving new meaning to the phrase "getting old before getting rich"; in 2018 China's income per head reached around US$15,000–US$16,000, precisely the point at which standard measurements show that economic growth tends to decline.[18]

Then, there is the issue of chronic misallocation of resources, which ranges from the "ghost cities" to the "bridges to nowhere". Major ecological problems also come into the agenda, such as the air quality in large cities, where foggy miasmas and invisible pollutants seriously impact quality of life and life expectancy itself. On the other hand, Naoyuku Yoshino, CEO of the Asian Development Bank Institute, argues that China's economy is showing worrisome signs that are reminiscent of Japan's in the 1990s. China is, indeed, experiencing the beginning of a housing bubble, expressed through the astronomical surge in property prices.[19] Clearly, China has yet to overcome the period a high vulnerability. From every perspective, this did not seem to be the most auspicious moment for a frontal test of strength with the United States.

WHY NOT WAIT FOR THE RIPE FRUIT?

If, however, China manages this transitional period well, the auspices could not be better. The Unites States' share of the global GDP is 16%, but in the next three decades it is expected to decline to just 11%. Meanwhile, China's percentage of the global GDP should be

[18] George Magnus, *Red Flags: Why Xi's China is in Jeopardy* [Kindle version], New Haven: Yale University Press, 2018, Amazon.com, locations 1535/6073, 1907/6073, 2217/ 6073, 2343/6073, 2345/6073 and 2588/6073.

[19] Karen Yeung, China's economy looks like Japan's in the 1990's, and that's not good, Inkstone, May 28, 2019, https://www.inkstonenews.com/business/will-chinas-economy-sink-recession-japans-did-1990s/article/3012107. Accessed May 28, 2019.

reaching 30% in 2040.[20] Moreover, China is growing at more than twice the speed of the United States; if the current trends persist, China is expected to surpass the U.S. as the world's top economic power in absolute terms in 2030. From that point forward, the gap between them will keep increasing to China's benefit with every passing year.[21] Since China's economy is the foundation of its military buildup, its technological development and its global power, this gap will translate into a new correlation of power between the two countries.

Within that frame of reference, several questions come to mind: Was it wise for China to speed through times at a critical junction while boasting prematurely about its own capacities? Was it sensible to openly challenge America's sphere of influence in the Pacific, its technological lead and even its overall lead so early, when time was clearly playing on its favor? Would it not have been smarter to keep building its capabilities and overcoming its economic problems, while maintaining a lower profile as they did until 2008? Would China's influence in its own backyard not have increased much more efficiently if its neighbors had not felt threatened? Both Michael Pillsbury and Jonathan D.T. Ward have argued that China's objective was to secure its global power without awakening the United States, or awakening it only when it was far to late to react appropriately.[22] If that was indeed the Chinese aim, it would appear that they failed.

If the strategic value of waiting had been maintained for a longer period, while playing, in the meanwhile, a more ambiguous game, the ripe fruit would have fallen into its lap. For the United States, it would have probably been to late to provide an adequate response, while the Chinese accomplishments would have imposed their weight. As Yi-Zheng Lian wrote in *The New York Times*: "The Hu Jintao

---

[20] Graham Allison, Robert D. Blackwill, and Ali Wyne, Lee Kuan Yew: The Grand Master's Insights on China, the United States and the World, Cambridge, MA: MIT Press, 2013., location 178/8462.

[21] Jonathan D.T. Ward, *op. cit.*, locations 294/6589 and 300/6589.

[22] Michael Pillsbury, *op. cit.*; Jonathan D.T. Ward, *op. cit.*

years, saw China's most tactful exploitation of American openness (and naiveté). Cheap Chinese imports created runaway bilateral trade deficits for the United States. The Confucius Institutes, a network of language schools cum influence agencies, began to take root in American universities and high schools. (Today, there are more than 100 throughout the United States.) Chinese venture capitalists flooded Silicon Valley with money raised in American financial markets — then quietly siphoned off cutting-edge American expertise and injected it into China's own high-tech hub".[23]

STRATAGEMS OF THE WARRING STATES

During that period, China, indeed, had the unrestricted opportunity to penetrate U.S. universities, laboratories and companies, gaining access to technology that enhanced its power. Meanwhile, it benefited from an expanding market and huge American investments and technology transfers — all of this, and much more, while discretely strengthening and organizing its armed forces, transforming itself into a military asymmetric superpower, and steadily advancing from imitator to innovator in the technology field. To top of it all off, China was able to enjoy the rewards of its global soft power stardom, and the advantage of having the U.S.' attention focused elsewhere. Until 2008, China played this game masterfully. From 2008 to 2012, it still tried to keep playing this game, but did so awkwardly. From 2012 onwards, it abandoned the game altogether.

For a nation like China, which measures time in a completely different scale from the West, keeping this strategy in place for a couple of decades more should not have been too difficult a task. Judged by its own standards and having the classical teachings of the Warring States Period as a political guide, China's behavior seems to have been not just precipitated but even clumsy. Let us just remember what wise leaders, according to historian John Lewis Gaddis' reading of Sun Tzu, should seek to do: "They'll sail with winds, not against

[23]Yi-Zheng Lian, Xi Jinping Wanted Global Dominance. He Overshot, *The New York Times*, May 7, 2019.

them. They'll skirt swamps, not slog through them. They'll avoid battles until they're sure they can win them".[24]

Contrary to the assertions of Pillsbury and Ward, if something seems to have characterized the post-2008 period it is a straightforwardness that goes against the subtle cleverness normally associated with such an ancient civilization. According to the classical book *Stratagems of the Warring States*, still considered as a manual for statecraft in China, the biggest mistake that a rising leader can commit is to provoke a confrontation with his most powerful rival before the point of maximum opportunity had been attained. One good example of the kind of things that should have been avoided were the defiant overtones of China's Minister of Defense General, Wei Fenghe, at the IISS Shangri-La Dialogue Summit of June 2019, in Singapore.[25]

ACRIMONY

While the possibility of being involved in a "Thucydides Trap" situation looms in the air, a Cold War between China and the United States has clearly taken shape. An action–reaction dynamic is now firmly in place. The simple fact that COVID-19 has become a new opportunity for acrimony and mutual accusations, instead of being a convergent moment for the common good of humanity, speak volumes of their distancing. Having provoked U.S. response, Beijing feels now constrained and contained by it. As a civilization-state with millennia of glorious history, the highest population, and a gigantic landmass, China feels entitled to have its own sphere of influence and to play a leading role in the concert of nations. Americans, on their part, feel challenged geopolitically, technologically and militarily.

---

[24] John Lewis Gaddis, *On Grand Strategy* [Kindle version], London: Penguin Books, 2019, Amazon.com, p. 86.

[25] Banyan, America's vision for the Indo-Pacific gets lukewarm reception, *The Economist*, June 6, 2019, https://www.economist.com/asia/2019/06/06/americas-vision-for-the-indo-pacific-gets-a-lukewarm-reception?cid1=cust/dailypicks/n/bl/n/2019065n/owned/n/n/dailypicks/n/n/LA/250150/n. Accessed June 6, 2019.

Not only challenged but betrayed: betrayed by the assertive turn that the Chinese behavior took after 2008, which did not recognize all the support given to them since 1972; betrayed, because Washington's static perception of their agreement, akin to a sort of *status quo,* is in stark contrast to China's fluid sense of it; betrayed because the Americans' "we know best" attitude led them to believe that by helping China's economic success they were promoting at the same time a freer society and economy in tune with their own values.

Surely there must have been a reason for China to put in motion the necessity for such an acrimonious situation against a still formidable potential adversary, especially so as this contradicted all the teachings of Sun Tzu and those given in the *Stratagems of the Warring States.* Perhaps the reason has to be sought in the paradoxical relationship that exists between economic growth and nationalism.

TWO KINDS OF LEGITIMACY

Indeed, both economic growth and nationalism provide the CCP with two different kinds of legitimacy in relation to its own society. This forces the regime to play both cards at the same time. Economic growth, which is synonymous with globalization and by extension of access to the American market and investments, has brought great prosperity to China. This identifies itself with the Mandate of the Heavens, which is an ancestral formula according to which prosperity, order and peace show that the gods still extend their protection upon the rulers. Nationalism, on the other hand, identifies itself with the belief that China's ancient history and it's never surpassed tradition of centrality entitles the country to a position of privilege. Moreover, a century of humiliation by foreign powers imposes upon them the need to stand tall and hold their head up high. As a result, they project the prominence they consider themselves to be worthy of, not allowing adversaries to humiliate them ever again.

The CCP has to move, therefore, within the constraints that these two contradictory forces impose. It has to keep moving forward with economic growth and globalization, which has allowed

China to lift 800 hundred million people out of poverty, while transforming the country into the most commercially interconnected center of the world. Consequently, like a prestidigitator, it has to maintain this virtuous circle in continuous movement.

As Tim Marshall wrote: "The deal between the Party leaders and the people has been, for a generation now, 'We'll make you better off — you will follow our orders'. So long as the economy keeps growing, that bargain may last. If it stops, or goes in reverse, the deal is off. The current level of demonstrations and anger against corruption and inefficiency are testament to what would happen if the deal breaks".[26] The globalizing route thus became a fundamental part of this societal deal.

But at the same time, Beijing has to show its nationalist resolve. Portraying the current Chinese emergence against the backdrop of its century of humiliation, Robert D. Kaplan says: "There was a latent fear that 'China was about to be dismembered, that it would cease to exist as a nation, and that the four thousand years of its recorded history would come to a jolting end' … China, having survived that nightmare, and having reached a zenith of land power and territorial stability not seen since the Ming dynasty of the sixteenth century and the Qing dynasty of the late eighteenth century, is now about to press outward at sea … China's very urge for an expanded strategy space is a declaration that it never again intends to let foreigners take advantage of it, as they did in the previous two centuries".[27]

China's nationalist resolve, though, has caused countless problems for the country, increasing the cost of its actions manifold while unleashing a containment process by the United States. More than foreclosing its access to America's markets, investments and technology, Beijing seems to be giving arguments to U.S.' call for an anti-China coalition. The Mandate of the Heavens, thus, runs the risk of being overwhelmed by its nationalistic impulses.

---

[26] Tim Marshall, *Prisoners of Geography: The Maps that Tell You Everything You Need to Know About Global Politics. London, UK: Elliot and Thompson Limited,* 2015, p. 51.

[27] Robert D. Kaplan, *Asia's Cauldron: The South China Sea and the End of a Stable Pacific.* New York, NY: Random House, (2014), p. 21.

GRABBING WITH BOTH HANDS

However, what makes China so especial is the fact that, as mentioned before, globalization and nationalism are not seen as antithetical forces, as it happens in many places of Europe and the United States. On the contrary, they are seen as interdependent expressions of State policy, which converge in the aim of legitimizing the regime in the eyes of its citizens.

As a matter of fact, this dual policy has been conceptualized under the aphorism of "grabbing with both hands". According to Christopher R. Hughes: "The policy of 'grabbing with the two hands' may succeed in providing security for the CCP Party-state through a combination of economic growth and rising nationalist expectations. Yet this nationalism remains a 'two edged' instrument ... and also enhances tensions with neighbouring states. Whether or not the CCP can maintain the right balance between nationalism and globalisation thus presents an interesting case study ...".[28]

Chinese culture naturally includes the complementarity of opposites. This is exemplified by the duality of *yin* and *yang*— seemingly opposing forces that actually belong to the same Oneness. As such, this balance between its domestic audience and the international one, and between openness and closeness, may probably be seen as natural as well. Not so natural though is the daunting task of keeping the proper equilibrium between these hugely conflicting aims. One false step, one overreach, one overreaction, and the Mandate of the Heavens might be blown to pieces.

Also, the risk of a false step increases with popular pressure. As stated by the Council on Foreign Relations: "Beyond the party's control, the emergence of the Internet in the last two decades has given nationalists more power to vent their anger at particular incidents

[28] Christopher R. Hughes, Globalisation and nationalism: Squaring the circle in Chinese international relations theory, The London School of Economics and Political Sciences, LSE Research Online, March 2009, p. 23, http://eprints.lse.ac.uk/23038/1/Globalisation_and_nationalism%28LSERO%29.pdf. Accessed September 18, 2016.

… 'It makes it much easier for the nationalistic rhetoric', says Minxin Pei (a senior associate in the China program at the Carnegie Endowment for International Peace). He says the young, urban and educated Chinese are more nationalistic and they are the ones using Internet (…) Pei says nationalism is certainly an obstacle in China's image as a responsible stakeholder. 'A very nationalistic public makes foreigners very wary of China and harms China's image', he says'… The Chinese leaders also fear nationalism could turn against them in the form of criticism if they failed to deliver on the nationalistic promises. *New York Times* columnist Nicholas D. Kristoff writes: 'All this makes nationalism a particularly interesting force in China, given its potential not just for offering legitimacy to the government but also for taking it away'".[29]

There may be though an inherent strategic value for the CCP in limiting its own room for maneuver by overplaying the nationalist card. The reason for this is that their neighbors and interlocutors are thus warned that if they do not bend to China's will, the government may have no other choice than to take drastic action in support of its claim, as otherwise it would be faced with grave domestic instability.

The result of this emerging Cold War will be a zero-sum relation between the two biggest international powers, where the rules-based multilateral order, the globalized economy and the workable international order could end up being badly shaken, if not entirely destroyed.

THE FURY OF THE WESTERLY WINDS

Against this background the main question appears to be if, indeed, China challenged the United States too hard and too soon, and by doing so seriously affected its chances to attain its aims? This leads by implication to another question: Can Washington still contain China's ascendancy and maintain its current leading status?

---

[29]Jayshree Bajoria, Nationalism in China, Backgrounder, April 22, 2008, https://www.cfr.org/backgrounder/nationalism-china. Accessed June 6, 2018.

There seems to be no doubt that by speeding times, heralding their ambitions and boasting about their capabilities, while at the same time hardening their geopolitical and military stance, the Chinese have made their aims more difficult to attain. They have created for themselves many unnecessary problems and, instead of sailing with the winds as used to be the case, they are now sailing against them. By giving the United States an early warning regarding their intentions, they awoke the fury of the westerly winds (the ones that blow from West to East).

Again, did this come too early for the Chinese or, conversely, is it already too late for the Americans to reverse the Chinese ascendancy? For a country as obsessed as China is in continuously measuring its Comprehensive National Power, it would seem to be out of context to have provoked such a U.S. reaction if they have felt unprepared for a measurement of forces. Hence, weighing the comprehensive national power of both countries, through a balanced power profile, may be the best way to answer the above questions. In order to do so, we propose the following route: ascertaining how well they rank in six different aptitude categories. These will be the convergence aptitude, the mistakes avoidance aptitude, the universality aptitude, the military aptitude, the economic aptitude and the technological aptitude.

After measuring those six aptitudes, in the following pages, we may be able to attain a better understanding of the situation.

Chapter Four

THE CONVERGENCE APTITUDE

In the final phase of World War II or in its immediate aftermath, a network of multilateral organizations and alliances began to take shape under the auspices of the United States. Under Franklin D. Roosevelt, the Organization of the United Nations and the Bretton Woods institutions (the International Monetary Fund, the International Bank for Reconstruction and Development and the International Trade Organization) came to existence.

Under his successor Harry S. Truman, the General Agreement on Trade and Tariffs emerged as a successor to the shortly lived International Trade Organization, while the World Bank would come into formal existence. Also under Truman, a system of defensive alliances that linked the U.S. with different regions of the world took shape. The construction of this international institutional set of relationships would continue under Dwight D. Eisenhower and was consolidated in John F. Kennedy's time. The latter's administration would see the strengthening of the North Atlantic Treaty Organization (which had been created in 1949 as the North Atlantic Treaty) and the creation of the Organization for Economic Cooperation and Development (derived from the Organization for European Economic Cooperation, which had been created in 1948 to implement the Marshall Plan).

AMERICA'S HEGEMONY

A sophisticated multilateral system was therein structured under the stewardship of Washington. Although the United Nations Organization would follow its own course, especially with the Cold War and the decolonization process, other organizations and mechanisms would essentially remain under the United States' umbrella. Such was the case for World Bank, the President of which has to be an American citizen and whose appointment remains in the hand of the White House, or the International Monetary Fund, where the U.S. is the only country that enjoys of a veto power.

On the other side of the spectrum, of course, the Soviet bloc established its own system of alliances and institutions. Although much smaller in size and scope, the latter imposed limits on and created challenges to the United States. At the same time, Washington and Moscow had a negative correlation of forces within the Security Council of the U.N., resulting from their respective veto powers. However, this duality just strengthened America's control over the broad sphere where it exercised hegemony.

The first years of the 1970s put that hegemony in jeopardy. Not only did U.S.' failure in Vietnam erode its international credibility, but the end of the gold-dollar parity that resulted in the fluctuation of the dollar called into question the Bretton Woods structure. However, the lack of alternatives to the U.S. hegemony within the Western World made its military failure inconsequential. Meanwhile, the debt crisis that emerged a couple of decades later with the fall of the Soviet Union and within the developing world allowed for a relaunching of the Bretton Woods structure.

With the collapse of the Soviet bloc, the whole community of nations had to find a rearrangement under the American hegemony, which henceforward became global. As a result, Francis Fukuyama would proclaim the homogenization of the world under a set of values of universal acceptance. According to him, the defeat of rival ideologies to liberalism implied the end of historical contradictions and a final point in the ideological evolution of humanity. As a consequence, liberalism was to be the "final form of government" and, as such, the "end of history".[1] Rhetorical overtones aside, Fukuyama's assessment contained many hints of truth. The Washington Consensus was a good example of the new prevailing ideological truth.

McWORLD

George H.W. Bush not only adroitly navigated the sea of economic liberalism, by launching far-reaching multilateral initiatives, but also set in motion new precepts in matters of collective security. Six months after the collapse of the USSR, 34 of America's brightest foreign policy strategists gathered at Stanford University with the aim of developing "a new organizing principle for thinking about the world and how to act in it". Their objective was to replace the Cold War doctrine of containment and deterrence, with new guidelines for a post-Cold War era. A new guiding principle was born out of this effort: To build a regime of "co-operative security". This meant building trust between nations through transparency and mutual surveillance.[2] George H. W. Bush's handling of the Kuwait invasion followed this multilateral approach to international security.

Clinton's arrival to the White House allowed further refinement of America's hegemony. His understanding of the significance of "soft power", which in Joseph S. Nye's terms co-opts instead of coerces, made that possible.[3] He not only adhered to co-operative security but followed multilateral cooperation as the basic route map for international affairs, whether of political or economic nature. Moreover, a globalization process that expressed itself under American symbols and habits reinforced the U.S.' hegemony. McWorld reigned unchallenged.

---

[1] Francis Fukuyama, The End of History?, *The National Interest*, Washington D.C., Summer 1989.

[2] Mark Leonard, What Does China Think?, New York: HarperCollins, 2008, p. 99.

[3] Joseph S. Nye Jr., *The Paradox of American Power*, Oxford: Oxford University Press, 2002.

The new millennium thus arrived under a set of global rules and an ideological consistency that had no parallel in history. Within this frame, the United States could be a discreet but incontestable power. Washington could, as a result, open the domestic markets of countless countries to its manufactures, investments and services in an indirect but inescapable way. The policies of the IMF or the World Bank, under its control and ideological guidance, allowed it to do so.

Indeed, after the fall of the Berlin Wall, a new pattern of international credibility had emerged — one in which following the prevailing ideological traits became the only way to be taken seriously. Deviating from them not only implied a loss of credibility but could also lead to a form of ostracism from the world's power centers and institutions. Whoever dared to question the legitimacy of the ruling order was inviting its own de-legitimation. Ideology, and not force, was the tool through which the United States attained this pinnacle of power. As Fareed Zakaria has argued, the U.S. hegemony in the post Cold-War era was like nothing the world had seen since the Roman Empire.[4]

DEFYING COMMON SENSE

Inexplicable under the light of common sense, George W. Bush's Administration arrived in government wanting to turn such a state of things upside down. That implied leaving behind a system which was not only designed to fit its country's image and likeness, but which had served it exceedingly well. In this manner, the newcomers began to disarticulate, precisely at the moment when it had reached its apex, a complex hegemonic structure that had taken decades to build.

As a result, they proclaimed the futility of multilateral cooperation, which in their eyes constrained the freedom of action to which American power was entitled. They set, directly and brutally, the

---

[4] Fareed Zakaria, The Self-Destruction of American Power: Washington Squandered the Unipolar Moment, *Foreign Affairs*, 2019, **98**(July/August).

prerogatives of the country's national interest. They made it clear that the overwhelming nature of U.S. power exempted it from compliance with international norms and rules.

A few examples come to mind. On numerous occasions before the 2003 invasion of Iraq, President Bush emphasized that even if such an invasion violated international law, "America will do what is necessary to ensure our national security … I will not wait on events, while danger gathers".[5] The Bush Administration not only showed that it was unconcerned by international law or by the United Nations rules but also refused to pay the fees owed to the Organization. Although home to just 5% of the world population, the U.S. was responsible for 25% of the global impact on the environment. However, the Bush Administration refused to adhere to the Kyoto Protocol, as that would have imposed restraints upon its sovereignty. For the same reason, it refused to submit to the International Court of Justice and pressured others to do the same when its soldiers were being accused of violating human rights in Iraq and Afghanistan. And examples like these go on and on. In sum, the United States was able to transit for free within the international system, benefiting from it but without assuming its cost.

Immersed in archaic notions of power, the Bush team abandoned the essence of hegemony. This, according to the classical definition by Antonio Gramsci, is based on the capacity to define the agenda and to determine the framework of the debate, which, by definition, implies consensual acceptance of others. In international relations, this requires the recognition by a substantial part of the community of nations of a prevailing set of rules and beliefs identified with the leading power. Hegemony demands, thus, that power be recognized as legitimate through ideological and cultural perception. Collective action becomes the best way to attain such legitimacy.[6]

---

[5] John Mearsheimer, Bound to Fail: The Rise and Fall of the Liberal International Order, *International Security*, 2019, **43**(4), https://www.mitpressjournals.org/doi/full/10.1162/isec_a_00342. Accessed May 5, 2019.

[6] David Fogacs, *Antonio Gramsci Reader*, London: Lawrence & Wishart, 2001.

UNDRESSING THE EMPEROR

The Bush Administration abandoned global values and cooperative multilateralism in pursuit of egoistic national interest and militant unilateralism. Its world was one of "satellites" and not of allies, one of *ad hoc* coalitions and not of multilateral institutions, one of "with us or against us", one of punishment to dissidence and not of encouragement to cooperation, and one in which preventive action prevailed over international law. As leading neoconservative Charles Krauthammer wrote, those who opposed the power of the United States simply represented "an axis of petulance ... whose main problem is its irrelevance".[7]

Undoubtedly, September 11 had much to do with this attitude. However, this set of beliefs preceded Bush's arrival to power. The founding in 1997 of the think tank "Project for a New American Century" had given expression to this wave of American *hubris*. Many of its founders, which included Cheney, Rumsfeld and Wolfowitz, would become central figures within the new Administration. Neoconservatives were, indeed, ready for action. Krauthammer's "unipolar moment", had been awaiting its opportunity since 1990.

Global governance was thus badly shaken, taking away from the United States the mechanisms that allowed it to control that process. Inexplicably, Washington disassociated power from the international structures that facilitated and legitimized its exercise. Neoconservatives named themselves "Democratic imperialists" so as to be unambiguously associated to hard power. The result being that, from representing the most successful hegemonic power ever, the United States moved into becoming a pitiful imperial power, incapable of prevailing in two peripheral wars. Neoconservatives undressed the Emperor, making it possible for everyone to witness his sorry frailty. The Chinese, as we saw in Chapter 2, took good note of this.

The Pew Global Attitudes Project 2004 formulated the following question at an international level: "Does the United States take into

[7] Charles Krauthammer, The axis of petulance, *Washington Post*, March 1, 2002.

consideration the interest of others"? It came as a surprise how many countries considered as good friend of the Unites States came back with a high percentage of negative replies: France, 84%; Germany, 64%; Turkey, 79%; Jordan, 77%; Morocco, 57%.[8]

The BBC World Service and Global Poll Research Partners conducted another global poll in January 19, 2005, asking the question "How do you perceive the influence of the U.S. in the world?". Amid Washington's closest allies, the question received a negative answer, with the following percentages: Germany, 54%; Canada, 60%; Mexico, 57%; Australia, 52%; Brazil, 51%; United Kingdom 50%.[9]

Again, in March 2007, the BBC World Service conducted another poll on the same subject, this time in partnership with GlobeScan. According to this poll, traditional close friends of United States had the following negative perceptions of that country: United Kingdom, 57%; Germany, 69%; France, 69%; Portugal, 55%; Greece, 69%; Egypt, 59%; United Arab Emirates, 57%, South Korea, 54%; Indonesia, 71%; Australia, 60%; Mexico, 53%; Brazil 57%; Argentina 64%; Chile, 51%.[10]

It is obvious that with such a negative perception of the U.S. among its closest allies, hegemony had no ground on which to stand. All the goodwill towards that country and a friendly international institutional architecture had been tested to their limits. Had this trend continued, Washington would have become a very lonely power — sufficiently powerful as a force to be reckoned with, but insufficiently so as to be followed as a leader.

TRYING TO REGAIN THE LOST GROUND

Fortunately for the United States, the next tenant of the White House, Barack Obama, was ready to move in a totally different direction. Times had changed though. Both China and Russia had taken

---

[8] Alfredo T. Hardy, *Hegemonía e Imperio*, Bogotá: Villegas Editores, 2007, p. 59.

[9] Stephen Walt, *Taming American Power* New York: W.W. Norton and Company, 2005, p. 72.

[10] *Time*, March 26, 2007.

their own course and were ready to challenge Washington's leadership in their own spheres. This was compounded by the huge financial crisis with which Obama inaugurated his term in office and which clouded America's claim for undisputed primacy even more.

Moreover, China, whose economy had taken a huge jump during those past eight years, was strategically positioning itself in areas that hitherto had been essentially a United States preserve. Hence, to the U.S.' loss of hegemonic standing a new factor had to be added: a Chinese economic influence coming out of the blue in many parts of the world. Latin America was a good example of this.

In Kevin P. Gallager and Roberto Porzecanski words: "In the recent boom, Latin America export growth, which was considerably faster than GDP growth, was being driven by a commodities boom. Indeed, 70 percent of the growth of Latin America was due to the growth in commodities exports, and commodities exports comprised 70 percent of all Latin American countries' growth. China had both indirect and direct effects in this trend. Directly, Latin American countries exports to China have increased 370 percent since 2000 ... Indirectly, Chinese consumption of global commodities was making them scarcer and boosting global prices ...".[11]

As a result, growth rates soared in countries that represented 69% of Latin America's GDP, which were precisely those increasingly connected with China or dependent on commodities. Between 2004 and 2007, regional growth was more than 5%.[12] This state of affairs generated a clear consequence: the pendulum of economic influence in many Latin American countries began to shift from the United States to China. Indeed, "China could be said to have jumped the fence into the United States' backyard in an attempt to capitalize on the impressive inventory of natural resources that the region has to offer".[13]

---

[11] Kevin P. Gallager and Roberto Porzecanski, *The Dragon in the Room*, Stanford: Stanford University Press, 2010, p. 37.

[12] World Bank, *Latin America and the Caribbean's Long Term Growth: Made in China?*, Washington D.C.: September 2011.

[13] Lauren Paverman, China looks to Venezuela for energy security, *Worldpress.org*, October 11, 2011, https://www.worldpress.org/Americas/3820.cfm. Accessed June 25, 2012.

PINK TIDE

The political consequence resulting from this economic change was clear: It provided a previously unknown liberty of action to Latin America. Not surprisingly, the pink tide covered most of the region during those years. Moreover, the United States leadership was challenged to the bones in its own backyard, as the case of Hugo Chávez in Venezuela made it very clear. But more than simply Chávez, a whole array of Latin American governments contested the U.S.' primacy in the region, putting an end to the extension of the Free Trade Agreement of the Americas, which had begun in 1994.

This in itself was a remarkable turn of events in the history of the relationship between Latin America and the United States. After all, one of the reasons, besides isolationism, that after World War I had stopped Washington from accepting the collective security the League of Nations represented was precisely because it collided with its control over Latin America, as expressed by the Monroe Doctrine.[14] That would have undoubtedly created serious problems for the United States. Indeed, since 1903 (when it propitiated the separation of Panama from Colombia) and for the next three decades, the U.S. invaded the Caribbean Basin countries 34 times in order to impose its will upon them. Needless to add that after World War II, and for many decades, Latin America kept being seen by Washington as its undisputed fief.

So, both the fact that China had "jumped the fence into the United States' backyard", and the fact that many of the countries of that "backyard" felt empowered to assert their freedom of action in such a direct and even confrontational manner, was unprecedented. Would this have happened if the Emperor hadn't been shown to be naked? Probably not. Naked and, of course, also distracted. Latin America's case illustrates well how the eight years of the Bush Administration had seriously eroded the U.S.' prestige and leadership.

---

[14] Henry H. Kissinger, Diplomacy. New York, NY: Simon & Schuster, 1994, p. 372.

OBAMA'S COURSE OF ACTION

Consequently, the challenge faced by Obama was immense. It was not possible to go back to a bygone era, when Washington had enjoyed an undisputed hegemony. But, at least, it seemed feasible to rebuild its leadership and standing in the international scene. In order to do so, Obama embarked his Administration on a dual course: one of cooperative multilateralism and collective action, and the other that prioritized America's presence where it was most needed.

In pursuit of the first action, Obama seemed to have followed Richard Hass' prescription on the nature of influence. According to Hass, power as an end in itself is not very helpful. What really counts is the possibility of turning that power into influence. In other words, power alone is simple potentiality, and the role of a successful foreign policy is to transform such potentiality into real influence.[15]

His role in the Paris Agreement on Climate Change, in the Joint Comprehensive Plan of Action in relation to Iran, in the newly created G20, in the OTAN summits, or in the summits of the Americas, among other instances, were good evidence of this perception. Without being overbearing, and maintaining a respectful attitude toward other countries' positions, he aimed at exerting a leading influence within a process of collective action.

The Paris Agreement and the Comprehensive Plan of Action, commonly known as the Iran Nuclear Deal, were perfect examples of cooperative multilateralism. The former was negotiated within the United Nations Framework Convention on Climate Change by its 196 state parties. However, Obama's active support of the negotiations and his cooperation with China became major factors in the convention's success that led to the Paris Agreement. In the latter, the U.S., jointly with the other four permanent members of the United Nations Security Council and the European Union, negotiated with Iran an agreement that limited the country's

---

[15] Richard Hass, The Politics of Power, *Harvard International Review*, Cambridge, MA, Summer 2005.

nuclear program. Although theoretically just one of the many parties involved, the U.S. played the leading role in the negotiations with Iran.

On the other hand, he clearly understood that the Asia-Pacific region needed to go back to being a priority. China had benefited from the U.S.' lack of attention that prevailed during the Bush years, asserting its footprint in that part of the world. Obama's "pivot to Asia" emerged as a result, and within it the dual policy of security and economic prosperity. In both cases, his Administration followed a careful strategy of coalition building. The TPP, identified with the economic leg of this dual policy, searched for a type of partnership where the U.S. would be first among equals.

Obama also presided over the gradual withdrawal of U.S. soldiers from Iraq and Afghanistan (although during his first term, American presence increased in Afghanistan). His approach to warfare was, again, dual in nature. In the first place, military action had to be covered by the umbrella of collective security, as was the case with the NATO-led intervention in Libya. In the second place, military action had to be as circumscribed and narrow as possible. Obama understood well that his predecessor's "boots on the ground" approach had been exceedingly costly, not only in terms of American lives or dollars but also in terms of international credibility. As a result, he emphasized on limited, stealthy and, often, long-distance warfare, within the so-called "light-footprint" concept.

TRUMP'S DRAW BACK

All of the above helped the U.S. in regaining an important degree of international credibility and standing. This achievement was seriously compromised, however, with the arrival to power of Donald Trump, a president who was not only imbued with George W. Bush's unilateralism but curiously combined it with what appears as a pre-World War II isolationist approach to foreign policy — A tremendous drawback. His administration practically abandoned all the initiatives undertaken by his predecessor under the banners of collective action and cooperative multilateralism.

According to Richard Hass: "When great powers fade, as they inevitably must, it's normally for one or two reasons. Some powers exhaust themselves through overreach abroad, underinvestment at home, or a mixture of the two. This was the case of the Soviet Union. Other powers lose their privileged position with the emergence of a new, stronger power. This describes what happened to France and Great Britain in the case of Germany's emergence after World War I and, more benignly, with the European powers and the rise of the United States during and after World War II. To some extent America is facing a version of this -amid what Farid Zakaria has dubbed 'the rise of the rest' — with China's ascendance as the most significant development. But the United States has now introduced a third mean by which a major power forfeits international advantage. It is abdication, the voluntary relinquishing of power and responsibility. It is brought about more by choice than by circumstances either at home or abroad (…) Abdication is as unwarranted as it is unwise. It is a basic fact of living in a global world that no country can insulate itself from much of what happens elsewhere. A foreign policy based on sovereignty alone will not provide security in a global, interconnected world".[16]

INTERPRETING EVENTS

Richard Hass later coined the term "withdrawal doctrine" to describe this abdication. Daniel Quinn Mills and Steven Rosefielde labeled this introspective process as "democratic nationalism". According to them, this conception assumes that America is a large family in which the needs of the members of the family should not be sacrificed for those of people abroad, or to a U.S. establishment in tune with such cosmopolitan interests.[17] Robert Kagan elucidates

[16] Richard Hass, America and the Great Abdication, *The Atlantic Magazine*, December 28, 2017.

[17] Daniel Q. Mills and Steven Rosefielde, *The Trump Phenomenon and the Future of US Foreign Policy*, New Jersey: World Scientific, 2016.

the reasons why American withdrawal would be the worst possible response to disturbing events around the world, especially so since it is based on a fundamental and dangerous misreading of such events. He talks about a "jungle growing back", to describe that situation.[18] Fareed Zakaria, for his part, refers to the hollowing out of U.S. foreign policy, as Trump's Jacksonian instincts have led him to believe that the rest of the world is largely uninteresting. Uninteresting, except for the fact that, as he believes, most countries just want to screw the United States.[19]

As a result of these different interpretations of the same phenomenon, Trump not only withdrew his country from the Paris Agreement, the Iran Nuclear Deal and the TPP but also from the United Nations Human Rights Commission. The list, though, is significantly longer than that. Not only has he imposed tariffs on Chinese goods amounting to US$550 billion, he has also targeted Washington's own allies by various means. He impetuously withdrew American troops from northeastern Syria, leaving Washington's Kurdish partners and European allies in the dark. This led to a betrayl of the first and dissuaded the second from further participation in U.S.-led coalitions.

Finally, he has dealt with the COVID-19 pandemic with a "America First" mentality, without any attempt to provide global leadership to the crisis. Moreover, amid this terrifying pandemic, he attacked and halted American funding to the only multilateral institution able to coordinate global efforts against it: the World Health Organization. This deprived the 70-year-old institution from its major budgetary source, without any consideration being given to the worldwide implications of such a decision. Worst of all, this was made for mere domestic political gains. At the same time, no effort was made to provide any form of international coordination to counter the dramatic global economic downturn resulting from the coronavirus.

[18] Robert Kagan, *The Jungle Growts Back: America and Our Imperiled World*, New York: Knopf Publishing Group, 2018.
[19] Fareed Zakaria, *op. cit.*

Trump believes that national sovereignty, and not international cooperation, is the foundation of international relations. This is why he prefers bilateral meetings and negotiations, where U.S. power can be exerted. By the same token, he has "weaponized" economic tools by equating economy and national security. In doing so, he has targeted not only China but also its main allies. Dusting off Section 323 of the 1962 Trade Expansion Act, which allows tariffs on national security grounds, he has been able to impose penalizations at will. Moreover, he has been using the leverage of U.S.' large market, with the intention of bullying up other countries into submission. As a result, not only China but also close allies such as Japan, South Korea, Canada, Mexico, and the European Union have all been affected.[20]

BULLYING AROUND

He imposed sanctions on steel and aluminum upon America's allies, in a move reminiscent of the infamous Smooth–Hawley Act of 1930. He threatened to pull out from NAFTA, forcing a tough renegotiation of the treaty that humiliated his partners for no sensible reason, as the final result was more fanfare than substance. He has made his anti-European Union sentiments sufficiently clear, labeling this institution as an economic "foe" to the United States, while actively supporting Brexit. He threatened to impose a 25% tariff on the automotive imports coming from the European Union, which represent more than 28% of all European exports to the United States. Although this "weaponization" of trade tools has allowed him to skirt around WTO rules, he has also threatened to withdraw his country from this institution, while aiming to kill its dispute settlement mechanism.

[20] Ana Swanson and Paul Mozur, Trump Mixed Economic and National Security, Plunging the U.S. into Multiple Fights, *The New York Times*, June 8, 2019; Edward Alden, Trump Hired Robert Lighthinzer to Win a Trade War. He Lost, *Foreign Policy*, August 2, 2019, https://foreignpolicy.com/2019/08/02/trump-hired-robert-lighthizer-to-win-a-trade-war-he-lost/. Accessed August 7, 2019.

Meanwhile, he has threatened to reduce U.S.' participation in NATO, has referred to Germany as a "captive of Russia", and has called some of America's closest NATO partners "delinquents". He has irked West European liberal democracies by cheering the slide into autocracy of East European populist regimes. He abruptly cancelled a meeting with the Prime Minister of Denmark because she refused to discuss the sale of Greenland to the United States. This is akin to the use of national power to acquire territory against the will of its sovereign government and people, something expressively forbidden by the 1975 Helsinki Final Act, which is the cornerstone of European stability. Moreover, when the Danish Prime Minister declared that "thankfully, the time when you buy other countries and populations is over", Trump responded: "You don't talk to the United States that way. At least not under me".

Moreover, in October 2019, the U.S. imposed tariffs on European Union products as a result of an underlying dispute over plane-manufacturing subsidies that had been dragging on for 15 years. It was a highly complex technical issue that Trump tried to settle overnight through one of his typical ultimatums. Trump, as usual, acted as a wild card, creating the conditions for the situation to spiral into a trade war.

He has abused Mexico time and again, threatening it with the Emergency Powers Act for allowing Central American migrants to reach the U.S. border. This act is an outgrowth of the Trading with the Enemy Act, frequently used during the Cold War to impose sanctions on the Soviet Union. He has described multiple developing countries, particularly in his own hemisphere, as "shitholes".

NOT EVEN THE INDO-PACIFIC REGION

Not even in the key Indo-Pacific region has Trump taken care of his country's partnerships. He declared that cars coming from Japan were a risk for American security and had to be treated accordingly; he then forced both Japan and South Korea to renegotiate their trade agreements with his country. In 2019, he asked Japan for a dramatic increase in payments for hosting 50,000 American troops there, quadrupling its annual contribution for that purpose. The same year, he requested South Korea to pay 400% more for the privilege of hosting U.S. soldiers, which comes on top of a demand in 2018 for a 50% increase. Moreover, Trump has made a habit of sending lower-level delegations to regional meetings.[21]

In Steven Metz words: "Trump has questioned many of America's alliances, and ominously, there are few signs that he is fully committed to sustaining or expanding vital U.S. security partnerships in the Indo-Pacific. He seems more concerned with America's trade balance than with the region's security architecture. He does not appear to back the regional economic integration that helped provide a soft power bulwark against Chinese assertiveness. He has given little sign of expanding American ties with Taiwan or aligning American policy with other key regional states … No matter how sound a National Defense Strategy [might be], it cannot succeed in isolation from tightly integrated political and diplomatic efforts".[22]

India, a fundamental U.S. ally in any China containment policy, is a good example of the above. The country has not only been bullied around by Trump, but fundamental geostrategic considerations have been subordinated to trade ones. Donald Trump has been attacking New Delhi on the basis that it is unfairly limiting American manufacturers from access to Indian markets, and the possibility of a trade war between both nations looms in the air. Sensitivities run high in India, as there is the prevailing public perception that Washington is bullying this proud country into submission.[23] Not surprisingly, as Hugh White wrote when referring to how the United States was distancing itself from Australia and its partners in Asia: "The new [Autralian] foreign policy White Paper went further than

[21] World Politics Review, Trump Works Overtime to Shake Down Allies in Asia and Appease North Korea, November 20, 2019.

[22] Steven Metz, Is the New National Defense Strategy The Right Way to Deal With China's Rise, *World Politics Review*, February, 2018, https://www.worldpoliticsreview.com/articles/24112/is-the-new-national-defense-strategy-the-right-way-to-deal-with-china-s-rise. Accessed November 18, 2018.

[23] World Politics Review, Can Modi Steer India Back to Relevance?, October14, 2019.

Canberra has ever gone before, in acknowledging uncertainty about America's commitment to Asia".[24]

THE ALLIES' REACTION

Consequently, Trump's relations with its main allies have become atrocious. As James Kirchick explains: "Donald Trump ascended to the presidency challenging the basic precepts of America's relationship with Europe: NATO he proclaimed, was not only 'obsolete', but Washington should make its security commitment contingent upon alliance members paying 'their fair share'. The European Union was not an ally but a competitor that had 'been formed, partially to beat the United States on trade'. Against the express wishes of every European government — including, at the time, Britain's — Trump cheered along Brexit and conveyed ambivalence as to whether the European Union should continue to exist".[25]

It hardly came as a surprise, therefore, when the U.S.' three closest allies in Europe, the UK, Germany and France, issued an official statement on April 2018, saying that they would forcefully defend their interests against Washington's protectionism. Moreover, on May 10, 2018, Angela Merkel declared in Aquisgran that the time during which Europe could trust the United States had ended. By the same token, Canada and Mexico, the partners of U.S. at NAFTA, expressed their outrage on May 31, 2018 at being targeted by the steel and aluminum taxes. According to the BBC News: "Mr. Trump has justified the tariffs by arguing that US steel and aluminum producers are vital to national security ... The Canadian Prime Minister Justin Trudeau described that claim as an affront. 'That Canada

[24] Hugh White, Canberra voices fears but who will contain the dragon?, *The Straits Times*, November 25, 2017.

[25] James Kirchik, Europeans want to break with America: They'd do so at their peril, Brookings, May 25, 2018, https://www.brookings.edu/blog/order-from-chaos/2018/05/25/europeans-want-to-break-up-with-america-theyd-do-so-at-their-peril/. Accessed May 26, 2018.

could be considered a national security threat to the United States is inconceivable' he said".[26]

As a result of his actions, the G7 fractured in two groups: on one side, the United States; on the other, all the rest. In relation to the June 2018 summit of the group, *The New York Times* reported: "Earlier Thursday, President Emmanuel Macron of France and Prime Minister Justin Trudeau of Canada lashed out at Mr. Trump for imposing tariffs on their steel and aluminum industries ... 'The American President may not mind being isolated, but neither do we mind signing a 6 country agreement if need be'".[27] And, indeed, that was exactly what happened, as the six other members signed the final G7 document, while the U.S. abstained from doing so. No wonder that in the following year's G7 summit, in August 2019, the summit's traditional joint agreement communique was altogether eliminated, "as an attempt to avoid the inevitable clash with Mr. Trump".[28]

In an interview to *The Economist* on November 2019, President Emmanuel Macron warned European countries that "they could no longer rely on America to defend NATO allies", which implied the "brain death of NATO". According to him: "I'd argue that we should reassess the reality of what NATO is in the light of the commitment of the United States". America, in his view, shows signs of "turning its back on us". In the case of Donald Trump, Europe is now dealing for the first time with an American President who "doesn't share our idea of the European project", Macron said. As a result, he argued, Europe should regain "military sovereignty" and "resume dialogue with Russia".[29] In other words, Europe is finding its own path independently of the United States, as this country had become untrustworthy.

[26] Trade tariffs: Chorus of condemnation intensifies, May 31, 2018.
[27] Michael D. Shear, Anger Flares Up as Group of 7 Heads to Quebec, *The New York Times*, June 7, 2018.
[28] Michael D. Shear, Trump Aides Slam French for Focusing on 'Niche Issues' at G7, *The New York Times*, August 24, 2019.
[29] Emmanuel Macron warns Europe: NATO is becoming brain-dead, November 7, 2019.

DYNAMICS OF NATIONALISM AND DESTABILIZATION

To make matters worse, Trump's behavior towards the U.S. allies is putting in motion dynamics of nationalism and destabilization. Robert Kagan has argued that Germany today is the product of the postwar order that implies Washington's security commitment to Europe, free trade, democracy and multilateralism. All these identity traits are currently being questioned by the Trump Administration. Kagan worries that an American-induced failure of the European project might see the return of the "German question". This would entail a dangerous return to a historic nationalist assertiveness.[30]

Another consequence of Trump's actions is the resurgence of old quarrels among U.S. allies. Without the cohesive and mediating presence of Washington, Japan and South Korea are now at odds with each other. As Bonnie S. Glaser and Oriana Sylkar Mastro explained: "For more than half a century, U.S. power in Asia has rested on the alliance system that Washington built in the years after World War II. Now, a dispute between Japan and South Korea — the two most important pillars of that system-threatens to undo decades of progress. But instead of seeking actively mediate between its allies, Washington has largely watched from the sidelines — leaving the field to China, which has moved quickly to benefit from U.S. inaction (…) Instead (China), it has tried to cast the tensions between Japan and South Korea as evidence of poor U.S. leadership — if the United States cannot serve as an effective mediator between its allies, what good is it- and present itself as a proactive peacemaker and more reliable partner than the United States".[31] As *The Economist* explained in relation this situation: "President Trump has called the two allies to

---

[30] The New German Question, *Foreign Affairs,* May–June, 2019, https://www.foreignaffairs.com/articles/germany/2019-04-02/new-german-question. Accessed August 24, 2019.

[31] Bonnie S. Glaser and Oriana S. Mastro, How an Alliance System Withers: Washington is Sleeping Through the Japanese-Korean Dispute. China Isn't, Foreign Affairs, September 9, 2019, https://www.foreignaffairs.com/articles/china/2019-09-09/how-alliance-system-withers. Accessed September 10, 2019.

'get along', but done precious little to mediate in the dispute, complaining that he has too much on his plate already".[32]

Donald Tusk, President of the European Council, expressed his bewilderment with this whole situation in the following terms: "What worries me the most is the fact that the rules-based international order is being challenged, quite surprisingly not by the usual suspects, but by its main architect and guarantor, the US ... Undermining this order makes no sense at all, because it will only play into the hands of those who seek a new post-West order...".[33]

Mark Leonard finds, however, a sense in the great disruptor's acts. As he argues: "Trump's response is one of creative destruction and his aim is to undermine existing institutions — such as the World Trade Organization, Nafta and Nato- as a first step towards bilateral renegotiations of world order on terms more favourable to Washington D.C. He wants to do this while the US is still the dominant power and can deal with others from a position of strength".[34]

Little does it matter, though, whether Trump's acts are senseless or respond to something akin to a strategic sense. The result is the same: By wanting to bully its trade partners and allies into acquiescence of U.S. dominance, he is only humiliating and pushing them away. At the end, the U.S. remains lonelier and becomes increasingly isolated. From the point of view of American interests, there seems to be much destruction and little creation in this process.

A THIRD OPPORTUNITY?

During George W. Bush's final year at the White House, Zbigniew Brzezinski wrote an important book in which he asserted that the

[32] An old grudge between South Korea and Japan is getting out of hand, *The Economist*, August 28, 2019.

[33] Julian Borger and Anne Perkins, Donald Trump calls for the G7 to readmit Russia, *The Guardian*, June 8, 2018.

[34] Britain's lonely future in the age of clashing empires, *New Stateman*, October 30, 2019, https://www.newstatesman.com/world/2019/10/britain-s-lonely-future-age-clashing-empires. Accessed November 6, 2019.

United States had lost much of its international legitimacy. He found that particularly disturbing, as the combined impact of the global political awakening and modern technology was leading to "an acceleration of political history". In his view "what in the past took centuries, now takes decades, and what before took decades now happens in a single year". As a result, the primacy of any world power was subjected to strong pressures of adaptation, change and fall.[35]

Although the U.S. had seriously eroded its international standing and was confronting the challenges imposed by the acceleration of history, Brzezinski believed that a "second chance" was still possible as "no other power can play the role that the United States *potentially* could and should play".[36] He also believed that recuperating what had been lost would be extremely difficult: "It will take years of sustained effort and true ability to restore the political credibility and the legitimacy of the United States".[37] It was thus essential, according to his view, that the second chance should not be missed, "as there will not be a third opportunity". [38]

Although Obama did his best to regain the space lost during the preceding eight years, there was not enough time. It would have required many more years "of sustained effort and true ability to restore the political credibility and the legitimacy of the United States". It seems crystal clear now that the second chance given to the United States has been totally squandered under Donald Trump.

The combination of George W. Bush plus Donald Trump is simply too much for the allies and friends of America to handle, since they have come to mistrust them as much as the country where the ideas they represent enjoy such a wide support. In an article in *National Interest*, Nikolas K. Gvosdev argues precisely about such ideas gaining ground: "Across both parties, there is a sense among Americans, as a recent report issued by the Carnegie Council for

---

[35] Zbigniew Brzezinski, *Second Chance*, New York: Basic Books, 2007, p. 206.
[36] *Ibid.*, p. 191.
[37] *Ibid.*, p. 192.
[38] *Ibid.*, p. 216.

Ethics on International Affairs concludes, that U.S. involvement in international system must be amended — with a renew focus on how American policy abroad connects to the doorstep issues of average Americans. There is also a renewed suspicion of losing American sovereignty or decision-making to bodies that are beyond the reach of American voters".[39] If a nation as close to the U.S. as Germany can no longer trust it, as Angela Merkel said in Aquisgran in 2018, which country can? The fact that foreign investments in the United States fell to almost zero in 2018 is evidence of a sentiment that goes beyond simple governments.[40]

The window of opportunity that the U.S. enjoyed is thus closing, especially since there is now a competing power. The fitting question then to be asked would be: Where does China stand in terms of its convergence capacity?

A COMPETING POWER

The answer is simple. China's unstoppable drive to a position of leadership in the expansion of globalization has simultaneously broadened its convergence capacity. This route has not been easy, obvious, or linear. It began in 2001 as the natural by-product of its explosive international commercial interconnectedness, after its access to WTO. It continued as an expression of the country's willingness to create a parallel institutional framework to the Western controlled multilaterals. It went on, finally, as a way of transforming the country to become the center of an expanding supply chain and the nucleus of the Asian economic integration process.

In 2011, the United Nations Economic Commission for Latin America and the Caribbean, ECLAC, pointed out that South–South exchange, headed by China, was the main driving force of global trade growth: The volume of exports from developing countries

---

[39] Nikolas K. Gvosdev, Can a 'Trumpian' Foreign Policy Stick?, November 9, 2019, https://nationalinterest.org/feature/can-trumpian-foreign-policy-stick-95196. Accessed November 13, 2019.

[40] Kishore Mahbubani, What China Threat?, *Harper's Magazine*, January 16, 2019.

had, indeed, grown by 17% in 2010 compared with 13% in developed countries.[41]

The year before, Gordon Brown had written: "This weakening of the European, American and Japanese growth rate also reflects the fundamental shift taking place across the world in the location of production and the direction of trade ... And with China leading the growth of South–South trade, globalization will no longer be dominated by trade between today's developed countries".[42] In 2012, indeed, China had already become the first or the second trade partner for 78 countries representing 55% of the global GDP.[43]

Some good examples of the above were the trade expansions between China and Latin America and the Caribbean and China and Africa. The former had risen from US$8.3 billion in 1999 to US$257 billion in 2017, while the latter rose from US$10 billion in 2000 to US$127.97 in 2016. In 2011, China had already surpassed the United States as the largest trade partner with Africa, while its trade with Latin America at that point was growing at nearly twice the level of the one the region had with the United States.[44]

The increase in trade between China and the Arab world was also impressive. In Ben Simpfendorfer words: "The door between the Arab world and China, which was shut for centuries, is now open

[41] ECLAC, Exports from Latin America and the Caribbean will increase in 27% in 2011, Santiago de Chile, August 31, 2011, https://www.cepal.org/en/pressreleases/exports-latin-america-and-the-caribbean-will-increase-27-2011. Accessed March 27, 2013.

[42] Gordon Brown, *Beyond the Crash: Overcoming the First Crisis of Globalisation*, London: Simon & Schuster, 2010, p. 136.

[43] *Sistema Económico Latinoamericano, Las relaciones entre China y América Latina y El Caribe en la actual coyuntura económica mundial*, Caracas: Ediciones SELA, Septiembre, 2012.

[44] John Naisbitt and Doris Naisbitt, *China's Megatrend*, *op. cit.*; Ruth Morris, China: Latin America trade jumps, LBC Latin Business Chronicle, May 9, 2011; *Comisión Económica para América Latina y El Caribe, La República Popular China y América Latina y el Caribe: Diálogo y Cooperación ante los Nuevos Desafíos de la Economía Mundial*, Santiago de Chile: Junio de 2012; China, Africa trade increase in 2010, Africa News.com, http://www.africanews.com/site/list_message32503. Accessed January 12, 2012; Jonathan T. D. Ward, *op. cit.*, locations 2626/6589, 2801/6589 and 2807/6589.

again". In 2000, China's exports to Arab countries were worth US$6 billion, while in 2010 they had reached US$60 billion. In the process, China had overtaken the United Kingdom in 2002, Germany in 2006 and the United States in 2008, as the larger exporter in this region.[45]

Edward Luce provided the proper context to understand what was happening: "From barely a statistical rounding error in 1978, with less than 1% of global trade, China rose to become in 2013 the world's leading trading nation with almost a quarter of its annual flows ... Nothing on this scale or speed has been witnessed before in history".[46]

BYPASSING THE CABAL

At that time, unsurprisingly, China accounted for 13.6% of the global GDP. What was surprising, though, was the lack of connection between this figure and its share percentage at the IMF, which remained at just 3.8%. In fact, in 2014 China had surpassed the U.S. in GDP measured in Purchasing Power Parity (PPP).[47] Indeed, while the U.S. accounted for US$17.4 trillion, China had reached US$17.6 trillion. Nonetheless, China's paltry voting power of 3.8% stood against 17.9% for the United States, which was nothing short of absurd.

China's attempts to increase this unfair ceiling to reasonable levels proved unsuccessful. In the words of Joseph Stiglitz: "To maintain a cabal among developed countries, whereby the U.S. appoints the World Bank president and Europe picks the International Monetary Fund's head, seems particularly anachronistic and perplexing today, when the bank and the fund are turning to emerging-market countries as a source of funds".[48] It must be added, though,

---

[45] Ben Simpfendorfer, *The New Silk Road*, New York: Palgrave Macmillan, 2011, p. 160.

[46] Edward Luce, *The Retreat of Western Liberalism* [Kindle version], London: Little, Brown, 2017, Amazon.com, location 219/4115.

[47] The PPP exchange rate states that exchange rates between currencies are in equilibrium when their purchasing power is the same in each of the two countries.

[48] Joseph Stiglitz, Picking the next chief: Whose World Bank is it?, *The Straits Times*, April 12, 2012.

that in 2016 the IMF reform was finally achieved giving China a bigger share percentage and, as a consequence, more voting power. However, the U.S. remained as the only country with enough votes to block any major reforms in the future. Well before that date though a group of emerging economies, with China at its head, had attempted to bypass that frustrating situation.

Indeed, the leaders of the BRICS member countries (Brazil, Russia, India, China and South Africa) agreed to create a new development bank. In their March 2012 summit, they moved to create a financial institution that would improve access to capital for developing nations while allowing them to make deals with one another in their local currencies.

As Radhika Deasi explained, the main emerging economies began to bypass the economic institutional architecture of the West, and all this without fanfare: "The BRICS and emerging economies have already set in train a wider set of changes in the institutional architecture of the world order. Since Western powers maintain their grip on its major institutions, these rising powers have simply side-stepped them, setting up new institutions and using old minor ones in new ways. The result is a decentralised institutional structure that doesn't look like a rival to Western-dominated centralised and worldwide institutions at first sight. But it is. For example, it bypasses the US dollar-centered world monetary and financial regime ... Over this period, the International Monetary Fund's influence fell and it had to compromise key policy prescriptions — pre-eminently on capital controls — as regional development banks and arrangements between two or more developing economies to conduct trade in their own currencies undermined its monopoly".[49]

China was instrumental in the creation in 2014 of the BRICS' New Development Bank, whose headquarters are in Shanghai. The bank is called to support public and private projects through loans, guarantees and other financial instruments. Moreover, the bank aims at cooperating with international organizations and other

[49] Radhika Desai, The West must wake up to the growing power of the BRICS, *The Guardian*, April 2, 2012.

financial entities in order to provide technical assistance to projects supported by the bank. The initial authorized capital of the bank was US$100 billion, distributed in equal parts among its five members.

In 2015, the BRICS member countries established a Contingency Reserve Arrangement to provide protection against global liquidity pressures. This arrangement was seen as a competitor to the IMF. Within its capital of US$100,000 billion, the majority, US$39.95 billion, corresponded to China.

A FINANCIAL JUGGERNAUT

Even before becoming a vital player in the promotion of these initiatives, China had already been asserting an important international role through the China Development Bank. Created in 1994 as an engine called to empower the government's economic development, the Bank was involved in the international financial positioning of the country. Besides being the second bond issuer in China, after the Ministry of Finance, it became a key international lender. Solely in Latin America, Chinese loan commitments between 2005 and 2013 reached US$130 billion. That amount represented more than what the World Bank, the Inter-American Bank and the World Bank combined had lent to the region during that same period. The majority of those resources, dedicated to infrastructure and energy projects in commodity-exporting nations, came from the China Development Bank.[50]

At the same time, the country became a member of many multilateral institutions within emerging nations. In Erik Berglof words: "In fact, Chinese international engagement is now occurring on a scale and at a rate never seen before. China is a member of many multilateral institutions — including several regional

[50]Jorge Guajardo, A Latin American Perspective on China's Growing Presence in the Region in Riordan Roett and Guadalupe Paz, *Latin America and the Asian Giants: Evolving Ties with China and India,* Washington D.C.: Brookings Institution Press, 2016, p. 69.

players like the African Development Bank (AfDB) and the Inter-American Development Bank (IDB) — with which it is deepening its relationships, especially through co-investment in projects around the world. For example, China significantly ratcheted up its commitment to the AfDB last year through the $2 billion African Growing Together Fund".[51]

China was also behind the creation of the Shanghai Cooperation Organization (SCO), whose organizational charter was signed in June 2002, entering into force on September 2003. This is a multi-faceted organization that, beyond the mutually agreed economic support, covers security and political support as well. SCO has eight Eurasian member states that, in addition to China, include India, Russia, Pakistan and several Central Asian states. This organization superseded the Shanghai Five Group, which had been founded in 1996 under the stewardship of China.

Two other powerful organizations benefitted from having China as the driving force behind them: the Asian Infrastructure Investment Bank (AIIB) and the Silk Road Fund. The first is a multilateral development bank that aims at supporting the building of infrastructures in the Asia-Pacific region. The initiative gathered initial support from 37 regional and 20 non-regional members. Currently, AIIB lists almost 100 members from different parts of the world. To put things in context: the capital of the bank alone, US$100 billion, represents that of the Word Bank. China pledged US$50 billion to the AIIB special fund, which will help low-income countries in developing infrastructure projects. AIIB was proposed by China in 2013, and its launching initiative took place in Beijing in October 2014.

The Silk Road Fund is a different kind of initiative, not a multilateral financial institution but a State-owned investment fund. Its aim is to foster investments in the countries along the Belt and Road project. Established in December 2014, the Chinese government pledged US$40 billion for the creation of this fund. Another major

[51] Erik Burglof, Will China change the world's financial institutions?, World Economic Forum, November 25, 2015, https://www.weforum.org/agenda/2015/11/will-china-change-the-worlds-financial-institutions/. Accessed March 19, 2018.

difference from the AIIB is that recipients of its investments will not only be Asian countries but European ones as well. The Silk Road Fund will complement AIIB in relation to infrastructure developments along the Belt and Road route. These initiatives are bound to close the door to Washington'-based financial institutions in the Belt and Road project.

BELT AND ROAD

The Belt and Road Initiative, for its part, is a development strategy proposed by the Chinese government that focuses on connectivity and cooperation between Asian, African and European countries. President Xi Jinping unveiled this initiative in September and October of 2013. This mega infrastructure development plan covers more than 65 countries in Asia, Africa and Europe, and bears a price tag estimated at a trillion dollars.

The project, which comprises a land route (Silk Road Economic Belt) and a maritime route (Maritime Silk Road), aims at building highways, railways, pipelines, ports and industrial ports. The land route will go from Lianyungang in China to Rotterdam in the Netherlands, while the maritime one will depart from Quanzhou in China and end in Venice, Italy. The Belt and Road Initiative combines several land and maritime corridors that would link Central Asia; Southeast Asia; West Asia; the Indian Ocean; the Arabic Sea; the Persian Gulf; the Middle East; the Red Sea; the Mediterranean Sea; Eastern, Central and Western Europe; and the Horn of Africa.

In relation to China's reasons behind the Belt and Road Initiative, Hugh White states: "China wants to consolidate its position at the centre of the global supply and manufacturing networks which will be the key to the global economy over the coming decades. Beijing understands that as China's economy matures and its income levels rise, the lower-wage industries which have fueled China's growth so far, will migrate to less-developed countries where labour costs are lower. China's economic planners don't want to fight that trend, but turn it to China's advantage by building itself an inexpugnable place at the centre of the expanding supply-chain web which will result from it".[52]

The Belt and Road project encompasses 65% of the world's population, about one-third of the world's gross domestic product, and about a quarter of the world's trade.[53] Making this bold vision a reality will require an extraordinary alignment of financial resources, political commitment, technical skills and international cooperation. It is by no means an easy task. However, the benefits that it may bring to so many are extremely significant that numerous countries have shown interest in this project. It comes as no surprise that 110 countries were represented, some of them at the highest level, at the Beijing May 2017 meeting to discuss the initiative. With commodities being at their lowest prices in more than a decade, the incentive to build an intercontinental web of infrastructure and trade links has been greatly enhanced.

Anabel Gonzalez, from the World Economic Forum, provides an overly ambitious picture of the Belt and Road initiative and of its expansive possibilities: "It is the most ambitious initiative to improve regional economic integration and connectivity on a transcontinental scale: involving 'hard' infrastructure along six overland corridors, and the 21st Century Maritime Silk Road; 'soft' infrastructure, such as the financial system, to enhance efficiency and facilitate economic flows; and policy reforms and institution-building to promote trade and foreign direct investment among the 70 or so BRI countries. There is talk now of expanding it to Latin America or to shipping routes across the Artic, dubbed the 'Polar Silk Road'".[54]

However, the relevance given to the Belt and Road Initiative in the above quote pales when compared to the significance assigned to it by Parag Khanna: "When we look back from 2100 at the date on which

---

[52] Hugh White, China's One Belt, One Road to challenge US-led order, *The Straits Times*, April 27, 2017.

[53] Goh Sui Noi, China makes tracks on modern Silk Road, *The Straits Times*, May 11, 2017.

[54] Anabel Gonzales, Brexit, the US, China and the future of global trade, *World Economic Forum*, February 12, 2018, https://www.weforum.org/agenda/2018/02/brexit-china-global-trade/. Accessed March 4, 2018.

the cornerstone of an Asian-led world order began, it will be 2017. In May of that year sixty-eight countries representing two-thirds of the world's population and half of its GDP gathered in Beijing for the first Belt and Road Initiative (BRI) summit. This gathering of Asian, European, and African leaders symbolized the launch of the largest coordinated infrastructure investment plan in human history (...) The Belt and Road Initiative is the most significant diplomatic project of the twenty-first century, the equivalent of the mid-twentieth century founding of the United Nations and the World Bank plus the Marshall Plan all rolled into one. The crucial difference: BRI was conceived in Asia and launched in Asia and will be led by Asians".[55]

Thus, according to Khanna, the Beijing-led BRI is equivalent in magnitude and transformational nature to the Washington-led world order that emerged after World War II. By extension, this means that the 21st century will be as Asian as the second half of the 20th was American. But even if this grandiose vision proved to be an exaggeration, the fact remains that at this point the Belt and Road Initiative includes 900 projects at a cost exceeding US$1.4 trillion, which, after adjusting for inflation, amounts to 12 Marshall Plans.[56]

FREE TRADE

Beijing's wide-ranging initiatives, though, don't stop there. China has also been playing a major role in the proposed free trade agreement known as the Regional Comprehensive Economic Partnership (RCEP). This would include the ten member states of ASEAN (Brunei, Cambodia, Indonesia, Laos, Malaysia, the Philippines, Singapore, Thailand and Vietnam), plus the six states with which ASEAN has existing free trade agreements: Australia, China, India Japan, South Korea and New Zealand.

[55] Parag Khanna, *The Future is Asian: Global Order In The Twenty-First Century* [Kindle Version], London: Weidenfeld & Nicolson, 2019, retrieved from Amazon.com, locations 30/6214 and 36/6214.

[56] Graham Allison, *Destined for War: Can America and China Escape the Thucydides' Trap.* Boston, MA: Mariner Books, 2018, p. 23.

Formal negotiations for RCEP began in November 2012. RCEP member states together account for a population of 3.4 billion people and a combined GDP of US$49.5 trillion, which is approximately equivalent to 39% of the world's GDP. It will become the largest trading bloc in the planet, and its importance will keep increasing in direct relation to the GDP increase of its member states. Moreover, once in force RCEP will be open to new members, essentially to Central Asian nations and the remaining countries in South Asia and Oceania. As a conventional free trade agreement, it will have a lax structure.

Even more widely, Beijing is pushing forward for the Free Trade Area of the Asia-Pacific (FTAAP), whic will include countries from both sides of the Pacific Basin. At the 2014 APEC Economic Leaders' Meeting in Bijing, Xi Jinping urged the group to approve a roadmap for achieving such an initiative. As a result, a so-called Beijing Roadmap was adopted. A collective strategic study of this plan was subsequently approved at the 2016 APEC summit in Lima, Peru.

In Lima, President Xi delivered a keynote speech in which he urged the building of the FTAAP, as protectionism had dented global trade and economic integration. Moreover, he urged APEC members to stay committed to taking economic globalization forward and to transform the Asia-Pacific region into a growth engine within an "innovative, invigorated, interconnected and inclusive world economy".[57]

On the other hand, in a long report to the National Congress of the CCP, in October 2017, Xi developed his concept of a Community of Common Destiny, which searches a world defined by mutual cooperation. This common destiny is to be achieved through a community of shared interests and shared responsibilities. This implies the search for economic interdependence by means of win–win relations. Both at Davos and later at a keynote delivered at the U.N., Xi had previously talked about the goal of building a community of

[57] *Xinhua*, Highlights of President Xi's attendance at the Lima APEC Meeting, November 21, 2016, https://chinareportasean.com/2016/11/22/highlights-of-president-xis-attendance-at-the-lima-apec-meeting/. Accessed October 30, 2019.

shared future for mankind, which emphasized mutual cooperation between countries.

TWO DIFFERENT DIRECTIONS

As seen, then, the convergence aptitude of the United States and China has evolved in two completely different directions. Washington evolved from being the epitome of globalization and the stand bearer of the most successful hegemonic system ever into becoming a unilateralist and isolationist country. Conversely, China went from the total closeness of Mao's days into being the undisputed leader of globalization and, according to Parag Khanna, the main promoter of a 21st century Asian-led order.

As concepts go, the contrast between "America First" and the "Community of Common Destiny" could not be stronger. While the U.S. emphasizes protectionism, isolationism and the primacy of national interest, China promotes free trade and economic interdependent and win–win international relations. Indeed, Beijing, with a vision of a global village, confronted Washington's emphasis of a small village vision. Not surprisingly, while the convergence capacity that the United States can show today is quite low, China's is not only vast but keeps growing.

It should be noted that China's nationalist outreach has certainly obstructed its leadership in this area. However, its economic clout still carries much weight. Lee Kuan Yew, who was probably the greatest interpreter of China's and East Asia's political realities, explained the situation in the following terms: "China is sucking the Southeast Asian countries into its economic system because of its vast market and growing purchasing power. Japan and South Korea will inevitably be sucked as well. It just absorbs countries without having to use force … China's economic sway will be very difficult to fight".[58] The same goes for Australia and other Asian countries, which even converging with the U.S. over the common denominator of wanting to

[58] Graham Allison, *Destined for War, op. cit.*, p. 23.

contain China's geopolitical expansion, do not seem ready to sacrifice the benefits deriving from its gigantic economic footprint.

This is especially so, as from now until 2030 China's consumption growth is expected to exceed that of the United States and Western Europe combined. Already, between 2010 and 2016, it represented 38% of the global consumption growth, while in some sectors like automobiles and mobile phones it reached 68%.[59] While this happens, U.S.'s protectionism and retirement from the TPP have turned this country in a shallow option for Asian economies.

As Jonathan D. Pollack and Jeffrey A. Bader have correctly assessed: "China is now the world's lead trading state, deeply integrated in supply chains involving allies and partners. It is increasingly active in infrastructural funding across Asia, Africa and Europe, including as a multilateral lender. Its products (including in some high-technology sectors like telecommunications) are competitively priced and welcomed in global markets. Perhaps most important, there is no meaningful support outside the United States to exclude China from an even larger role in global and regional economics".[60]

STICK AND CARROT

It seems reasonable to assume, therefore, that its leading role in globalization and its economic growth perspectives have been able to shield China, to a significant extent, from its nationalistic

[59]Wang Huiyao, China's role in the Asian century of globalization, World Economic Forum, https://www.weforum.org/agenda/2019/07/the-dawn-of-the-asian-century/. Accessed August 2, 2019; McKinsey Global Institute, China and the world: Inside the dynamics of a changing relationship, July 2009 Report, https://www.mckinsey.com/~/media/mckinsey/featured%20insights/china/china%20and%20the%20world%20inside%20the%20dynamics%20of%20a%20changing%20relationship/mgi-china-and-the-world-full-report-june-2019-vf.ashx. Accessed August 2, 2019.

[60]Jonathan D. Pollack and Jeffrey A. Bader, Looking before we leap: Weighing the risk of US–China disengagement, Brookings, July 2019, https://www.brookings.edu/research/looking-before-we-leap-weighing-the-risks-of-us-china-disengagement/. Accessed July 29, 2019.

excesses. Notwithstanding those excesses, Beijing still enjoys quite a bit of international support. This is consistent with the concept of "geoeconomics" developed by Robert Blackwill and Jennifer Harris, according to which the use of economic instruments allows for the achievement of geopolitical goals. For these authors, China is the world's leading practitioner of geoeconomics.[61]

Within its regional sphere, Howard W. French believes that China is reenacting its ancestral strategy to co-opt client states. In his words: "Today, as in the past, the ideals of the *tin xia* system are being put into effect. This means building up dependency on China among its far smaller neighbors, the better to dominate them peacefully".[62] Whatever the name given to the strategy in motion, the truth remains that China's economic carrots have been effective in containing the stick's effects. Conversely, the United States has only shown the stick to its allies, making extremely difficult for them to follow Washington in a containment strategy against China.

Any attempt to decouple China from America's allies faces a dim prospect. Not even such a close ally to the U.S. as Australia seems ready to follow that route, as Hugh White explains: "No one in Canberra wants to risk that, because Australia's economy has flourished thanks to a boom trade with China".[63] And, as Jeff Bader of the Brooking Institution correctly formulates, what if America presses its allies, who strongly depend on China's economy, to disengage from that country and they simply refuse?[64]

As a matter of fact, even in Obama's time the U.S. was unable to muster such support when it asked its allies' not to participate in the creation of the Asian Infrastructure Investment Bank. Much less,

---

[61] Robert D. Blackwill and Jennifer M. Harris, *War by Other Means: Geoeconomics and Statecraft*, Cambridge, MA: Harvard University Press, 2016.

[62] Howard W. French, *Everything Under Heaven: How the Past Helps Shape China's Push for Global Power* [Kindle version], New York: Alfred A. Knopf, 2017, retrieved from Amazon.com, p. 66.

[63] Hugh White, Canberra voices fears but will contain the dragon?, *The Straits Times*, November 25, 2019.

[64] David Zweig, Tussle for tech supremacy powers US–China animosity, *Financial Times*, December 5, 2018, https://www.ft.com/content/ddbe9522-f878-11e8-a154-2b65ddf314e9. Accessed December 25, 2018.

and for obvious reasons, is attainable now. A good example of it was Southeast Asia's flat rejection of the U.S. ultimatum against Huawei.[65] Even its fellow members within the so-called Five Eyes intelligence sharing community (the closest thing to a true alliance that Washington still posseses) have been reluctant to embark on its crusade against China's 5G technology. This turns out to be particularly relevant as Washington has threatened not to share classified intelligence with them if they do not disengage from Huawei.

Referring to Europe, Andrea Kendall-Taylor and Rachel Rizzo explain the situation as follows: "European leaders remain convinced they can uphold the values and norms they share with Washington while benefitting economically with a greater engagement with China ... The United States has done little to help move Europe off the fence. Instead, the Trump administration has actively pushed the continent away ... While Washington has been antagonistic, Beijing has been careful to strike all the right chords. The CCP talks about harmonizing civilizations, invokes 'values' when discussing European and Chinese commonalities, and extols the values of multilateralism. Because China and Europe increasingly find themselves on the same side of conflicts with Washington, this administration has made it easy for Beijing to present itself as the reliable and responsible global partner".[66]

In order to increase the political footprint that derives from its economic leverage, China promotes its image and points of view within the political debate of democratic societies themselves. Through an organization called the United Front Department, China aims at shaping favorable views of itself within the politics of those countries by helping friendly voices. The best examples to date have been its efforts to shape domestic political debates in New Zealand and Australia, which have included the funding of

---

[65] Meaghan Tobin, The US ultimatum over China's 5G giant falls flat in Southeast Asia, Inkstone, April 22, 2019, https://www.inkstonenews.com/tech/us-fails-make-southeast-asia-abandon-chinas-5g-giant-huawei/article/3007139. Accessed April 26, 2019.

[66] Andrea Kendall-Taylor and Rachel Rizzo, The U.S. or China? Europe Needs to Pick a Side, *Politico Magazine*, August 12, 2019, https://www.politico.com/magazine/story/2019/08/12/us-china-europe-relations-227614. Accessed August 13, 2019.

politicians that support pro-China positions and funding pro-China media in those countries.[67]

Bush and Trump squandered one of Washington's biggest assets: its impressive list of allies. What could have been a clear advantage on their part at a time like this has essentially foundered. Washington is proving not to have the necessary leverage to be shouldered by its long time allies when confronting Beijing. China, on the other hand, can summon willing economic partners almost everywhere. The implications of this are clear: while the United States confronted the Soviet Union with an impressive array of friends and allies at its back, it now embarks into a new Cold War very much on its own.

A BEIJING–MOSCOW AXIS?

Another factor enters the fray: Russia. In addition to its leading role within the process of globalization and in the construction of a new economic order, China has gotten closer to Russia in an integral strategic association with a very wide spectrum. This is one scenario in which Beijing plays the dominant role. Although in its document "China's National Defense in the New Era", China advocates for partnerships rather than alliances, its relationship with Russia is clearly more an alliance than a partnership. As Frederick Kempe from The Atlantic Council correctly puts it: "It's time to start worrying more about what could become the most profound geopolitical shift of the post-Cold War years. China's Xi Jinping and Russia's Vladimir Putin are deepening their two countries' strategic alignment even as long-time democratic allies across the Atlantic grow more distant".[68]

Gilbert Rozman, a well-known scholar in this area, has argued that the Moscow–Beijing convergence transcends economic

---

[67] Evan S. Medeiros, The Changing Fundamentals of US-China Relations, *The Washington Quarterly*, 2019 (Fall), p. 104.

[68] Frederick Kempe, Xi and Putin's Budding Bromance, June 1, 2019, https://www.atlanticcouncil.org/blogs/new-atlanticist/special-edition-xi-and-putin-s-budding-bromance. Accessed June 15, 2019.

considerations. On the contrary, he says it is essentially based on the commonality of national identities defined by their opposition to the West. While Xi Jinping aims at a East Asian geopolitical order controlled by Beijing, Vladimir Putin pursues a EuroAsiatic Union, where his country is called to play a prominent role. Both leaders have accused the U.S. of maintaining a Cold War mentality at odds with their countries' natural leadership aspirations. It is not mere coincidence, hence, that China supports Putin's actions in Ukraine, while Russia supports Xi's vision of East Asia. The two parties have expressed their willingness to create a new geopolitical order where the West is excluded from their respective areas of influence. Rozman concludes that this is not a simple tactical alliance but a geopolitical bloc in the making.[69]

Since 1996, the idea of a Moscow–Beijing axis has been in the air. It is actually a doctrine that bears the name of the then Prime Minister who first formulated it: Yevgeny Primakov.[70] As an anti-U.S. bloc in the making, this alliance could potentially become a true nightmare for Washington. Having to confront a Beijing–Moscow axis would undoubtedly be the United States' worst geopolitical scenario. But more than what the future may hold, this combination is already challenging Washington's historical primacy in different parts of the world.

In Europe, as Andrew A. Michta writes: "The combination of Beijing's efforts to aggregate economically and financially dependent states in Europe and Moscow's pressure to disaggregate NATO and the European Union poses a clear and present danger to the security of the Transatlantic community".[71] In the Arab Gulf region, China and Russia are lending a hand to Iran, by proposing a regional security organization that counteracts Washington's

---

[69] *The Sino-Russian Challenge to the World Order: National Identities, Bilateral Relations, and East versus West in the 2010s*, Washington D.C.: Woodrow Wilson Center Press, 2014.

[70] Mahdi D. Nazemroaya, *The Globalization of NATO*, Atlanta: Clarity Press, 2012.

[71] Andrew A. Michta, As China Surges, Europe Is on the Menu, *The American Interest*, September 11, 2019, https://www.the-american-interest.com/2019/09/11/as-china-surges-europe-is-on-the-menu/. Accessed September 12, 2019.

"maximum pressure" to that country. As a result, Beijing is asserting itself politically in this traditionally U.S.-dominated security area. Until now, China had limited itself to an economic presence in that region, but as a result of Moscow's strategic reinforcement, China seems ready to take a step further.[72] Something similar could be said in relation to Venezuela. The aggregate leverage of Beijing and Moscow is helping the Maduro regime to withstand Washington's strong pressures for its ousting. This changes China's traditional position in Latin America as well, a region where so far it has acted as a simple economic interlocutor.

To summarize, in terms of converge aptitude, Washington's confusing "withdrawal" and Beijing's active international engagement are clearly leaning the scale in China's direction.

[72] China backs Russian proposal for Gulf security, *The Arab Weekly*, August 3, 2019, https://thearabweekly.com/china-backs-russian-proposal-gulf-security. Accessed August 6, 2019.

Chapter Five

THE MISTAKES AVOIDANCE APTITUDE

In this Cold War in the making, the country that commits less mistakes will undoubtedly hold the better position. At this point in time, both China and the U.S. have made serious ones: China by overreaching its nationalism, the United States by squandering one of its biggest assets, its allies.

CHINA'S OVERREACH

China's nationalistic overreach has increased the costs of attaining its objectives simultaneously on almost every front. This has created a powerful anti-China coalition within the United States, which not only transcends the current polarization in Washington but gathers the most diverse sectors of its society, including most of its business community. As a result, it has unleashed a China containment policy in the United States, while it has affected China's globalizing credentials and its regional economic integration process. Many of the Southeast Asian countries have gotten closer to the United States for balancing purposes, and Japan is beefing up its armed forces and sending its navy into the South China Sea. The United States, Japan, India, and Australia (the so called "Quad", short for quadrilateral), have forged a *de facto* coalition to contain China.

At the same time, Beijing's tough hand in Hong Kong has not only generated massive protests but may end up strangling China's only real financial alternative to Wall Street, with seamless access to Western markets, high credit rating, equivalent status for its stock exchange with those in America, Europe, and Japan, and so on. Even more importantly for Beijing, Hong Kong has been transformed in the best propaganda tool for Taiwanese pro-independence sentiments. On another front, its mass interment and harsh treatment of ethnic Uighurs of Muslim faith in Xinjiang runs the risk of alienating the Muslim countries that represent the spine of its Belt and Road Initiative.

At the other side of the Eurasian landmass, its European trade partners have become increasingly wary of China's assertive foreign and defense policies. As a result, they are beginning to distance themselves from the Belt and Road Initiative. The country's public image has suffered an important blow in the world's public opinion forum, greatly affecting the international goodwill that it once enjoyed.

The above brings to mind Isaiah Berlin's famous distinction between the hedgehog and the fox. While the spiky creature, as Berlin explained, subordinates everything to a single central vision, soft-hair foxes pay more attention to the swamps, deserts, and chasms that may appear along the way. By obsessively and impatiently fixating on 2049 and on the "resurrection" of their country, China's leaders are clearly acting like hedgehogs. In the process, they have neglected the many loose ends along the route. These, no doubt about it, are proving to be costly and could backfire in a big way. No wonder, as Isaiah Berlin remarked: "Foxes were better equipped to survive in rapidly changing environments ...".[1]

Fortunately for China's image, Xi Jinping showed restraint in the handling of the massive Hong Kong protests of 2019. Although promoted by Beijing's overbearing attitude towards the city, the crisis was handled well. According to an article by Andrew J. Nathan, President Xi Jinping concluded that protesters' support was eroding

[1]John Lewis Gaddis, *On Grand Strategy*. London, UK: Penguin Books, 2019, p. 32.

and would eventually die out, that economic problems (housing costs specifically) were driving discontent, and that Beijing could prevail by waiting patiently while addressing those concerns. Moreover, Xi assumed that Western opposition to China was a given, no matter what happened in Hong Kong. Hence, he did not overreact to Western criticism and took it calmly. As a result, a crisis that could have escalated was kept under control.[2]

Notwithstanding the many problems caused by Beijing's hedgehog behavior, at least thus far, much of the damage of this nationalistic overreach has been countered. This is the result of two courses of action: One of China's making, and the other the U.S.'. The first derives from the counterbalancing force represented by the China-led globalization process, as described in the previous chapter. Through its economic initiatives and actions, China has been able to contain the overflowing of the fear dam, generated by China's nationalism. Australia's former Prime Minister Tony Abbot once described his country's approach to China in three words: "Fear and greed".[3] For the time being, greed seems to matter more than fear, not only in Australia but also in Asia in general. How long this will go on for is another matter to consider.

AMERICA'S BIGGEST MISTAKE

The second course of action, the one of U.S.' making, has been the squandering of its allies. As mentioned earlier, this has been America's biggest mistake. This network of international partnership bolstered America's national security and helped to multiply the country's influence. Acting in tandem with its allies would have made Washington's containment of China much easier, as was the case in relation to the Soviet Union during the Cold War. However, not only does China provide neutralizing economic incentives, but

---

[2] Andrew J. Nathan, How China Sees the Hong Kong Crisis: The Real Reasons Behind Beijing's Restraint, *Foreign Affairs*, November/December 2019.

[3] Hugh White, Canberra voices fears but who will contain the dragon?, *The Straits Times*, November 25, 2017.

the U.S. provides clear discouraging reasons for its allies to follow suit.

Former U.S. National Security Adviser Susan Rice puts the situation in the following terms: "With the President increasingly alienating our allies and insulting potential partners as 'shithole' countries, America is hardly well positioned to call upon of the good will and cooperation of other states when next we need it most. Moreover, in our intensified competition with China for influence in Asia and in markets globally, we are hobbled by the contrast between a president who embraces white nationalist mantras and holds people around the world in disdain, and China, which is still perceived by many developing countries as more sympathetic to the world's underdogs ...".[4]

Referring to the possibility of fostering an anti-China coalition by the Trump Administration, Paul Krugman concurs with Rice's assessment: "What about a coordinated international response? That's unlikely, both because it's not clear what Trump wants from China and because his general belligerence (not to mention his racism) has left America with almost nobody to take its side in global disputes".[5]

WHO WILL SHOOT THEMSELVES IN THE FOOT NEXT?

Hence, up to this point both parties have made important mistakes. However, those of the U.S. seem to be greater. In this context, we need to think ahead: Who may win the next point in this very particular competition of mischiefs? Who may be more prone to shooting themselves in the foot?

An overview of the international arena leads to the presumption that the United States is much closer to doing so. Getting into what

[4]When the President Is a Bigot, the Poison Spreads, *The New York Times*, August 6, 2019.

[5]China Tries to Teach Trump Economics: But he doesn't seem to be learning, *The New York Times*, August 8, 2019.

Obama used to call a dumb war would be a perfect way to do so, and Iran seems the right place for such an undertaking. This would not only distract Washington's attention from East Asia once again but might bog down the country's military capabilities for a second time in a protracted war.

As Nathan Levine wrote: "Indeed, Trump's tough approach to China is the one area where he enjoys broad bipartisan support, as even in badly divided Washington there is a growing recognition that China will be the most formidable geostrategic competition the United States has ever faced. Yet at the very moment when the United States faces its greatest strategic challenge since the Cold War, if not ever, some in the administration appear utterly distracted, beating the drums of war over an entirely less relevant threat: Iran ... Iran Derangement Syndrome may thus end up being catastrophic to America's long-term national interest, extending the 'period of strategic opportunity' beyond Beijing's wildest dreams and leaving China free to fulfill its ambitions of surpassing the United States economically, securing military predominance in the Western Pacific, and achieving a leading role in the evolution of the global system".[6]

But, could such a dumb war actually happen? Some background information may help clarify the situation. In 2006, the Iranian-American scholar Vali Nasr published an interesting book entitled *The Shia Revival: How Conflicts Within Islam Will Shape the Future.*[7] There, he explained how the Shiite, who together with the Sunni shared the religious scenario of the Middle East, attained commanding heights in the region.

THE EMPOWERMENT OF IRAN

Three facts had contributed to this state of affairs: The fall of Saddam Hussein's regime, the democratization process in Iraq, and

[6]Nathan Levine, China Will be the True Winner of a U.S.–Iran War, *op. cit.*
[7]Vali Nasr, *The Shia Revival: How Conflicts Within Islam Will Shape the Future,* New York: Norton, 2006.

the profound Iranian influence upon Iraq. The first of them brought down the secular contention wall upon Iran, represented by Sunni controlled Iraq. The second one made possible for the 65% Shia population of Iraq to gain control of government through the ballots. The third one placed the Iraqi government and the power networks within the country under Tehran's direct influence.

All these gave a tremendous boost to the revalorization of Shia's self-esteem all around the Middle East. According to Nasr, Shiites represented 90% of the Iranian population, around 70% of the population of the Persian Gulf, and around 50% of the population of the Muslim arch that goes from Lebanon to Pakistan — in total, a population of more than 140 million people. In Nasr's words: "The Middle East that will emerge from the Iraqi drama is not going to be more democratic, but it certainly will be more Shiite and more contentious".[8]

Nasr resorted to Hosni Mubarak's words to explain the latter: "Shiites are essentially loyal to Iran and not to their own countries".[9] Hence, after turning Iran into the main regional power, by destroying the regional balance of power, the U.S. had no other choice, according to Nasr, but to try to build a constructive relation with Tehran. The reason being that a suddenly empowered Iran could either be part of the solution or a very important part of the problems of the region.

Nasr's book anteceded the Lebanon events of 2006, where Shia's Hezbollah attained what no other Arab force had attained since the creation of Israel: the longest and most effective confrontation to Israel's military forces. This increased the Shiite and Iranian influence within the region even more.

No other country had been more responsible than the United States for the increase of Iran's regional power. However, Washington remained reluctant to approach Teheran, preferring to demonize it. Finally under intense pressure from the European Union, National Security Advisor Condoleezza Rice offered to

---

[8] *Ibid.*, p. 59.
[9] *Ibid.*, p. 67.

open direct negotiations with Tehran on the condition that the latter ceased with immediate effect all nuclear enrichment and allowed international inspection of its nuclear facilities. To place what would have been considered as a successful outcome of the negotiation as a precondition for it to take place was tantamount to foreclosing any chance of it happening in the first place.

However, in March 2007 the Bush Administration accepted Iran's participation within a broader scope and a different kind of negotiation, aimed at reducing tensions in Iraq. Other participants included Bahrain, Egypt, the five permanent members of the U.N. Security Council, the Arab League, and the Islamic Conference Organization. Notwithstanding the opportunity provided by this first approach between the U.S. and Iran, the Bush Administration used it to accuse Iran, in front of the others, of destabilizing Iraq. Far from reducing tensions between the two countries, the occasion only soured their relations even more.

Iranian grievances derived in good part from the fact that, immediately after September 11, they had put their best efforts to help the United States, and to reduce the old tensions between them, but it had all fallen onto deaf ears. They made that clear during the above mentioned multi-party negotiation, while insisting that they had been a moderating influence upon the Iraqi Shiites. Whatever the situation had been, the fact remains that the then Iranian President Ayatollah Khatami was a pragmatic and moderate man, which was definitely not the case with his radical successor Mahmoud Ahmadinejad. Washington's reluctance to negotiate with the former, in no small measure, helped electing the latter. This, again, did not serve well American interests.

OBAMA'S APPROACH TO IRAN

During Obama's Administration, Iran's Natanz uranium enrichment facility was presumably sabotaged with the malicious computer worm Stuxnet. Both the U.S. and Israel were signaled as alleged culprits. Tensions between Iran and the United Stated remained high during that period. However, in November 2013 began a 20-month negotiation within the so-called Joint Comprehensive Plan of Action. This negotiation included Iran, the five permanent members of the United Nations Security Council, and the European Union.

American Secretary of State John Kerry was instrumental in bringing this negotiation to a successful outcome. This was reached on July 14, 2015, through a landmark comprehensive nuclear agreement. The final agreement was based upon "the rules-based nonproliferation regime created by the Nuclear-Non Proliferation Treaty (NPT) and including especially the IAEA safeguards system".[10]

As a result, and among other concessions made by Iran, the country agreed to eliminate its stockpile of medium-enriched uranium, cut its stockpile of low-enriched uranium by 98%, and reduce by about two-thirds the number of its centrifuges for 13 years. The International Atomic Energy Agency (IAEA) was given regular access to all of Iran nuclear facilities to assess compliance with the agreement.

Conversely, Iran was to receive relief from the sanctions imposed by the U.S., the European Union, and the U.N. Security Council. An important by-product of this deal was the confidence-building process that had taken place between Washington and Tehran. Henceforward, they could look at each other face to face. Having been released from this burdensome situation, Washington had one less headache to worry about and more time and energy to focus in its foreign policy priority: Containing China.

However, in May 2018, President Trump announced that the United States was retiring from the agreement, while in November of the same year, he made public that the U.S. sanctions upon Iran were back in motion. That, notwithstanding the fact that IAEA inspectors spent 300 calendar days per year in Iran, verifying its compliance with the agreement, and that IAEA Director had stated

---

[10] George Perkovich, Mark Hibbs, James M. Acton and Toby Dalton, Parsing the Iran Deal, Carnegie Endowment for International Peace, August 8, 2015, https://carnegieendowment.org/2015/08/06/parsing-iran-deal-pub-60942. Accessed August 12, 2019.

in March 2018 that Iran was fully implementing its nuclear-related commitments.[11]

Hence, Washington and Tehran were back at round one, and tensions began to build up again — tensions that triggered an escalation process within the whole Gulf region. Moreover, the Trump administration's official list of demands placed on the Iranian regime was tantamount to the Islamic Republic's unconditional surrender. With demands so oversized, not even the most punishing sanctions can yield concessions. On the contrary, they become an incentive for Iran to escalate its actions as its only way out. This implied putting enough pressure on the American government to change its cost–benefit equation in relation to Iran.

GOING BACK TO ROUND ONE

In response to the escalation resulting from its utterly unnecessary actions in relation to the agreement, the United States took several military steps, such as the following: sending more than 500 soldiers to Prince Sultan Air Base in Saudi Arabia, deploying an Air Force fighter jet squadron and a B-52 bomber strike group, deploying the USS Abraham Lincoln strike group, and sending manned and unmanned intelligence, surveillance, and reconnaissance assets to the Middle East. As a U.S. Central Command statement explained, "this movement of forces provides an additional deterrent, and ensures our ability to defend our forces and interests in the region from emergent, credible threats".[12]

Having reached that point, the possibility of getting involved in a direct conflict with Iran runs high. This is especially so as nothing would please Saudi Arabia or Israel more, and this factor might be instrumental in steering matters in that direction. Actually, in

[11] International Atomic Energy Agency, IEA director general: Press conference, March 5, 2018, https://www.iaea.org/newscenter/statements/iaea-director-generals-introductory-remarks-at-press-conference. Accessed August 12, 2019.

[12] S. G. Jones, D. Newlee, N. Harrington, and J. S. Bermudez, Iran's Threat to Saudi Critical Infrastructure, CSIS, August 8, 2019, https://www.csis.org/analysis/irans-threat-saudi-critical-infrastructure-implications-us-iranian-escalation. Accessed August 9, 2019.

addition to his obsession with undoing President Obama's legacy, Trump had two reasons for retiring from the nuclear agreement and establishing punishing sanctions on Iran. The first one was siding with the Saudi Crown Prince Mohammed bin Salman. The second reason was siding with Benjamin Netanyahu. The former indicated that the U.S. supported Saudi's traditional rivalry with Iran, while the latter meant assuming as its own Israel's bellicose approach to Iran. In an interview with *MIT Technology Review*, Sean McFate asked himself what the purpose of the U.S. getting involved with Iran was: "Why is Iran a national security threat? We think of it as existential — and it is if you're like Israel or Saudi Arabia, but not the United States. We've forgotten what an existential threat is".[13] In other words, there are no reasons for the U.S. to get involved in this mess, other than doing Saudi Arabia's and Israel's job for them. Consequently, after having emboldened Iran as a result of a dumb war with Saddam Hussein, and when the main contentious issue with Tehran had already been solved, the U.S. might end up embarking itself in an even dumber war.

According to Thomas L. Friedman: "After Trump withdrew America from the Iran nuclear deal — even though Iran was abiding by its terms — his ambitious, sycophantic secretary of state, Mike Pompeo, gave a speech listing the 12 ways Iran had to change at home and abroad — demands that were tantamount to regime change ... And now Iran's countermove — in response to the U.S. withdrawal from the nuclear deal and reimposition of sanctions designed to drive Iran's oil sales to zero — has reportedly been to deploy proxies and covert operatives to attack oil and gas tankers passing through the Persian Gulf, forcing the U.S. to protect all of those shipping lanes ... For the moment at least, though, the Iranians, who are hurting economically, have chosen to call Trump's bluff. They've not only allegedly attacked the shipping lanes, but they've announced plans to resume higher uranium enrichment heading for weapons-grade levels. It's a dangerous escalation".[14]

[13]Janine di Giovanni, Why America isn't equipped for the new rules of war, *MIT Technology* Review (interview), October 24, 2019.

[14]Thomas L. Friedman, Trump's Only Consistent Foreign Policy Goal Is to One-Up Obama, *The New York Times*, June 18, 2019.

The one good thing that could have been said about Trump's isolationist impulses is that they could have prevented his country from getting involved in unnecessary foreign adventures. However, the Iran case proves otherwise. It appears then, that amid his many inconsistencies, the current guest of the White House can be at the same time an isolationist and a warmonger. Despite Trump's disavowal of America's global role, he has stocked his Cabinet with hawkish interventionists.

John Glaser, Christopher A. Preble and A. Trevor Thrall address this issue in a recent book. According to the authors, in a counter-intuitive way, as Washington's mandarins recoiled in horror while Trump dismantled their handiwork to pursue his "America First Agenda", Trump has doubled down, at the same time, on the imperial presidency. With inflated threat perceptions, defense spending, and the pursuit of global domination, Trump is setting course for continued interventionism.[15]

TIT FOR TAT

In addition to U.S. sanctions to Iran and to its main leaders, including the Supreme Leader Ayatollah Ali Khamenei, both parties have engaged in an action and reaction process. This has increased exponentially the tensions in the Persian Gulf. Iran's Revolutionary Guard has siezed oil tankers passing through the Gulf, while mine attacks have disabled oil tankers crossing the area. Iran destroyed an American drone entering its airspace, while a retaliatory missile strike by the U.S. was aborted within minutes of its launching. Washington directed a cyber-attack against Iran that wiped out the critical database of Iran's Revolutionary Guard. The Air Commander of the Iranian Revolutionary Guard warned the U.S. that its bases and aircraft carriers in the region were within range of Iranian missiles, after the American Secretary of State blamed Iran of an "unprecedented attack" on Saudi oil plants. President Trump

[15] John Glaser, Christopher A. Preble and A. Trevor Thrall, *Fuel to the Fire: How Trump Made America's Foreign Policy Even Worse (and How We Can We Recover)*, Washington D.C.: Cato Institute, 2019.

retorted that his country was "locked and loaded" and ready to respond to Iranian attacks on oil facilities in Saudi Arabia. This went on back and forth.

One of the most potentially dangerous of these tit-for-tat situations was the last one quoted. In September 2019, a drone and cruise missile attack struck two key oil installations inside Saudi Arabia, damaging facilities that processed the vast majority of that country's output. Although the pro-Iranian Shiite Houthi rebels claimed responsibility for the attack in Yemen, Washington pointed its accusing finger directly at Iran, calling this action an "act of war" by Tehran. While Secretary of State Mike Pompeo announced that the United States was working to build an anti-Iran coalition to deter further attacks, additional American forces and weapons were sent to Saudi Arabia.

According to *The New York Times* editorial board: "Whether conducted by Houthi rebels in Yemen, Shiite rebels in Iraq or by Iran itself, the drone attacks on Saudi oil facilities amount to a sharp provocation against the United States. And at this dangerous moment, President Trump has few options, few allies, a depleted national security team and little credibility ... Though Saudi Arabia was the target, the gauntlet was at Mr. Trump's feet, and the immediate question was how he would respond ... The United States is now facing a serious crisis for which there was no real reason other than Mr. Trump's compulsion to undo President Barack Obama's legacy by abandoning a nuclear deal that had broad international support".[16]

Analyzing the Iranian perspective on this matter, Suzanne Maloney, from *The Washington Post*, wrote: "Iranian leaders appear to have concluded that restraint will probably achieve little in extricating the country from its predicament. Restraint, after all, was Iran's first response after Trump exited the Iran nuclear deal in 2018 and began economic pressure. It achieved only misery. Unilateral U.S. sanctions dealt a catastrophic blow, eliminating expected inflows of foreign investments, slashing the value of Iran's currency (the rial) and

[16] *The New York Times* editorial board, 'Locked and Loaded', but for What?, *The New York Times*, September 16, 2019.

shrinking the economy. The rest of the world offered little more than commiseration and empty denunciations of Trump's 'maximum pressure' policy. Facing a financial blockade with no end in sight, the Islamic Republic changed its approach four months ago, shifting toward one that has served its interest best since its establishment 40 years ago: It launched a counterattack ... In May, Iran's leaders again concluded that countering American pressure required aggressive action that would change the cost-benefit calculus for Washington and the world ... An Iranian leadership steeped in mistrust for the international system bristled at the indignity of submitting to Washington's mandate, as well as the affront of indebtedness to Europe. It wonder: Could a bigger, bolder shock to the global economy generate a more favorable resolution of Iran's economic siege?".[17]

A COSTLY AND PROTRACTED WAR

In the September 2019 Democratic Party Presidential Debate, nearly every candidate agreed on at least one thing: The United States should reenter the Iran nuclear deal. This, certainly, would be the fastest way to end the conundrum and the risk of war the Trump Administration has placed itself in. This looks extremely difficult though. Not only because, for the most megalomaniac President that the U.S. has produced in decades, swallowing his own pride does not seem possible, but because the hardliners have been tremendously empowered in Tehran. As *Al-jazeera* pointed out, Trump's decision to withdraw his country from the nuclear deal, and his escalating anti-Iranian rhetoric, gave the hardliners in Iran the excuse they needed to discredit and corner Rouhani's moderate government.[18]

Not surprisingly, the worst was yet to come. On January 3, 2020, the United States shocked the world by killing General Qasem

---

[17] Suzanne Maloney, Why Iran's leadership thinks escalation can pay off, *The Washington Post*, September 18, 2019.

[18] Massoumeh Torfeh, Trump's threats are empowering hardliners in Iran, May 22, 2018, https://www.aljazeera.com/indepth/opinion/trump-jcpoa-decision-empowered-hardliners-iran-180518114306512.html. Accessed August 13, 2019.

Soleimani with a drone strike attack in Bagdad. In addition to being an iconic Iranian war hero, he was considered the second most powerful person of that country's regime. This assassination represented a leap forward of tensions, as it directly targeted a top official of a sovereign member of the international community. This led, in turn, to an Iranian ballistic missile on U.S. forces based in Iraq, five days later. Both events could have configured a state of war between Iran and the United States. Fortunately, the two countries restrained from further escalation at that point.

This could turn out to become a costly and protracted war. Since 2001, the United States has spent US$5.9 trillion in its wars in that region of the world. That total is almost US$2 trillion more than all the Federal Government spending during the 2017–2018 fiscal year.[19] Hence, of the current US$22 trillion national debt, approximately US$6 trillion is bill for the post-9/11 wars.[20] Such an amount not only busted America's public debt but left no budgetary space for countless development projects that could have placed the U.S. economy on a much better footing. However, Washington seems prone to stumble over the same stone, which would be particularly irrational at a moment when the federal budget deficit is expected to reach US$960 billion in 2019 and US$1 trillion in 2020.[21] That would accelerate America's economic decline, in relation to China's upward economic curve.

AN EXTENDED STRATEGIC OPPORTUNITY

As Nicholas Kristof writes: "A full war with Iran would be a catastrophe. Iran has twice the population of Iraq and would be a much

---

[19] Amanda Macias, America has spent $5.9 trillion on wars in the Middle East and Asia since 2001, CNBC, November 14, 2018, https://www.cnbc.com/2018/11/14/us-has-spent-5point9-trillion-on-middle-east-asia-wars-since-2001-study.html. Accessed August 12, 2019.

[20] Elliot Ackerman, Born into War, *Time*, October 21, 2019.

[21] Jim Tankersley and Emily Cochrane, Budget Deficit on Path to Surpass $1 Trillion Under Trump, *The New York Times*, August 21, 2019.

more formidable foe than Iraq was. So Trump has a genuine dilemma: Inaction may be perceived as weakness, while military strikes may escalate and drag us into cataclysm. But this dilemma is of Trump's own making. We are in this mess because Trump abandoned the landmark 2015 Iranian nuclear deal ... Instead, I'm afraid we risk slipping into conflict. Nobody wants a war, but getting out of this will require skillful diplomacy, which isn't something the Trump team has much demonstrated".[22]

If the U.S. were to enter in a war with Iran, China would certainly receive a fabulous and unexpected gift. In his book *Fire and Ashes: Success and Failure in Politics,* Michael Ignatieff argues how politics is more often than not a tale of grasping luck. He referred to the stories by ancient Roman statesman Cicero, according to whom *Fortuna,* the goddess of fate, shifts unexpectedly from one side to another.[23] China's luck could indeed turn out to be immeasurable, if suddenly the Americans decided to jump into a swamp of their own making.

According to Beijing's self-conceptualized "strategic opportunity", the first two decades of the new millennia were to be a relatively benign period, in which China could increase its power without serious challenges from abroad. Experts, however, have concluded that such a period of strategic opportunity ended earlier than originally estimated.[24] If the U.S.–Iran conflict materializes, China's strategic opportunity could not only be greatly revitalized but extended well beyond its original estimation. With Washington's attention and priority focused elsewhere, China may be able to replicate the gigantic opportunity that it enjoyed during George W. Bush's years.

As an established superpower that plays the geopolitical game in different fields at the same time, the risks of distraction and dispersion are much higher for the United States. Hubris plus its characteristic

---

[22] Nicholas Kristof, We're not the Saudis' Mercenaires, *The New York Times,* September 18, 2019.

[23] Michael Ignatieff, *Fire and Ashes: Success and Failure in Politics,* Toronto: Vintage Canada, 2015.

[24] David Gitter, Is China Period of Strategic Opportunity Over?, *The Diplomat,* May 28, 2016, https://thediplomat.com/2016/05/is-chinas-period-of-strategic-opportunity-over/. Accessed August 13, 2019.

short spans of attention can do much damage to the country. Conversely, with a much less developed sense of hubris as yet, more localized and closer to home geopolitical ambitions plus a single minded sense of purpose, China is much better prepared to remain in focus. Although responsible for alerting Washington ahead of time, the explicit purpose of becoming number one at mid-century provides Beijing with a solid strategic compass.

Distraction and dispersion are not the only mistakes that the two parties can make, as we saw at the beginning of this chapter. However, in the context of a long-term strategic competition, maintaining a steady course within a preexisting route map becomes a clear advantage.

Former Australian Prime Minister Kevin Rudd captured this succinctly when he wrote: "Since the fall of the Soviet Union there has been little strategic direction about the idea of the West itself, and the core elements of the liberal democratic and capitalistic project. Instead, the West is increasingly self-absorbed, self-satisfied and globally complacent. China is marching towards its perception of its global destiny. It has a strategy. The West has none".[25] Having seen the populist uprisings of Europe and the United States and the disarray in which liberal democracy finds itself on both places, Rudd's remarks become clear a more poignant.

The above situation is particularly critical in the United States, given the divide between the two different societies that coexist within it — a divide that expresses itself in different contexts, mainly social, regional, and political.

THE SOCIAL DIVIDE

The social divide materializes with harshly contrasting polarity. Since the end of the 1970s, the earnings of the upper 1% have increased 156%, and that of the 0.1% at the top by 362%, while the

[25] Kevin Rudd, Xi Jinping offers a long-term view of China's ambition, *Financial Times*, October 23, 2017.

40% at the bottom owes more than it owns.[26] Moreover, the top 1% owns almost as much wealth as the bottom 90%. The salary of the majority of the working population, meanwhile, has remained stagnant since the end of the 1970s.[27] Billionaires in the U.S. grew tenfold between 2000 and 2015. In 2000, the U.S. had 51 billionaires with a combined net worth of US$480 billion. In 2015, the country had a record-breaking 540 billionaires with a combined net worth of US$2.4 trillion. Moreover, the 20 wealthiest Americans own more wealth than the bottom 150 million Americans.[28]

Jonathan Gruber and Simon Johnson explain this situation in graphic terms: "From 1993 to 2015, more than half of all the income growth in the United States went to the total 1 percent of the income distribution, that is, if you took all the growth in US incomes over that entire period, you could divide into two piles: a slightly larger one going to the top 1 % of all Americans, and a slightly smaller one going to the other 99 %".[29]

The mind-blowing extent of this economic inequality is described by Martin Ford in the following terms: "While inequality has been increasing in nearly all industrialized countries the United States remains a clear outlier. According to the Central Intelligence Agency's analysis, income inequality in America is roughly on par with that of the Philippines and significantly exceeds that of Egypt, Yemen and Tunisia".[30]

As a result of this economic polarization, only two types of jobs have increased in number in the last few years. On the one hand,

---

[26] Alvin Powell, The cost of inequality: When a fair shake isn't, *Harvard Gazzete,* February 1, 2016, https://news.harvard.edu/gazette/story/2016/02/the-costs-of-inequality-when-a-fair-shake-isnt/. Accessed January 27, 2017.

[27] Nicholas Kristof, 'Occupy Wall Street' and inequality, *The New York Times,* October 15, 2011; Bernie Sanders, *Our Revolution: A Future to Believe,* London: Profile Books, 2017, p. 207.

[28] *Ibid.*, pp. 207, 208.

[29] Jonathan Gruber and Simon Johnson, *Jump-Starting America: How Breakthrough Science Can Revive Economic Growth and the American Dream,* New York: Public Affairs, 2019, p. 127.

[30] Martin Ford, *The Rise of Robots: Technology and the Threat of a Jobless Future,* New York: Basic Books, 2015, p. 46.

Wall Street financiers, Silicon Valley entrepreneurs, corporate managers, doctoral engineers, physicists and the like are doing extremely well. On the other hand, there are the low-end services undertaken by nurses, domestic aides, food preparers, janitors, auto repair workers, nutritionists and such. Between both types of jobs is a gap that has been labeled as the missing middle.

THE REGIONAL DIVIDE

The regional divide is directly linked to the social one. Fundamental differences exist between large coastal cities, essentially global cities, and inland United States. In Paul Krugman's words: "On the economic side, some parts of America, mainly big coastal cities, have been getting much richer, but other parts have been left behind ... In the most part I'm in agreement with Berkeley's Enrico Moretti, whose 2012 book *The New Geography of Jobs*, is must reading for anyone trying to understand the state of America. Moretti argues that structural changes in the economy have favored industries that employ highly educated workers — and that these industries do best in locations where there are a lot of these workers. As a result, these regions are experiencing a virtuous circle of growth: Their knowledge-intensive industries prosper, drawing even more educated workers, which reinforces their advantage. And at the same time, regions that started with a poorly educated workforce are in a downward spiral, both because they're stuck in the wrong industries and because they're experiencing what amounts to brain drain".[31]

On the one hand, then, there are busy, favored coastal cities. On the other hand, there are areas that are left behind that are beginning to show alarming signs of social decay. A Harvard University analysis of 1.4 billion Internal Revenue Service records on income and life expectancy showed amazing differences in life expectancy between the richest and the poorest. People living in wealthy cities such as New York City, Boston, Los Angeles, or San Francisco have

---

[31] Paul Krugman, What's the Matter with Trumpland?, *The New York Times*, April 2, 2018.

significantly longer life expectancies than that those in poorer inland regions. Life expectancy in the latter is now equal to places like Sudan or Pakistan. When data was laid over maps of the United States, low life expectancy was concentrated not in the Deep South but across the Midwest Rust Belt. People in New York or San Francisco have longer lifespans than those in the industrial Midwest. Among men, the gap is around 15 years.[32]

Paul Krugman gets into further detail as to the reason of this life expectancy gap between big coastal cities and the Midwest Rust Belt. In his words: "To be sure, social collapse in the white working class is a deadly serious issue. Literally. Last fall, the economists Anne Case and Agnus Deaton attracted widespread attention with a paper showing that mortality among middle-aged white Americans, which had been declining for generations, started rising circa 2000. This rising death rate mainly reflected suicide, alcohol and overdoses of drugs, notably prescriptions opioids ... And other signs of social unraveling, from deteriorating health to growing isolation, are also on the rise among American whites. Something is going seriously wrong in the heartland".[33]

THE POLITICAL DIVIDE

This social and regional divides translate into a third divide: the political one. Republican areas of the country rely on lower-skill and lower-productivity traditional sectors like manufacturing and resource extraction. Democratic areas, mostly urban districts, exhibit large concentrations of the country's higher-skill and higher-tech professionals and digital services. This polarization generates an important degree of political turbulence.

According to a Brookings report: "Not only are red and blue America experiencing two different economies, but those

[32] Peter Reuell, For life expectancy, money matters, *The Harvard Gazette,* April 11, 2016, https://news.harvard.edu/gazette/story/2016/04/for-life-expectancy-money-matters/. Accessed January 27, 2017.

[33] Anne Case and Angus Deaton, Republican elite's reign of disdain, *The New York Times,* March 18, 2016.

economies are diverging fast. In fact, radical change is transforming the two parties' economies in real time (...) Turn to our economic and demographic data, however, and it's clear that a series of genuine, penetrating shifts have been happening at warp speed through the last decade. These shifts are massively altering the two parties' economic identities. For one thing, the two parties have in just 10 years gone from near-parity on prosperity and income measures to stark, fast-moving divergence (...) The concentration of more than 70% of the nation's professional and digital service economy in the territory of one party would seem to register an almost unsustainable degree of polarization (...) If that's how the politics of the decade's changing economy are going to play out, then political analyst Ron Brownstein may be right that the nation may be heading deeper into an era of sustained turbulence that 'pits what America has been against what it is becoming'".[34]

The three aforementioned divides lead to a high degree of political volatility. The United States has become a highly unpredictable place. While it is impossible to ascertain in which direction the country is heading, it is almost certain that it will keep shifting its route every time that a change of political parties occurs in the White House. Zigzagging becomes natural when completely different societies compete for political power. This is well exemplified by the notoriously divergent approach towards COVID-19 by blue and red states or, in general, by Democrats and Republicans.

Moreover, such a divided country becomes natural prey for demagogues who may easily proliferate as a result of the acute resentment of the left-behinds. This, by extension, leads to political extremes. Trump and the populists' control of the Republican Party may not be the exception, but the expression of an emerging normality.

The rigid two-party system and the existence of the Electoral College seemed to act as contention barriers against populism,

[34] Mark Muro and Jacob Whiton, America has two economies — and they are diverging fast, September 19, 2019, https://www.brookings.edu/blog/the-avenue/2019/09/10/america-has-two-economies-and-theyre-diverging-fast/. Accessed September 25, 2019.

simply because it took away any chance of success by a populist party. Even Ross Perot, who ran two of the strongest presidential showings by a third party or an independent candidate in U.S. history, had no chance of success. In the 1992 election, he received 18.9% of the popular vote, about 19,741,065 votes, but did not get any Electoral College vote. In 1996, after having founded the Reform Party, he received 8% of the popular vote, but again not a single Electoral College vote. While he showed that populism had quite a good support in the country, he also made evident the impossibility of winning the presidency from outside the two-party system.

Hence, the only chance that populism had was by conquering the two traditional political parties from the inside. The first recent populist movement that tried to do that was the Tea Party. Although its grasp on the Republican Party proved to be very important, it remained clearly insufficient to obtain control of the party. The 2016 Presidential Election was to become a landmark in American politics, as both Bernie Sanders and Donald Trump emerged as formidable populist candidates within the two-party system. Thus, from then on, populism was able to operate at ease within the two major parties, leading them further away from the center and killing any remaining possibility of consensus building.

Strategic consistency, hence, ranks low in the case of the United States. The contrast with China in this area could not be higher. While China knows well where it wants to go, and by extension can more easily avoid mistakes along the road, the U.S.' polarized vision of society and its lack of route map makes it prone to get lost en route. This is an easy way to commit mistakes.

Chapter Six

THE UNIVERSALITY APTITUDE

Referring to the contrasting ways in which China and the West see their roles in the world, Martin Jacques expressed: "They both, in a sense, regarded themselves to be universal ... Europe interpreted this proposition essentially as an evangelizing mission to transform the world. To take the message of civilization to those who were not civilized through the colonial mission, through Christianity, through the language, through the culture, and so on. China's interpretation of universality was entirely different. China did not see it in terms of externalizing itself. Because the Chinese idea of universalism was we are the Middle Kingdom. We are the land under Heaven. We are the highest form of civilization. So, why leave China? What's the point of leaving China when is it where we are all that could be? So the Chinese interpretation of its universalism was essentially a stay-at-home universalism, whereas the European version was to go overseas, to go around the world".[1] Kishore Mahbubani agrees with this vision, saying: "The Chinese mind has always focused on developing Chinese civilization, not developing global civilization".[2]

---

[1] Martin Jacques, What China will be as a great power, *op. cit.*

[2] Kishore Mahbubani, *The New Asian Hemisphere: The Irresistible Shift of Global Power to the East,* New York: Public Affairs, 2008, p. 239.

WHAT MIGHT HAVE BEEN

The Chinese version of universalism, though, might have followed a more similar pattern to that of the West. If Admiral Zheng He's experience during the Ming dynasty had not been aborted in a radical and definitive manner, another historical evolution might have taken place. Between 1405 and 1424, indeed, Zheng He undertook six epic voyages that led his fleet to Southeast Asia, India the Persian Gulf and the East coast of Africa. However, according to Gavin Menzies' assertion in his book *1421: The Year China Discovered America*, Admiral Zheng He went much further than has been conventionally accepted. This thesis, which is not subscribed by historians, affirms that in his 1421–1423 trip, the Admiral's fleet reached America and circumnavigated the globe.[3]

As it stands, nonetheless, conventional history presents a sufficiently breathtaking picture. Over 60 of the 317 ships on his first voyage were enormous vessels that were over 400 feet long, 160 feet wide, several stories high and had 9 masts and 12 sails. The likes of these ships had never been seen before, and it would take until World War I to assemble an armada of such proportions again. Nearly 28,000 people participated in this first expedition, which besides sailors and soldiers, also included astronomers and scholars.

At the time, the Ming court was divided between the pro-expansionist voices led by Admiral Zheng He and the traditionalist Confucian advisers, who argued for introspection and frugality. Emperor Zhu Di, better known as the Yongle Emperor, sided with the former. His aim was to overwhelm foreign peoples with China's advanced technology and richness, which would render the addition of new tributary countries. According to traditional arrangements, China regularly received gifts of tribute in exchange for benefiting such countries with military posts and trade treaties.[4] The

[3] Gavin Menzies, *1421: The Year China Discovered America*, London: Bantan Books, 2003.

[4] The Ming Voyages, Asia for Educators, Columbia University, http://afe.easia.columbia.edu/special/china_1000ce_mingvoyages.htm. Accessed 10 July, 2019.

wide geographical scale covered by Zheng He's trips was an obvious testimony to the Emperor's expansive and ambitious aims.

Upon the Yongle Emperor's death, however, this chapter ended as suddenly as it had begun. In Niall Ferguson words: "But then, in 1424, this ... was shattered. Yongle died — and China's overseas ambitions were buried with him ... The *haijin* decree definitively banned oceanic voyages. From 1500, anyone in China found building a ship with more than two masts was liable to the death penalty; in 1551 it became a crime even to go to sea in such a ship. What lay behind this momentous decision? We may never be sure. But the consequences of China's turn inwards seem clear."[5]

The tributary system, of course, did not disappear but remained confined to China's neighbors. The idea of projecting China's might over faraway lands was never again part of its vision. The country, thus, kept itself within its Great Wall and its conservative Confucianism, thus leading to an inward looking status quo power.

The same Ming dynasty, under which Admiral Zheng's expeditions took place, was responsible to a great extent for a very significant event in the history of China: the building of the Great Wall of China (whose original more primitive version had begun during the Qin Dynasty, in the second century BC). The Ming dynasty, like every other regime in Chinese history, was obsessed with the need to hold China together and shield it from foreigners. As Mark Leonard explains: "The Chinese have labelled this obsession with boundaries the 'Great Wall mentality'".[6]

PORTUGUESE AND SPANIARDS

The history of European sailing contemporary to that of the Chinese, unassertive in size though it was, virtually changed the conception that mankind had of the planet where it lived. It took two routes, and two sets of very different sailors, from two countries that

[5] Niall Ferguson, *Civilization: The West and the Rest* [Kindle version], London: Penguin Books, 2011, retrieved from Amazon.com, location 971/8539.

[6] *Op. cit.*, p. 132.

shared the same peninsula — Portugal and Spain — to achieve this momentous result. Their sailing practices differed accordingly: The Portuguese took small prudent steps while the Spaniards took the full plunge.

While Admiral Zheng He was making his majestic voyages, the Portuguese who were at the vanguard of European overseas explorations began their very modest West African expeditions. Beginning with the islands of Azores and Madeira, the Portuguese would keep pushing south along the coasts of West Africa. They explored the land and the seas down below while diligently establishing a system of slave and ivory trading posts, never venturing inland. In the late 15th century, they discovered a sea route to the East around the Cape of Good Hope.

As Parag Khanna wrote: "With the Ming having withdrawn their Indian Ocean fleets, Europeans took advantage of the latest technologies in shipbuilding and weaponry to advance trade among Europe, Africa, the Americas and Asia".[7] Between 1497 and 1499, the explorer Vasco da Gama led the first Portuguese fleet around Africa, arriving to current Calcutta in India. It just included four small ships and 170 men. The instructions given to him by his king were to go in the search of spices. Since 1453, when Constantinople fell to the Ottoman Turks, the control of the spice trade was placed entirely in their hands. They soon raised taxes and increased tariffs to the point of virtually shutting off the spice supply to "infidel" Europe. As a result, sailing became the only obvious way of reaching the distant lands where the spices came from.

In 1510, the Portuguese had already founded the colony of Goa on the western coast of India and, a few years later, the Malacca peninsula (current Malaysia) had become its strategic base for trade expansion towards China and Southeast Asia. Subsequently, they seized cities in today's Indonesia where they constructed fortified settlements seeking to dominate and control the spice trade. The Portuguese Empire of the East, with its capital in Goa, had strongholds in all of the Asian sub-continents, East Africa and the Pacific.

[7] *Op. cit.*, location 643/6214.

Christopher Columbus proposed to reach the East Indies by sailing westwards instead of taking the long coastal sail eastwards. Building on the knowledge that the Portuguese had gather on the so-called trade winds, he daringly proposed to sail through the open sea. The Spanish Crown, seeing the chance to reach the lands of cloves, cinnamon, pepper, nutmeg and ginger, through what Columbus insisted on was a shorter route, decided to finance his expedition. The result is well known. In 1492, believing he had arrived at the East Indies, he found himself in lands previously unknown to the Europeans.

Cosmographer Martin Waldseemuller coined the term America in 1507 to name those lands. This was done to honor Amerigo Vespucci, who was the first to establish that the lands encountered by Columbus were not the Indies easternmost but a separate and previously unknown land mass. Vespucci himself, in a letter to his patron Lorenzo di Pierfranceso de Medici, called it "Mundus Novus", that is, New World.[8]

When the Portuguese King John II found out about the successful voyage of Columbus, he sent a threatening letter to King Ferdinand and Queen Isabella of Spain. He reminded them that according to a previous agreement between their countries, ratified by a Papal bull, all lands south of the Canary Islands, in the western part of Africa, belonged to Portugal. Hence, King John II announced that he was making arrangements for a Portuguese fleet to take possession of his new lands. This led to a new Papal bull and further negotiations between Spain and Portugal, which concluded with the so-called Treaty of Tordesillas. This divided the New World territories between them.

REACH VERSUS GRIP

Spain and Portugal felt empowered to do as they wished in their "America". But as Portugal had a deliberately contained

[8] Germán Arciniegas. *Cuando América Completó la Tierra*, Bogotá: Villegas Editores, 2001.

expansionist strategy in that part of the world, the Spaniards reacted swiftly to the new opportunities. The Portuguese saw those territories as low priority ones when compared to its Far East colonial enterprise and took their time in holding them properly. For the Spaniards, on the other hand, a span of 50 years was enough to discover, explore, and subdue those lands. Moreover, for urban-minded Spaniards, founding "cities" was a civilizing imperative, which soon produced a whole network of towns and urban settings around their part of the Americas.

As a matter of fact, the first Portuguese trip to their American territories happened by accident. In 1500, an expedition headed by Pedro Alvares de Cabral, en route to South Africa, drifted westward and landed somewhere along the Brazilian coast. Those lands were soon called by the name of a local dye tree, the "Pau Brasil".

The Portuguese had a global reach unknown to the Spaniards (whose only Asian possessions were The Philippines and The Marianas, which became simple extensions of its American Empire through its Galleon Trade with Mexico inaugurated in 1565). But whereas the Spaniards had their American possessions under firm grip, the Portuguese were highly vulnerable in their overstretched territories. According to historian Bernard Vlekke: "...the Portuguese empire in the East was decayed, rotten and tottering, a structure which would collapse if given even a moderate blow".[9] Such a blow was provided by the Dutch through their East India Company, which all through the late 1600s and 1700s displaced the Portuguese from Hormuz to Malacca.

According to Niall Fergusson: "But the Spaniards rebellious and commercially adept Dutch subjects came to appreciate the potential of the new spice route; indeed, by the mid-1600 they had overtaken the Portuguese in terms of both number of ships and tonnage sailing around the Cape. The French also entered the lists. And what of the English...? How could they possibly sit on the sidelines with news coming in that their arch-foes the Spaniards and the French were making their fortunes overseas? Sure enough, it was not long before

[9] Stephen R. Brown, *Merchant Kings*, New York: Thomas Dunne Books, 2009, p. 25.

the English joined the race for overseas commerce".[10] The competition between European countries, in possession of this dog eat dog mentality, led to the worldwide expansion of their expeditions and commercial undertakings. And with it, the seeds of colonialism and imperialism were sown.

PAX BRITANNICA

Fast forward to 1914, and we see the United Kingdom the unmistakable master of this game. Between 1815 and 1914, 10 million square miles of territory and 400 million people had been added to the British Empire. This was to be known as the Second British Empire: The first one had been established between 1583 and 1783. Scattered around five continents (Ireland and Malta also in Europe), Britain had the greatest empire ever known. However, more relevant than the empire itself was its hegemony. The latter broadly coincided in time with its second empire, and it was normally accepted that it had expanded during the period after the Battle of Waterloo in 1815 and the beginning of World War I in 1914.

Hegemony, as explained in Chapter Four, requires recognition from a wide group of nations of a prevailing set of rules and values, identified with the leading power. Hegemony requires, thus, that power must be recognized as legitimate through ideological and cultural perception. Empire, conversely, does not require of the recognition given by others nor of any kind of legitimacy. Strength is the word normally associated with this last concept. Neither the Russian, the French or the Austro-Hungarian empires, to name but a few, ever required of the acceptance or the willingness of the people under their dominion. Most empires, nonetheless, aspired at attaining some kind of justification for their supremacy.

As expressed by Senator J. William Fulbright in 1968, in each case that justification not only varied but also had different names. The British called it the "White Man Burden", the French "The Civilizing Mission" and the 19th century Americans used notions

[10] Niall Fergusson, *Civilization: The West and the Rest,* op. cit., location 1027/8539.

such as "Manifest Destiny" or the "Promotion of Liberty".[11] With the probable exception of the Belgians in Congo and the Germans in Namibia, who felt no need to provide any kind of justification for the enslavement of their populations, Western metropolis tended to give a meaning to such a rule.

"Pax Britannica", the name under which British hegemony was known, was a totally different proposition. Curiously enough, British hegemony emerged and developed in an era dominated by balance-of-power notions, as proclaimed by great political figures such as Klemens von Metternich and Otto von Bismarck. Despite this, Britain was able to take advantage of the synergy resulting from a group of policies and undertakings of varied nature, to become the central, organizing, great power of the time.

Thanks to the Royal Navy, secure transit on the oceans was guaranteed. British steamboats revolutionized transport and shortened distances. Its submarine telegraphic cables crisscrossed a good part of the globe, interconnecting human beings in every nook and corner of the world. Taking advantage of this network of telegraph cables, the so-called All Red Line, their news agencies were able to project an Anglo-centric imprint to newspapers around the world.

The fixed parity between the Sterling Pound and gold preserved international monetary stability. Economic liberalism, which emerged from its land, became the ruling paradigm, defining the rules of world trade. Their practices of management and accounting became universal. Their investments projected worldwide, giving shape to numerous financial institutions, railroad networks and infrastructural developments.

Thanks to British initiative, the first group of international organizations emerged, chiefly among them the International Telecommunication Union. The British concept of civilized life was to become a "soft power" juggernaut, and this was being copied by elites around the world. No other contemporary power was able to shine in so many different fields, attaining the kind of global impact and recognition that the United Kingdom did.

---

[11] Niall Ferguson, *Colossus: The Rise and Fall of the American Empire*, op. cit., p. 23.

Moreover, together with its hegemony, and in many cases merging with it, the UK became the undisputed leader of the so-called First Globalization — the period between 1870 and 1914. This came as a natural extension of its championing of free trade around the world and by its holding of the global reserve currency, the British pound. This gave Great Britain the ability to set international economic rules and norms, which in turn reinforced its hegemonic power. At the time, being the world's largest Empire, the hegemonic power of the day and the leader of the first globalization wave was no small attainment. Not surprisingly, Anglo-centric contents became universal.

AMERICA'S EMERGENCE

By 1918, with the end of World War I, Britain's hegemonic power had evaporated, as had globalization itself. The UK just remained an imperial power, but a decaying one. At this point in time, the United States was the obvious candidate to take the hegemonic torch from Britain. After its bloody and costly Civil War, the country had spent the remaining three decades of the century settling and incorporating its western frontier. At the same time, the Industrial Revolution boosted the nation's economy. The American steel industry, its immense oil resources and its revolutionary methods of production, together with the sudden expansion of its consumer base, resulting from immigration, expanded its economy at an exponential rate.

In Henry Kissinger's words: "By 1885, the United States had surpassed Great Britain, then considered the world's major industrial power, in manufacturing output. By the turn of the century, it was consuming more energy than Germany, France, Austria-Hungary, Russia, Japan, and Italy combined. Between the Civil War and the turn of the century, American coal production rose by 800 percent, steel rails by 523 percent, railway track mileage by 567 percent. Immigration contributed to the doubling of the American population. And the process of growth was likely to accelerate".[12]

[12] Henry Kissinger, *Diplomacy*, op.cit., p. 37.

Export markets came as a natural extension. With American manufactures aiming at foreign markets, the first steel ships appeared. This was followed by innovations in steam propulsion, hydraulics and electricity. And so the innovation and expansion spiral followed, transforming the U.S. into the largest and most dynamic economy on the planet.

America's participation in World War I, which overflowed the war theater with men, equipment and food, leaned the scaled in favor of the Allied powers. Moreover, through President Woodrow Wilson's participation in the negotiations that led to the Treaty of Versailles, the U.S. exhibited the right ideas at the right time. Theirs were the most universal and far-reaching proposals on the table, giving birth to the League of Nations and to the new international order.

Nothing would have seemed more logical at that point than for the United States to hold the hegemonic torch in its hands. However, this was an isolationist time for Washington. Charles P. Kindelberger has argued that this undefined period, in which the United Kingdom could no longer sustain its hegemonic leadership and the United States refused to accept it, created the conditions for the 1929 economic recession to turn into a long and painful depression.[13]

CIVILIZATIONAL CONTINUITY

At the end of World War II, the U.S. could no longer abstain — nor was it willing to — from assuming the hegemonic role. Its overwhelming economic strength, its technological edge, and its convictions in regard to values such as liberal democracy, free trade and multilateral security, naturally drove Washington into the center stage.

While referring to the convergence aptitude, in Chapter Four, we gave an in-depth explanation on how America's hegemony developed and how it reached its zenith after the fall of the Berlin Wall.

---

[13] Charles P. Kindelberger, *The World in Depression, 1929–1939*, Berkeley: Berkeley University Press, 1973.

At its inception, this process included several convergent layers. Chief among them was the creation of an institutional framework allowing for the nations of the world to diplomatically work out their differences together, the creation of an international financial system with common rules and procedures and the creation of a geographically diverse group of multilateral security arrangements.

The fact that the United States inherited the hegemonic torch from a country from which it had also inherited its language and civilization had profound implications. As a result, the world continued to relate across Anglo-centric contents. Nothing similar to this had been seen in history since the commanding heights of the Greco-Roman civilization. But even then, the cultural traits between Greeks and Romans were not as similar, nor did they share a common language.

Given that kind of continuity, Britain has been able to retain a residual level of influence that otherwise would have been very difficult to keep. The following few examples can attest to this: present-day London has been able to retain its position at the head of the global cities and financial centers, together with New York; the BBC, *Financial Times* and *The Economist* maintain the world's top media ranks, jointly with America's most prestigious media conglomerates such as Time-Warner-CNN, *The New York Times* and *The Washington Post*; Oxbridge has joined forces with the Ivy League, and they are at the zenith of the academic universe; Chatham House competes with Brookings for the title of the most respected international think-tank; Penguin Random House and Macmillan, for their part, are among the five largest international publishers. The United Kingdom has thus been able to retain an important degree of world influence. Much more relevant though was the fact that the United States civilizational imprint did not have to begin afresh. On the contrary, as a natural continuation of the British one, it allowed for the Anglo-centric contents to remain at first rank for a much longer period.

Perhaps it would be useful to ascertain whether, after formally detaching itself from The Philippines, the U.S. would still remain an empire? According to Niall Ferguson it clearly remained one, although a reluctant one that did not want to recognize itself as such.[14] Clyde Prestowitz accepts the premise of the American Empire, and submits it to the duck test: "If it looks, it walks and it sounds like a duck, most probably it's a duck".[15] Certainly in Latin America, although it was not called such a thing, it looked, walked and sounded very much like a duck. But what about distant places? Marcos, Suharto or Reza Pahlevi regimes, to mention but a few, seemed palpable expressions of it, in the same manner in which leaders such as Lumumba, Mosadegh or Sukarno, looked like clear examples of the cost of dissension. Although the American flag did not wave in their countries, the silhouette of the duck seemed visible enough. However, as mentioned earlier, what really matters in terms of global influence is hegemony not empire. The United States, clearly so, became the most successful hegemonic power ever.

THE TIP OF THE ICEBERG

Following the metaphor developed by Michelle Le Baron and Jarley Cooker, culture can be symbolized as an underwater iceberg.[16] That is, a gigantic body of meanings, convictions and beliefs, not visible from the surface of the water. Hence, the interconnection between human beings of different cultural backgrounds, induced by globalization, only takes place at the tip of the iceberg that emerges out of the water. Underwater, the reign of complexity, ambiguity and diversity prevails.

Thomas L. Friedman took a totally different approach to this subject when arguing that a flat world, conformed by Anglo-centric cultural elements, prevailed. These elements, in his view, not only transcended borders but homogenized the planet.[17] Reaching a

[14] Niall Ferguson, *Colossus: The Rise and Fall of the American Empire*, op.cit.

[15] Clyde Prestowitz, *Rogue Nation: American Unilateralism and the Failure of Good Intentions*, New York: Basic Books, 2003, p. 26.

[16] Michelle Le Baron and Jarley Cooker, Why the 'Foreign' Matters in Foreign Affairs, *Harvard International Review*, Cambridge, Autumn 2000.

[17] Thomas L. Friedman, *The World is Flat: A History of the Twenty-first Century*, New

compromise between both theses, it could be argued that the tip of the iceberg — in this case a flat one — was indeed defined by Anglo-centric cultural elements. McWorld reigned at the tip.

This certainly was the case a few years ago. But is it still the case? Much has changed since Friedman proclaimed the existence of a flat world. On the one hand, the convergence aptitude of the United States has been deeply eroded, as explained in Chapter Four. On the other hand, while the West has entered into a declining phase, the rest of the world has been economically empowered, particularly Asia. The Asian continent has indeed become the new epicenter of globalization. It is there that this movement meets all the right opportunities: large funds, huge projects and a shared conviction of its merits by both governments and populations. It is there, too, that the emergence of a potent middle class has opened the largest opportunities for regional expansion.

Asian middle classes became the main beneficiaries of globalization, obtaining the lion's share of the economic growth that this process generated. Branko Milanovic explains it well: "People at point A had the highest real income growth: some 80% during the twenty-year period ... Who are the people in this group, the obvious beneficiaries of globalization? In nine of ten cases, they are people from the emerging Asian economies, predominantly China, but also India, Thailand, Vietnam and Indonesia ... They are the people around the middle of the distribution in their own countries (...) These groups were the main 'winners' of globalization between 1988 and 2008. For convenience, we call them the 'emerging middle class'".[18]

Moreover, according to the Organization for Economic Cooperation and Development (OECD), the number of people in the world's middle class will increase from 3,300 million in 2020 to 4,900 million in 2030. Also, 80% of the increase will take place in Asia. As a result, a big share of global consumption and investment

York: Farrar, Straus and Giroux, 2005.

[18] Branko Milanovic, *Global Inequality: A New Approach for the Age of Globalization* [Kindle version], Cambridge, Mass.: The Belknap Press of Harvard University Press, 2016, retrieved from Amazon.com, location 329/4560.

will move to Asia.[19] China and India will experience the largest increase, but other countries of the region will the see their middle classes grow at a significant pace as well.

MULTIPLE MODERNITIES

As Martin Jacques explains: "In the future, then, instead of there being one dominant Western modernity, there will be many distinct modernities. It is clear that we have already entered this era of multiple modernities ... Hitherto, we have lived in a Western-made and Western-dominated world, in which the economic, political and cultural traffic has been overwhelmingly one-directional, from the West to the others".[20] He also adds: "The emergence of new modernities not only mean that the West no longer enjoys a virtual monopoly of modernity, but that the histories, cultures and values of those societies will be affirmed in a new way and can no longer be equated with backwardness or, worse, failure. On the contrary, they will experience a new sense of legitimacy".[21]

This takes us back to an enlightening exercise of scenarios realized by Shell in 2002. When envisaging year 2020, the exercise defined two alternative routes: the first was represented by the "Executive Class" scenario, and the second by the "Prism" scenario. The first scenario envisaged a continuation of the market economy rules, i.e., a world characterized by a single modernity, where an all-powerful and cohesive international elite supported those rules. The "Prism" model, as its name suggests, disperses different colors. This symbolized a multicultural world economy in which a plural sense of modernity prevailed, thus placing heavy emphasis on cultural, national and/or regional diversities.[22]

---

[19] Homi Kharas, The Emerging Middle Class in Developing Countries, Working Paper N. 285, 2010, http://www.oecd.org/dev/44457738.pdf. Accessed 12 June, 2018.

[20] Martin Jacques, *When China Rules the World.* London, UK: Allen Lane, 2009, p. 142.

[21] *Ibid.*, p. 144.

[22] Shell Group of Companies, *Peoples and Connections: Global Scenarios for 2020*, London: 2002.

A group of successive circumstances played against the "Executive Class" scenario. One of these was the economic emergence of two powerful civilization-states: China and India. Some of the others included the spectacular success of the economic opening process in China, the social and political disruptions brought about by the implementation of the Washington Consensus in different parts of the world, the contrast between the flexibility of the so-called Beijing Consensus and the rigidity of the Washington Consensus, the relative decline of the West (in particular after the 2008 financial crisis) and, last but not least, the emergence of Western populism.

As Edward Luce points out: "At some point during the 2008 global financial crisis, the Washington Consensus died. In truth, that economic model had been declared a 'damaged brand' back in 2003 by John Williamson, the man who coined the term in the late 1980 (...) Most of the world has since chosen China's more pragmatic path of opening slowly and in its own terms. China's unorthodox route to development exposed the limits of the Washington Consensus".[23]

However, these new modernities, and particularly the one represented by China, have proven to be more adept at eroding many of the values associated with the American hegemony. Together with America's failures in its convergence aptitude, these emerging modernities have been instrumental in degrading Washington's primacy. However, they are still nowhere close to being able to substitute the civilizational imprint left behind by 200 years of continuous Anglo-Saxon hegemony.

COMMON DENOMINATORS

English is the closest thing to a *lingua franca* in modern days, being the common language spoken in airports around the world as well as the global language of business; the dollar still retains its rank as

---

[23] Edward Luce, *The Retreat of Western Liberalism.* London, UK: Little, Brown, 2017 location 315/4115.

the planet's prevailing currency; one billion people from every corner of the globe watch the Oscar Awards ceremony every year, in the same manner in which two billion people from around the world watched the wedding of Prince William and Kate Middleton; the world's most influential media is based either in the U.S. or the UK, and when aiming at global coverage, Chinese, Russian or Qatari media resort to the English language; the three largest financial centers of the world are based in English-speaking countries, while the fourth (Hong Kong) retained many of the characteristics of its colonial past; the ten highest ranking universities of the world are located in the United States or the United Kingdom, while most of the top 20 are in English-speaking countries (including Singapore); the world's top publishing houses are in English-speaking nations as well. And on the list goes on.

From Shakespeare to J.K. Rowling, from McDonald's to Facebook, from Walt Disney to Marvel Comics, from jazz to rock, from Twitter to Google, from Kennedy to Lady Diana, from CNN to LinkedIn, from Elvis Presley to John Lennon, from Hollywood to Broadway, from Coca-Cola to the ketchup Heinz, from HBO to Netflix, from Marylin Monroe to Michael Jackson, from Amazon to Apple, from Batman to Game of Thrones, from John Glenn to Neil Armstrong, from Thomas Edison to Steve Jobs, from ESPN to Nike, from Henry Ford to Bill Gates, from Uber to Airbnb, from Cassius Clay to Tiger Woods, and from hamburger to hotdog, the symbols of universal interconnection have been and still remain very much Anglo-centric. "Green tea, Jackie Chan and Confucius", as Mark Leonard points out, "are no match for McDonald's, Hollywood and the Gettysburg Address". To this, he later adds: "The twenty-first century will not be a Chinese century where McDonald's is replaced by *mantou* (steamed buns) as the world's favourite fast food, CNN is subordinated by CCTV, or Hollywood by the Chinese New Wave".[24]

[24]Mark Leonard, *What Does China Think.* New York, NY: HarperCollins, 2008, pp. 97 and 133.

LIMITED SPACE

Notwithstanding the emergence of new forms of modernity, and the renewed strength of old identities, the tip of the iceberg is a space enclosed by boundaries. It can only accommodate on its surface common denominators with an aptitude to interconnect numerous cultural backgrounds. If overcharged with multiple "modernities" and cultural backgrounds, the tip will simply sink, becoming part of a gigantic submerged body. In other words, if connectivity at the top is to be maintained, it can only be through meanings and symbols understandable to all. It is here where the comparative advantage derived from a long hegemonic standing acquires its true meaning.

The above applies to the West as well. Take the case of Germany, for instance. Despite being the economic locomotive of Europe, its media and venerable universities simply cannot aspire to compete with the Anglo-Saxon ones, remaining to a large extent encapsulated by language barriers. Another telling example is Castilian, the Spanish language spoken by 400 million people across three continents, boasting many internationally loved writers, and yet remaining within its own confines. Spanish-speaking people (including the author of this book) who want to connect with the outside world do so in English. The examples could go on and on. To overcome the language barrier and open themselves to an international audience, universities around Europe have chosen to teach bachelor, master and doctoral degrees in English. In 2017, just the number of B.A.s offered in English language within Continental Europe reached 2,900.[25]

Even in China, English has been a major part of the high school exit test, to help determine which school students will move on to at university level. This bilingual policy is now paying out, with young Chinese scientists being able to publish their research in English, which has become their ticket to make their work known

[25] Pamela Druckerman, Parlez-Vous Anglais? Yes, of Course, *The New York Times Sunday Review*, August 10, 2019.

internationally. This is simply because the world's leading journals are still published in English.[26]

It could be argued, yes, that the strength of the Chinese business system should allow it to have a share of the space at the tip of the iceberg, together with the Anglo-Saxon universal common denominators. However, Joseph Healy points out that "The 'commanding heights' of the global business system, as Professor Nolan argues, are occupied almost entirely by firms from high-income countries. Whilst Chinese firms are second only to US firms in terms of market capitalization within the *FT 500*, and *Fortune 500* large-firm index, these firms are mostly SOEs and owe their size to the benefits of a protected, often monopolistic, position within their domestic market rather than to their management competences, cultural adaptability, or competitive advantage-based success in the global economy".[27]

Of course, names such as Alibaba, Tencent, Baidu or Huawei, among others, cannot be left aside. In terms of competitiveness, they are at the top of the game. The problem is that such firms are too few in number for China's business system to reclaim a leading place in the realm of universality.

INWARD LOOKING SELF-SATISFACTION

Thousands of years of self-centered, inward looking self-satisfaction owing to the "Great Wall mentality" imposes a huge burden on China's possibility of giving shape to a Sino-Centric World. Its civilization, as its business system, remains domestically encapsulated to a large extent, with only a few parts of it having attained true universality. China's sophisticated and potent civilization, second to none

---

[26]John Richard Schrock, American science in decline as China's rises, *University World News*, December 7, 2018, https://www.universityworldnews.com/post.php?story=20181207064734679. Accessed October 1, 2019; *The Economist*, Looking to beat the World, November 17, 2018.

[27]Joseph Healy, *Chinese Firms Going Global: Can They Succeed?*, New Jersey: World Scientific, 2018, p. 9.

in its antiquity and strength, still remains unintelligible to most of humanity, as does its official language — Mandarin. Although the world has caught glimpses of this extremely rich culture, they are still mere glimpses, most probably stereotyped and Western-filtered glimpses.

Throughout history, China's culture was projected thanks to the osmosis resulting from its tributary system. The range of its projection thus remained mostly within the boundaries of its Middle Kingdom universe, which was a far cry from real universality. In the rest of the world, this has been compounded by the prevailing Eurocentric patterns of transmitting history. As Parag Khanna explains: "However, as Sebastian Conrad persuasively argued in his *What Is Global History?*, the discipline still suffers from Eurocentrism and a nation-state centered lens, diminishing the role of non-European civilizations".[28] This not only applies to Western knowledge about China, but to Asian knowledge about China as well. Again, in Parag Khanna's words: "... Asian history will not be familiar to most readers, both because of the Eurocentric nature of Western historical narratives but also Asia itself has been fragmented for so long that many societies have lost touch with the bonds that once tied them together".[29] Five hundred Confucius Institutes around the world try to address that limitation today. This is but a grain of sand on a very large beach, the task ahead remains immense.

Under such circumstances, the universality aptitude of China is inadequate, and can, in no way, aspire to compete with the American one. If that is indeed the case, not even the prevalence of the other remaining aptitudes would help China succeed in materializing a Sino-Centric World. Conversely, just the retention of this aptitude to a certain extent would help the U.S. remain highly relevant in the global scenario.

[28] Parag Khanna, *op. cit.*, location 396/6214.

[29] *Ibid.*, location 953/6214.

Chapter Seven

THE MILITARY APTITUDE

The military capacity of both parties becomes increasingly relevant for two important reasons. First, because one party can impose its will upon the other without going to war. Second, because one party can defeat the other in proper armed conflict.

In order to approach this highly complicated subject, it would be useful to analyze four different setups already outlined in Chapter Two. These setups are as follows: the control of the South China Sea, the control of the first and the second island chains, the Blue-water navy competition and their overall military capabilities.

SOUTH CHINA SEA

According to Humphrey Hawksley: "The South China Sea, which Oson calls the West Philippine Sea, is the main shipping route between the Indian and Pacific Oceans. It carries $5 trillion worth of trade a year. Its fishing produces 12% of the global catch and is the lifeblood for Southeast Asia's 620 million people and others far beyond. The South China Sea lies at the heart of Chinese global expansion. As China's tentacles spread around the world, the South China Sea and the building of islands there has become a test of how far China can push the boundaries of international law and get away with it".[1]

In other words, this area not only represents the heart of the Chinese geopolitical expansion but is also the biggest test to the United States' ability to impose limits to such an expansion, in accordance with international law. Hence, this is the most geographically sensitive space in the contest between both countries. China's aim is to expand its military presence in the area, generating a *fait accompli* situation that would force the United States to accept China's revisionism upon the regional *status quo.* This would entail leading Washington to accept Beijing's control of the area as the lesser of two evils. The other option would be a military confrontation with China under disadvantageous conditions. This remains consubstantial with China's way of thinking, as by Mark Leonard elucidates: "From the days of Sun Zi's 'Art of War', Chinese thinkers have regarded war as a failure of strategy, preferring to manipulate situations so that they can get their way out without a single shot being fired".[2]

The U.S. pursues the opposite policy: It contests every inch of the Chinese expansion so as to avoid the consolidation of its *fait accompli* strategy. Protecting the right of free passage in international waters with periodic shows of force, it aims at making clear that it will not yield its presence in the area. It is thus important to ascertain how well prepared both parties are in terms of their warfare capacity, to sustain their respective positions.

Two curious situations emerge from this test of wills between both parties in the South China Sea. The first one is that China, a signatory of the United Nations Convention of the Rights on the Sea, ignores the treaty by alleging superior rights, while the U.S., which is not a signatory of such a U.N. convention, presents itself as its guarantor. The second situation arises from the fact that both countries approach this contention by looking at the rear-view mirror — in other words, having the past as its frame of reference.

---

[1] Humphrey Hawksley, *Asian waters: The Struggle over the South China Sea & the Strategy of Chinese Expansion* [Kindle version], New York: The Overlook Press, 2018, retrieved from Amazon com., location 332/2370.

[2] Mark Leonard, *What Does China Think?*, New York: HarperCollins, 2008, p. 87.

In the case of China, having put behind the historical parenthesis represented by its hundred years of humiliation, it now aspires to reclaim the central role it once had. Within this context, it ignores the aforementioned U.N. convention by appealing to ancestral rights, while it contests a *status quo* shaped during its period of historical weakness. Overcoming the inequities of the past has, thus, become its route to the future. To confront China's assertiveness, the U.S. resorts to three old notions: balance of power, contention and a refusal to accept appeasement — in other words, three approaches shaped in the past. Balance of power (by way of counterbalancing China with other regional powers) puts in motion a policy designed by Admiral Alfred T. Mahan and President Theodore Roosevelt to deal with Asia during the dawn of the 20th century. The contention with China reproduces the policy devised to confront the URSS on the onset of the Cold War. The refusal to appease China aims at avoiding the policy applied by Britain and France towards Hitler, before World War II. Hence, a fixation with the past still commands the actions of both China and the United States.

It is true, as John Mearsheimer has explained, that China was not the first in undertaking the construction of artificial islands on the South China Sea. It might also be true as he argues that it was in China's neighbors' interests to elevate the noise of the South China Sea contention, before China could transform itself into the superpower that it is called to be.[3] However, the fact remains that China completely dwarfed its neighbors in the island construction process. In 2014, it had built 17 times more than of all the rest put together.[4] At the same time, it transformed those artificial islands into fortresses armed to the teeth, with advance radars, missile batteries and tactical fighters. This means forward-deployed bases hundreds of miles from its own shores, with the obvious intention of forcing its opponents to give up contentions and presence in the South China Sea.

---

[3]John Mearsheimer, *The Great Tragedy of Great Power Politic* [Kindle version], New York, NY: W.W. Norton, 2014, retrieved from Amazon.com.

[4]Robert D. Kaplan, *Asia's Cauldron: The South China Sea and the End of a Stable Pacific*, New York, NY: Random House, 2014, pp. 34.

GREAT WALL OF SAND

John Mearsheimer has written about what he calls "the stopping power of water", meaning water as a forbidding barrier to a navy that attempts to take control of a well-defended land.[5] The military building spree undertaken by China in the South China Sea has had the tangible result of increasing that stopping power exponentially. These artificial islands not only significantly increase the cost possibility of the U.S. Navy accessing military targets in Mainland China but also impose a significant distance barrier between themselves and an approaching enemy navy by way of its missiles deployment. Not surprisingly, in 2015, Admiral Harry Harris, Commander of the U.S. forces in the Pacific, coined the term "Great Wall of Sand" to describe China's artificial island building in the South China Sea.[6] This wall not only becomes a space-denying sea tool but also one for sea controlling.

China has 20 outposts in the Paracel Islands and 7 in the Spratlys. Since 2014, it has created more than 3,200 acres of new land in the Spratlys, along with a substantial expansion of its presence in the Paracels. It has also built two airfields, one of them in Fiery Cross Island in the Spratlys, and the other one in Woody Islands in the Paracels. It has deployed, in those 27 outposts, intermediate-range missiles in massive numbers as well as other modern military equipment. Many of these advanced missiles are designed to attack the aircraft carriers and the bases that form the backbone of U.S. military dominance in the region. China has threatened to further fortify its man-made islands as tensions with the U.S. escalate.[7]

According to the U.S. Department of Defense, in 2015, China possessed about 1,200 conventional short-range ballistic missiles with a 300–1000-km range, 200–300 conventional medium-range

---

[5] John Mearsheimer, *op. cit.*, location 2042/11417.

[6] Michael Fabey, *Crashback: The Power Clash Between the U.S. and China in the Pacific*. New York, NY: Scribner, 2018, p. 231.

[7] Michael Fabey, *op. cit.*; Michael Martina, *op. cit.*; John Sharman, China threatens to further fortify its man-made islands in disputed region as tensions with US escalates, *The Independent*, January 9, 2019; China Island Tracker, Asia Maritime Transparency Initiative, https://amti.csis.org/island-tracker/china/. Accessed August 29, 2019.

missiles with a 1,000–3,000-km range, an indeterminate number of conventional intermediate-range missiles with a 3,000–5,500-km range and 200–300 ground-launched cruise missiles with a range of 1,500 km or greater.[8]

Not only has the number of Chinese missiles increased significantly since 2015, but a significant portion of them are located in the outposts of the South China Sea. These include "carrier-killer" ballistic missiles capable of sinking premier U.S. power projection tools as well as its unmatched fleet of aircraft carriers. The accuracy and range of the missiles posted in these artificial islands make them deadly efficient. China has prioritized what is known as anti-access/area denial. This allows to push American power projection forces outside their effective combat ranges. China's DF21/CSS-5 ballistic missiles can hit aircraft carriers more than 1,500 mi away. The synergy resulting from the combination of these kinds of weapons and the 27 sea outposts generates an immense *de facto* exclusion zone.[9]

SHORT-RANGE APPROACH

The United States is at present particularly vulnerable to this pushing out pressure, as it has moved in a totally different direction from that of China. The reason for this is that its Air Force and Navy in fact stopped working together since the end of the Cold War. To make matters worse, each of these forces decided to prioritize short-range missions over long-range ones. The Air Force shifted the balance from long-range strategic bombing aircraft to short-range tactical fighters, while the Navy pulled of the long-range strike

[8] CDR Thomas Shugar, USN, First Strike: China's Missile Threat to U.S. Bases in Asia, Center for a New American Security, June 28, 2017, https://www.cnas.org/publications/reports/first-strike-chinas-missile-threat-to-u-s-bases-to-asia. Accessed July 13, 2019.

[9] Jerry Hendrix, Filling the Seams in U.S. Long-Range Penetrating Strike, Center for a New American Security, September 10, 2018, https://www.cnas.org/publications/reports/filling-the-seams-in-u-s-long-range-penetrating-strike. Accessed July 13, 2019; Michael Pillsbury, *op. cit.*, location 2922/7620.

missions altogether. U.S. campaigns in Kuwait and Kosovo, which were waged using aircrafts flying short distances from their airfields and aircraft carriers, helped craft these new policies. Hence, the assumption that proximity to targets would be the natural way of fighting wars generated an emphasis on short-range, high sortie rates and precision strikes.[10]

Accordingly, while China has developed an intermediate-range area denial strategy that can be accurately implemented from its South China Sea outposts, the United States needs to come near its targets in order to be effective. This is compounded by the F-22 and F-35A aircraft's innate design as short-range fighters and the U.S. Air Force's dramatic cutting back of its long-range strike component as a percentage of its overall force. Moreover, U.S. fifth-generation stealth strike aircrafts do not have sufficient range to reach their targets without the assistance of "big wing" oil tankers, which are vulnerable to attack by China. At the same time, the U.S. Navy weapons inventory, from its AIM-9 Sidewinders to its Tomahawk Land Attack Missile, depend on designs that are nearly 50 years old.[11] In other words, China has developed a layered defense-in-depth that presents itself like an indomitable fortress for America's short-range air and naval approaches. This means they have the capability to keep the United State out of the region always at hand.

ISLAND CHAIN SCENARIOS

The first island and second island chain setups, as previously mentioned, are the major archipelagos out from the East Asian continental mainland coast. In Jonathan D.T. Ward words: "... China's naval strategy is focused on what planners call the 'two island chains' of the West Pacific. These are the locales that Mao envisioned would be someday stripped of American power".[12] China's aim is to exert its control within them and, by extension, to keep the U.S. Navy out.

[10] *Ibid.*

[11] *Ibid.*

[12] Jonathan D.T. Ward, *op. cit.*, location 1317/6589.

The first of those island chains, it is worth remembering, is principally comprised of the Kuril Islands, the Japanese Archipelago, the Ryukyu Islands, Taiwan, the northern Philippines and Borneo. Within this chain we find not only the South China Sea but also the East China Sea and the Yellow Sea. While this first chain is the main priority, China also aspires to be able to maintain the U.S. Navy out of the Second Island Chain as well. The latter is located within the middle portion of the Pacific Ocean, formed by the Ogasawara Island and Volcano Island of Japan, in addition to the Mariana Islands, which are a U.S. territory.

Admiral Liu Huaquing, often called the "father of modern Chinese navy" and "China's Mahan" (in reference to America's main naval strategist, Admiral Alfred T. Mahan), envisaged in the 1980s China's "offshore defense" naval strategy. This strategy still is the fundamental guideline of the People's Liberation Army Navy (PLAN), and it has three phases. Phase 1 was to be achieved by 2000 and implied control of the First Island Chain by the PLAN. Phase 2 was to be achieved by 2020, when China's naval control would be extended out to the Second Island Chain. Phase 3, finally, was to be achieved by 2050, by which time the PLAN would have evolved into a true global navy.[13] Obviously, the time frame is skewed in relation to phase 2, since phase 1 is itself yet to be fully achieved. Moreover, phase 2 may be unachievable short of a direct military confrontation with the United States, given that in the Second Island Chain also has the U.S.' Mariana Islands, which include Guam.

CONTROLLING THE FIRST ISLAND CHAIN

It could be argued that China has several reasons for its aspirations to control the First Island Chain, two of which are fundamental. Not only does Taiwan fall within the chain, but China's control could

---

[13] Daniel Hartnett, The Father of the Modern Chinese Navy — Liu Huaqing, Center for International Maritime Security, October 8, 2014, http://cimsec.org/father-modern-chinese-navy-liu-huaqing/13291. Accessed September 10, 2019.

minimize the impediments of certain maritime chokepoints literally capable of sealing it.

The importance of Taiwan is incommensurable to Beijing, as it is considered as an integral part of the Chinese territory. The PLA continues to prepare for contingencies in the Taiwan Strait and, if necessary, will compel Taiwan to abandon moves toward independence. It is also likely that the PLA is preparing for the contingency of a forced union between China and Taiwan, while simultaneously deterring, delaying or denying any third-party assistance to Taiwan — namely that of the United States.

The maritime chokepoints are those vulnerable to interdiction by a number of other countries, chiefly by the United States. This could represent a formidable barrier in and out of the China Seas and the Yellow Sea. As such, they represent clear limitations to China's expansion into the broader maritime spaces and, at the same time, endanger funnels into China's supply and trade.

In a piece written by James R. Holmes, we can read the following: "Each annual Pentagon report on Chinese military power, moreover, includes a map that traces the island chain from the Philippines westward to central Vietnam. Interpreted thus, and sealed off by the occupants of the islands, the chain would present a formidable barrier to exit from or entry into the China Seas. This is an ideal opportunity for mischief-making at the PLA Navy's expense. Contingents scattered on and around the islands and straits comprising the first island chain could give Beijing a bad day should things turn grim over the Senkaku Islands, Taiwan, or some other geopolitical controversy".[14]

For China, overcoming such gigantic vulnerabilities means guaranteeing its supply and trade lanes and having free access to the oceans of the world. Not surprisingly, Beijing aspires to maintain the U.S. Navy out of the First Island Chain, so as to keep those fundamental maritime passages under control. However, one country's

[14] Defend the First Island Chain, U.S. Naval Institute, April 2014, Vol. 140/4/1,334, https://www.usni.org/magazines/proceedings/2014/april/defend-first-island-chain. Accessed September 11, 2019.

search for absolute security always translates into absolute insecurity for others — in this case for Japan and the Philippines, among others.

It goes without saying that in order to obtain control of the First Island Chain area, China has to be able to intimidate, bend and neutralize Japan and the United States' adamant opposition. In order to do this, the Chinese must overwhelm them with superior forces in place so as to make the cost of intervening against them prohibitively high. This is by no means an easy task.

For this, China can count on its array of intermediate missiles, which have been previously described, and a powerful navy firmly in place. Andrew S. Erickson describes the latter in the following terms: "But China's shipbuilding industry has already produced a fleet of several hundred increasingly advanced warships capable of 'flooding the zone' along the contested East Asian littoral, including increasingly large amphibious vessels well-suited to landing on disputed features, if they can be protected sufficiently. This is also where China's large, conventionally-powered submarine fleet can be particularly deadly. When several hundred easy-and-cheap-to-build ships from China's coast guard and its most advanced maritime militia units are factored in, Beijing's numerical preponderance becomes formidable for the 'home game' scenarios it cares about most. And that does not even include the land-based 'anti-navy' of aircraft and missiles that backstops them".[15]

Beyond Japan's modern Maritime and Air Self Defense Forces, and the potent U.S. Navy, the Chinese have to also bear in mind the U.S. bases in Okinawa and the Philippines, which they consider to be within the First Island Chain. Are the PLA forces up to a task of that magnitude? We should listen to what CDR Thomas Shugar has to say in that respect: "But does China have the missile forces to execute a preemptive missile strike, and would it work against U.S. and allied missile defenses in Asia? We conducted an analysis to

[15] Chinese Naval Shipbuilding: Full Steam Ahead, The Maritime Executive, January 18, 2019, https://www.maritime-executive.com/editorials/chinese-naval-shipbuilding-full-steam-ahead. Accessed August 30, 2019.

attempt to answer these questions. The result of our modeling and simulation, which show the potential for devastation of U.S. power projection forces and bases in Asia, are deeply concerning (...) By marrying great accuracy with numerous ballistic missiles, China may have developed a capability that the Soviet armed forces never had: the ability to strike effectively, in a manner of minutes, U.S. and allied bases, logistical facilities and command centers without resorting to the use of nuclear weapons, and without having established air superiority".[16]

SECOND ISLAND CHAIN

China's rationale for controlling the Second Island Chain is much more tenuous and difficult to attain as well. With islands scattered amid the open ocean, establishing an anti-access/area denial strategy remains a highly complex task. In James R. Holmes words: "And indeed, as Alfred Tayer Mahan points out, the open ocean is like a featureless plain. It's hard to string a picket line across such emptiness. As Admiral Koda observes, Imperial Japan's outer defense perimeter [during WWII] proved unenforceable with the resources Japan's navy had to deploy".[17] Moreover, as mentioned earlier, the U.S.' Mariana Islands, which include the Guam base, are located within the Second Island Chain.

However, Admiral Mahan wrote those lines at a time when submarines were not around, in the same manner in which World War II's Imperial Japan did not have the kind of naval and missile resources that China has mastered. Guam, though, seems to be a totally different proposition. Or is it not? Until recently, and unlike the range up to Japan or the Philippines, China did not have missiles with the capacity to cross the 3,058 km (1,900 mi) to strike Guam. Only its Intercontinental Ballistic Missiles, which can also hit U.S. mainland cities, possessed that capacity. However, with only a

---

[16] Thomas Shugar, *op. cit.*

[17] James R. Holmes, *op. cit.*

few hundred nuclear warheads, compared to the thousands that the United States possess, Beijing would have not dared to attack Guam and provoke nuclear retaliation. And although Chinese H-6 bombers and PLA Navy ships and submarines could approach Guam and launch cruise missiles, this would have led to the destruction of valuable Chinese assets. Nowadays, that situation has changed.

The new DF-26 missile, which has been called the Guam killer, gives China the capability of striking that island with a conventional weapon. With an estimated range of about 3,000–4,000 ki (1,900–2,500 mi) and up to 3,300 pounds of conventional warhead, China can hit Guam without going nuclear or exposing its forces in a highly risky blue water confrontation. Missile defenses in Guam, reinforced by U.S. Navy ships missile interceptors, could bring down some but not all DF-26 missiles. Hence, although control of the Second Island Chain is still out of reach for China, they are on the right track to obtain it.[18]

In order to counter the situation currently faced in the South China Sea and within the first and second island chains, the U.S. is investing in a new generation of long-range missiles such as the hypersonic missiles and the electromagnetic rail guns. Unfortunately for the U.S., investments do not go far enough to be effective against China's predominance. This is one of the main reasons why, in July 2019, Washington pulled out from the Intermediate-range Nuclear Forces Treaty with Russia. Such a treaty bans ground-launched nuclear and conventional ballistic missiles and cruise missiles with ranges of 500–5,000 km. As a result, the United States will be able to deploy such missiles in the region. China, which was not part of the treaty, had previously refused to join it as this would have implied renouncing its main strategic advantage in that area. In August 2019, shortly after putting an end to the pact with Russia, U.S.

[18] Sebastien Roblin, Why China's DF-26 Missile is a Guam Killer and a Nuclear Killer, *The National Interest,* November 9, 2018, https://nationalinterest.org/blog/buzz/why-chinas-df-26-missile-guam-killer-and-nuclear-killer-35847. Accessed November 1, 2019.

Defense Secretary Mark Esper announced the intention of placing ground-launched intermediate-range missiles in the region within months.[19]

Although the U.S. wants to place some of those missiles in allied countries in the region, such as Japan or South Korea, this may not be easy to accomplish. Not only Washington's underestimation of alliances will bear its cost, but there would be few countries willing to relinquish the benefits of its dealings with China or to incur in Beijing's wrath. Hence, having abandoned the TPP and belittling its regional allies, as mentioned earlier, translates into clear limitations for Washington.

BLUE WATER NAVY

Blue water navies are those capable of operating in the oceans of the world. A clear competition between the U.S. and China has emerged in this area as well. This transpires as a consequence of Beijing's intention to construct its own global expeditionary capabilities, which for decades have been a U.S. monopoly. Hence, the Chinese Navy, which has grown into a giant in surrounding seas, now wants to become a blue water navy with the capacity to extend the country's influence by operating continuously in major oceans. Xi Jinping and other Chinese leaders have indeed called for the transformation of China into a "maritime great power" capable of guarding against all contingencies as its economic interests grow.

China's modern shipyards crank out around a dozen large, new ships a year. This has produced 20 large modern multirole cruisers and destroyers already in service, while 17 more are awaiting completion. Since 2010, it has also put into service 23 frigates, with three more under construction. Destroyers, cruisers and

[19] Michael Martina, China wans of countermeasures if U.S. puts missiles in its 'doorstep', *Reuters*, August 5, 2019, https://www.reuters.com/article/us-china-usa-defence/china-warns-of-countermeasures-if-u-s-puts-missiles-on-its-doorstep-idUSKCN1UW044. Accessed August 7, 2019.

frigates have been supplemented by 41 corvettes (essentially for "close seas"). Chinese shipyards are busy building submarines as well. However, their efforts to maintain this underwater fleet secret make it difficult to ascertain how many submarines are currently under construction. It has been estimated, nonetheless, that in the next few years China will be operating 75 submarines, outpacing in numbers the U.S. submarine fleet. From that set group, China currently operates four nuclear-powered ballistic missile submarines. Moreover, since 2010, China has commissioned seven large replenishment ships and built five large amphibious assault ships. In addition to the stock above, other recent constructions include electronic intelligence-gathering ships, mine-warfare vessel and vessels required for logistical support. To top it all off, these are supplemented, as we shall see next, by aircraft carriers. In total, these provide China with a well-rounded fleet, thus making it capable of enforcing claims close to home while deploying a long-range presence.[20]

MAJOR CHALLENGES

For Beijing, however, things are not so easy because deploying a blue water navy involves several major challenges or, indeed, problems. The first challenge/problem is that in order to operate effectively in distant seas it needs aircraft carriers. These vessels are in fact the only ones that provide both air protection to a fleet and the kind of power projection that China is aiming at. The People's Liberation Army Navy (PLAN) has a two-combat ready aircraft, with one more

---

[20] Shahryar Pasandieh, China's Naval Buildup is a Real Challenge to the U.S. Navy's Dominance, *World Politics Review*, July 2008, https://www.worldpoliticsreview.com/articles/25290/china-s-naval-buildup-is-a-real-challenge-to-the-u-s-navy-s-dominance. Accessed July 25, 2019; Robert D. Kaplan, *op. cit.*, pp. 35–36; Greg Torode and David Lague, China's furtive fleet of nuclear missile-laden submarines tests the Pentagon, *The Japan Times*, May 7, 2019, https://www.japantimes.co.jp/news/2019/05/07/asia-pacific/chinas-furtive-fleet-nuclear-missile-laden-submarines-tests-pentagon/#.XZPBWi8ZNmA. Accessed October 1, 2019.

under construction. It is projected that China will be in possession of five or six aircrafts by 2030s.[21]

The problem herein involved is that in order to avoid the mistakes that the USSR made by getting involved in a ruinous competition with the U.S. for military parity, China has emphasized the buildup of an asymmetric arsenal. At a fraction of the cost of America's arsenal, it aims at neutralizing their weapons' superiority. Good examples of these are its anti-aircraft carriers' intermediate-range missiles and its hypersonic missiles. Costing just a few million dollars, they can destroy a Gerald R. Ford–class aircraft carrier with a price tag of US$13.2 billion and the more than 65 F-35C air fighters that it carries inside, each at a cost of US$107 million. According to retired American navy captain Jerry Hendrix, China could build over 1,200 DF-21D anti-aircraft carrier missiles for the cost of one American carrier.[22]

However, developing aircraft carriers is the opposite of asymmetric expending. This is a costly undertaking with a high maintenance fee attached. Moreover, having put in motion the era of asymmetric weapons, they could now become their next victims. Their costly aircraft carriers with airplane fighters could, at some point in the future, become targets of aircraft carrier killer missiles developed by others. Thanks in good measure to Chinese asymmetric weapons, the aircraft carrier is in danger of becoming, in the words of Jerry Hendrix, "expensive, vulnerable — and surprisingly irrelevant to the conflicts of the time".[23]

---

[21] Nick Childs, China's carrier-aviation developments: making a difference, IISS, June 3, 2018, https://www.iiss.org/blogs/military-balance/2018/06/china-carrier-aviation-development. Accessed September 1, 2019; Kyle Mizokami, In the Age of the Aircraft Carrier at and End? Thanks to Drones Maybe Not, Jalopink, March 14, 2019, https://foxtrotalpha.jalopnik.com/is-the-age-of-the-aircraft-carrier-at-an-end-thanks-to-1833297085. Accessed August 5, 2019.

[22] Kyle Mizokami, *op. cit.*; Michael Fabey, *op. cit.*; Jerry Hendrix, Aircraft-carriers are big, expensive, vulnerable- and popular, *The Economist*, November 14, 2019.

[23] Jerry Hendrix, Aircraft-carriers are big, expensive, vulnerable- and popular, *op. cit.*

CHINESE OVERSEAS NAVAL BASES

The second challenge/problem confronted by China is its lack of naval bases around the world, outside of China, that are capable of providing dock space to and restocking facilities and maintenance for its fleets. This represents a huge disadvantage when compared with the more than 30 bases and installations that the U.S. Navy possesses worldwide. In 2017, as mentioned before, the first, and thus far only, Chinese overseas naval base was opened in Djibouti, in the Horn of Africa, in 2017.

Many sensitive politicians, particularly African ones, and Western analysts have spoken about a Chinese debt-trap diplomacy. According to this phenomenon, China deliberately extends excessive credit to some countries, with the alleged intention of extracting economic or political concessions when the debtor country becomes unable to honor its obligations. This debt-trap diplomacy has been presented as an integral part of China's geostrategic vision. The case of the Djibouty's PLA naval base has been quoted as an example of this. If this turns out to be truthful, China could end up extending its military footprint in Africa and establishing future naval bases in that continent.

Sri Lanka's Hambantota Port has been cited as yet another example of the Chinese debt-trap diplomacy. The country's failure to pay its debt obligations led to a 99-year lease of this port to China. Again, if true, the so-called "string of pearls" Chinese strategy would converge with the alleged debt-trap one. The several port infrastructures built by China in the Indian Ocean could end up being used as military facilities, just as many analysts have been forewarning about. Ports like Kyaupyu in Myanmar, Chittagong in Bangladesh or Gwadar in Pakistan, together with Hambantota in Sri Lanka, could at some point start hosting Chinese naval bases.[24]

---

[24] Mark Green, China's Debt Diplomacy, *Foreign Policy*, April 25, 2019, https://foreignpolicy.com/2019/04/25/chinas-debt-diplomacy/. Accessed September 1, 2019.

Moreover, in July 2019 the *Wall Street Journal* reported that China and Cambodia had signed a secret agreement allowing the Chinese navy to use a military facility near Ream, along Cambodia's southern coast. Although the Cambodian government denied the report, images have shown the construction of important military installations at the site.[25] Given the close relations between both countries, and the subsidiarity role to China that Cambodia plays within ASEAN, this is a highly plausible situation. Therefore, although the PLAN cannot compete as yet with the U.S. Navy in this area, the ground may have been sufficiently tilled to give shape to a whole array of Chinese naval bases in the Indian Ocean, Africa and the South China Sea. Allegedly then, China could not only extend its naval presence to several maritime scenarios but also might reach a competitive position with the U.S. Navy in terms of overseas naval bases.

STRIKE CARRIER GROUPS

The third challenge/problem faced by China stems from its lack of experience in operating complex strike carrier groups. In the U.S. Navy case, such groups are composed of an aircraft carrier, at least one cruiser, a destroyer or frigate squadron, and a carrier air wing of 65–70 aircraft. On occasions, they also include submarines, attached logistic ships and a supply ship. Their relevance is in their capacity to act together as a coordinated force and their flexibility to operate in diverse scenarios.

The U.S. Navy has been operating aircraft carriers for 100 years and, as a result, has developed great experience in this field. In Gene I. Rochlin, Todd R. La Porte and Karlene H. Roberts' words: "In order to keep this network alive and coordinated, it must be kept connected and integrated horizontally (e.g., across squadrons),

[25] Timothy R. Heat, The Ramifications of China's Reported Naval Base in Cambodia, *WPR, World Politics Review*, August 5, 2019, https://www.worldpoliticsreview.com/articles/28092/the-ramifications-of-china-s-reported-naval-base-in-cambodia. Accessed December 6, 2019.

vertically (from maintenance and fuel up through operations), and across command structures (battle group-ship-air wing)".[26] While the aircraft carrier and its fighters provide the primary offensive firepower, the other ships may provide defense and support or undertake offensive operations as well (as launching cruise missiles). A single super-carrier strike group may possess more firepower than many nations.

The U.S. Navy had 12 carrier strike groups, recently reduced to 11, while the latest defense budget calls for the aircraft carrier fleet to be reduced to 10. Although the PLA Navy is an impressive and ever-growing force in terms of both quality and quantity, it still lacks the experience to operate such complex groups. In November 2017, the coordinated operations of three U.S. Navy carrier strike groups in the Western Pacific gave a stunning example of America's accrued expertise in this field. On that occasion, the strike groups of carriers USS Nimitz, USS Ronald Reagan and USS Theodore Roosevelt, with around two dozen U.S. warships, gathered together in the show of the biggest naval force to stream into these waters since World War II[27] As long as China fails to match the U.S. Navy's abilities in this area, it will remain in a disadvantaged position.

OFFSET STRATEGIES

The overall military capabilities of both countries present a more complicated picture. During the Cold War, the United States was able to "offset" the Soviet Union's advantages in force size by

---

[26] Gene I. Rochlin, Todd R. La Porte and Karlene H. Roberts, The Self-Designing High-Reliability Organization: Aircraft Carrier Flight Operations at Sea, *Naval War College Review*, **40**(Autumn 1987), https://digital-commons.usnwc.edu/cgi/viewcontent.cgi?referer=https://www.google.com.sg/&httpsredir=1&article=4373&context=nwc-review. Accessed August 24, 2019.

[27] Michael Fabey, *op. cit.*, p. 254; U.S. 7th Fleet Public Affairs, Three-Carrier Strike Force Exercise to Commence in Western Pacific, U.S. Indo-Pacific Command, November 13, 2017, https://www.pacom.mil/Media/News/News-Article-View/Article/1370838/three-carrier-strike-force-exercise-to-commence-in-western-pacific/. Accessed September 1, 2019.

maintaining a technological edge. The First Offset Strategy came in the 1950s during President Eisenhower's time in office. While the USSR pursued a deterrent approach based on its conventional forces overwhelming superiority, Eisenhower refused to pay the economic penalty of matching Moscow man-for-man or tank-for-tank. Instead, he aimed at confronting Soviet numerical superiority with a smaller but technologically superior army. To such an end, he turned to the battlefield with atomic weapons (missiles, rockets and artillery shells tipped with low-yield atomic warheads) to deter the Warsaw Pact greater conventional forces.

The Second Offset Strategy came at the end of the 1970s, during Jimmy Carter's years at the White House. Since the beginning of that decade, it became evident that the First Offset Strategy had run its course. Two reasons were responsible for this. On the one hand, the Soviet nuclear arsenal had become as powerful as that of the U.S., which made the early use of tactical weapons a weak deterrent and an unnecessary invitation to nuclear escalation. On the other hand, the Soviets had matched their quantity superiority in conventional assault forces, with a quality equal to those of the NATO forces.

As a result, the U.S. pursued the development of conventional weapons capable of "near-zero miss" through the ability to "look deep and shoot deep". This implied the operational merging of several weapon systems: Airborne targeting radars, missiles and air-delivered bombs, guided anti-armor sub munitions, and ground-based data processing stations. Under this military-technical revolution, conventional guided munitions could achieve battlefield effects comparable to those of tactical nuclear weapons. Operation Desert Storm in 1991 showed for the first time the power of this guided munition battle networks: Iraqi heavy formations were reduced to scrap during a 100-hour ground battle. And although only 8% of all conventional weapons employed by the U.S. in that battle were guided, it could be said that a new military paradigm had emerged.[28]

[28] Robert O. Work and Greg Grant, Beating the Americans at Their Own Game, Center for a New American Security, June 6, 2019, https://www.cnas.org/publications/reports/beating-the-americans-at-their-own-game. Accessed July 10, 2019.

BEATING THE U.S. AT ITS OWN GAME

In little more than two decades, the Chinese military have accomplished technological achievements that risk beating the United States at its own game. Although never stated in such a manner, China decided to develop its own offset strategy — one that aims at overcoming the American technological advantages and superior military budget. This Chinese military-technological strategy is supported by a sustained and robust increase in military spending. Annual Chinese defense spending, indeed, jumped by at least 620% in real terms between 1996 and 2015, representing an annual average increase of 11%.[29]

Among the characteristics of China's offset strategy, three features stand out: Its asymmetrical strategy of finding and exploiting the U.S.' soft spots, its directing and executing large-scale cyber-espionage campaigns on U.S. military technology (as a way to leap-forward in its own military developments) and its civic-military fusion, based on dual-use technologies with both civilian and military applications.

In the first place, China is investing a disproportionate amount of its defense resources on asymmetric capabilities. As Mark Leonard says, China is attempting to become an "asymmetric superpower", outside the realm of conventional military power.[30] So, similar to the first American offset strategy of the 1950s, which refused to pay the economic penalty of matching the Soviet Union man-for-man and tank-for-tank, China refuses to match the U.S. military machine, plane-for-plane or bomb-for-bomb.

Conscious that Moscow spent itself to bankruptcy by accepting a ruinous competition for military primacy with Washington, Beijing is on the lookout for cheaper ways to compete. As a result, China is investing billions of dollars in an attempt to make a generational leap in military capabilities, to become capable of neutralizing and trumping the superior conventional forces of the United States.

Making reference to ancient Chinese folklore, Michael Pillsbury wrote about a legendary hero who was able to knock down a more

---

[29] *Ibid.*

[30] Mark Leonard, *op. cit.*, p. 106.

powerful enemy with the single blow of a mace. The element of surprise and the hero's knowledge of his enemy's weakest point allowed him to defeat a superior adversary. Roughly translated into English, the hero's weapon can be called the Assassin's Mace: One that ensures victory over a stronger foe. Referring to the frequent use of this term in current Chinese military doctrine, Pillsbury says: "After further investigation, I realized that in the military context the Assassin's Mace refers to a set of asymmetric weapons that allow an inferior power to defeat a seemingly superior adversary by striking at an enemy's weakest point".[31]

In other words, instead of rivaling the Americans on their own ground, China wants to engage them at a different game. One that they can win. A novel by P.W. Singer and August Cole depicts how, through surprise and a whole array of asymmetric weapons, China defeated the superior forces of the United States.[32]

ASYMMETRIC WEAPONS

In essence, these weapons are dual focused. On the one hand, they emphasize long- and intermediate-range precision missiles and advanced targeting systems capable of providing a high probability of penetrating U.S. battle network defenses during the opening stages of a conflict. The aircraft carrier killer missile or the Guam killer, which were mentioned in this chapter, are just two examples of this type of weapon. Admiral Harry Harris, then Commander of the U.S. Pacific Command, testified in 2017 that China controlled the largest and most diverse missile force of the world, with an inventory of more than 2,000 ballistic and cruise missiles.[33]

---

[31] Michael Pillsbury, *op. cit.*, location 2588/7620.

[32] P.W. Singer and August Cole, *Ghost Fleet: A Novel of The Next World War*, Boston: An Eamon Dolan Book, 2016.

[33] Andrew S. Erickson, China's Massive Military Parade Shows Beijing is a Missile Superpower, *The National Interest*, 1 October, 2019, https://nationalinterest.org/blog/buzz/chinas-massive-military-parade-shows-beijing-missile-superpower-84731. Accessed 2 October, 2019.

On the other hand, they aim at systems destruction warfare, able to cripple the U.S.' command, control, communication and intelligence battle network systems. As such, their objective is to paralyze America's high-tech ability to conduct war. Good examples of this would be the following: Electromagnetic pulse weapons, susceptible of knocking out all electronics over a wide area; land-based lasers, able to blind or blow out American satellites; microsatellites, able to push American satellites out of orbit through electronic jamming.

The two aforementioned directions are convergent. Their objective is to coordinate actions against the enemy's operating forces (and their logistic support) and the command and control centers that guide them. In both cases, the objective is to target U.S. military soft spots, with weapons priced at a fraction of the systems that they aim to destroy or render useless.

In the end, the idea is to find ways of exploiting what they see as American weaknesses (like their dependence on the information highways or space satellites that handle a huge percentage of all military communications), while neutralizing American strengths (like their fleet of aircraft carriers). Michael Pillsbury describes this situation in graphic terms: "For two decades, the Chinese have been building arrows designed to find a singular target — the Achilles' heel of the United States".[34] Graham Allison also describes this very graphically: "Just as technology start-ups like Facebook and Uber have used the concept of disruptive innovation to upset previous dominant firms, the Chinese military is developing new technologies that can counter ships, planes, and satellites that the US has developed for decades — and for a fraction of the cost".[35]

CYBER-CAMPAIGNS

Second, China's offsetting strategy is based on directing and executing a large-scale cyber-espionage campaign on U.S. military technology. This is done as a way to leap forward in its own military

[34] Michael Pillsbury, *Op. cit.*, location 2939/7620.
[35] Graham Allison, *Op. cit.*, p. 19.

developments. Through industrial and military espionage, the Chinese aim at rapidly acquiring comparable military capabilities as those developed over decades by the United States.

According to Harry Krejsa and Hannah Suh: "As a result, Chinese cyber capabilities — and the laws and doctrine governing them — have benefited from a decade or more of formal, significant support and investment ... People's Liberation Army (PLA) Unit 61398, based in Shanghai, is thought to employ thousands of people and be responsible for the theft of advanced manufacturing techniques and trade secrets from hundreds of the United States' most successful companies, including those of the defense industry".[36]

In 2013, the *Washington Post* reported that, in accordance with a classified study by the Defense Science Board, Chinese cyber-intruders had accessed more than 24 American system designs. These included the Patriot missile system, the Aegis missile defense system, the F/A-18 fighter, the V-22 Osprey multirole combat aircraft, or the Littoral Combat Ship. Major General William Lord of the U.S. Air Force observed, on his part, that China had downloaded 10–20 terabytes of data from a Pentagon computer network.[37]

Through their cyber-theft, China's hackers have been instrumental in accelerating their country's military research at neck-breaking speed and enabling the development of a wide variety of copycat weapons. These include, in addition to the aforementioned details, vast amounts of information regarding America's F-35 and F-22, which has shortened the production timeline of China's own fifth-generation fighters. However, not only the United States but also Canada, Australia, United Kingdom, India, and NATO have seen their defense industry data stolen in large quantities by Chinese hackers.[38]

---

[36] Phishing in Troubled Waters, Center for a New American Security, 10 April, 2017, https://www.cnas.org/publications/reports/phishing-in-troubled-waters-1. Accessed 16 July, 2019.

[37] Michael Pillsbury, *op. cit.*, locations 2817/7620 and 2825/7620.

[38] Harry Krejsa and Hannah Suh, *op. cit.*

CIVIL–MILITARY FUSION

Third, China's military offsetting strategy has been helped by a civil–military fusion with dual-use technology. As mentioned in Chapter Two, according to the recent policy of "Civic Military Fusion", the Chinese Communist Party demands that new technologies developed by the private sector must be shared by the military. In January 2017, Xi Jinping created the Central Commission for Integrated Military and Civilian Development, a body for overseeing and coordinating civil–military fusion efforts.[39]

However, this fusion goes further back in time. In 1986, the so-called 863 Program (or China's National High-Technology Program) was inaugurated. Its aim was to overcome the country's shortcomings in national security through the use of science and technology. The 863 Program, still in progress, encompasses the development of technologies with dual use, like biotechnology, laser technology and nanotechnology.

China's "indigenous innovation" strategy, included in the National Medium- and Long-Term Plan for the Development of Science and Technology (2005–2020), derives from the above-mentioned program and follows the same guidelines. As such, China's indigenous innovation strategy pursues the development of technological capacities for both military and civilian uses. Within this Medium- and Long-Term Plan, 16 megaprojects, considered as national priorities, are being advanced, with 3 of them being classified. Hence, China's military programs are embedded in its civilian science and technology base.[40]

This fusion attests two fundamental things lacking in the United States: first, a synergistic relation between Government and the private high-tech sector. The cultural clash between Silicon Valley and the Pentagon is proverbial. This was proven by an open letter signed

---

[39] Council on Foreign Relations, Civil-Military Fusion: The Missing Link Between China's Technological and Military Rise, 29 January, 2018, https://www.cfr.org/blog/civil-military-fusion-missing-link-between-chinas-technological-and-military-rise. Accessed 9 November, 2019.

[40] Michael Pillsbury, *op. cit.*, locations 2616/7620 and 2621/7620.

by 3,000 Google employees who, in January 2019, demanded that the company cease working with the Pentagon's Project Maven machine-learning program.[41] As expressed by an Independent Task Force Report on Innovation and National Security: "A persistent cultural divide between the technological and policymaking communities threatens national security by making it more difficult for the Defense Department and intelligence community to acquire and adopt advanced technologies from the private sector and draw on technical talent".[42] This adversarial tradition goes back in time to the countercultural generation that came out of Stanford in the late 1960s and early 1970s. Since then, Silicon Valley's desire to think different and to question authority has only intensified. In Margaret O'Mara words: "Time and again, technologists pushed back when government tried to intrude".[43]

Second, the long range and broad approach of Chinese industrial policies is absent from the interplay of market forces prevalent in the United States. The space race in the U.S. allowed efforts funded and led by the government on long-term research and development (R&D) to thrive in close partnership with the private sector. This led to impressive results. However, high-tech in today's America is led by the search for commercial and short-term payoffs, very different in nature from the experience of the space race. Indeed, current technological developments in the U.S. are characterized by private companies' unwillingness to invest when commercial returns are not clear and by venture capitalists reluctant to take risks on large undertakings with potentially distant payoffs. This translates

[41] Aaron Mehta, Cultural divide: Can the Pentagon Crack Silicon Valley?, DefenseNews, 28 January, 2019, https://www.defensenews.com/pentagon/2019/01/28/cultural-divide-can-the-pentagon-crack-silicon-valley/. Accessed 4 October, 2019.

[42] James Manyika and William H. McRaven, Chairs and Adam Segal, Project Director, Innovation and National Security: Keeping our Edge, Independent Task Force Report No. 77, Council on Foreign Relations, September 2019, https://www.cfr.org/report/keeping-our-edge/. Accessed 14 October, 2019.

[43] Margaret O'Mara, Silicon Valley Can Still Beat China, Bloomberg, 14 July, 2019, https://www.bloomberg.com/opinion/articles/2019-07-14/silicon-valley-can-still-beat-china-in-technology-race. Accessed 4 October, 2019.

into high-tech generation shortcomings, a result that is particularly relevant in the case of defense R&D. Under those circumstances, the U.S. defense industry lacks the kind of strategic view in technology generation that China has. This is a subject that we shall further expand on in Chapter Nine.

The combination between its asymmetrical strategy, its cyber-espionage campaign on U.S. military technology and its civil–military fusion with a long-term view is projecting forward China's PLA in a very impressive manner. Not surprisingly, a 2015 Rand Corporation study called "The U.S.–China Military Scorecard" found that, by 2017, China should have "advantage" or "approximate parity" in six of the nine areas of conventional military capability.[44] Meanwhile, and notwithstanding its superior budgetary position, the United States military seems to have stalled.

IS THE U.S. MILITARY DECLINING?

As Steven Kosiak explains: "Concerns about the adequacy of the U.S. military frequently focus on two issues: whether its force structure has gotten too small, and whether U.S. forces are being modernized too slowly and are too dependent on an aging weapons inventory (…) Measured in terms of personnel and major weapons platforms, the size of the U.S. military has been on a generally downward trajectory for decades. The path has not been simple, uniform or smooth, and there have been important exceptions in certain areas. Nevertheless, the overall trend is unmistakable and, view from a long-term perspective, quite consistent (…) Despite this more complex pattern, however, the overall trend in numbers has clearly been consistently toward a smaller force, whether measured in terms of military personnel or major weapons platforms. Paralleling this downward trend have been trends in both the frequency with which new weapons are introduced and in the aging of the military's inventory of major weapons platform, reflecting a significant decline

[44] Graham Allison, *op. cit.*, pp. 19, 20.

in weapons production rates (…) Nevertheless, the overall trend has clearly been toward and older weapons inventory for U.S. military. Similarly, the path at which successive generations of new weapons platforms are developed and deployed, over time, slowed significantly (…) Despite widely held misconceptions to the contrary, neither a declining defense budget top line nor declining resources for weapons acquisitions explain the trends in size of the U.S. military or the aging of the weapons inventory. This is for a simple reason: Viewed from a long-time perspective, neither the defense budget top line nor overall acquisition funding has declined".[45]

In other words, the U.S. military has gotten smaller, it is being modernized too slowly and it is increasingly dependent on an aging weapons inventory. However, neither the overall defense budget nor the budget for weapons acquisition has declined. How to explain, then, this apparent contradiction? As Steven M. Kosiak details in the same paper, two elements have been responsible for it. On the one hand, the cost of operation and support activities has gone up substantially. On the other hand, new weapons systems cost far more than the systems that they are intended to replace.

Operation and support activities include everything from military and civilian pay to funding for health care and other personnel benefits, to food, fuel, utilities, most spare parts and other supplies. In this "everything goes" equation, increases in compensation for the Pentagon's military and civilian personnel have played a very important role, significantly exceeding the overall inflation rate. Salaries, housing and subsistence allowances, retirement pension and health care have gone up substantially, hence absorbing an increasing percentage of the overall defense budget. This is consistent with the fact that within an All-Volunteer Force, generous compensation packages have to be offered in order to be competitive with other professional activities.

---

[45] Steven Kosiak, Is the U.S. Military Getting Smaller and Older: And How Much Should We Care?, Center for a New American Security, 14 March, 2017, https://s3.amazonaws.com/files.cnas.org/documents/CNASReport-SmallerOlderMilitary-Final.pdf?mtime=20170310154527. Accessed 19 June, 2019.

But the cost of replacing older weapon systems plays another relevant part in the process. This intergenerational cost growth has been even more dramatic than the increase shown in the operation and support activities. A good example of this is the F-35 fighter, whose total development and acquisition cost is about US$350 billion. By comparison, the F/A-18 aircraft that the F-35 is intended to replace had total development and procurement costs totaling US$85 billion.

THIRD U.S. OFFSET STRATEGY

To counter the above decline as well as China's emerging military threat, the Obama Administration announced in November 2014 the so-called Defense Innovation Initiative. It represented a Third Offset Strategy, one aimed at following those launched by the U.S. in the 1950s and the end of the 1970s. This strategy recognized that the technological superiority, which had been the foundation of U.S. military dominance for decades, was not only eroding but was also being challenged by China. Both the pace of America's technological innovation in this area and the pace at which foreign technology was advancing meant that the U.S. technological superiority had just a small temporary advantage (assumed to be of no more than five years).

Competitors, namely China, were making significant advances in anti-access/area denial capabilities that threatened U.S. power projection abroad. At the same time, those competitors, again China, were making great strides in the space and cyber realms, which could jeopardize the advantage that the country had held for decades in fields such as Command, Control, Communications, Computers, Intelligence and Surveillance. A Third Offset Strategy was thus needed, according to the Department of Defense, for the U.S. to preserve its innovation leadership and its conventional deterrence capabilities. Hence, the Department of Defense had to focus on technological innovation while developing innovative operational concepts and managing innovative organizations.

Technologically, several areas were identified: autonomous learning systems, human–machine collaborative decision-making, advanced manned–unmanned systems operations, network-enabled autonomous weapons and high-speed projectiles. Advancements in these areas were called for to boost conventional military capabilities to a range beyond the competitor's capacity to counter them.[46]

Beijing became truly concerned by America's Third Offset Strategy, as Tai Ming Cheung made clear: "Chinese analysts think that the United States has the political, economic, geostrategic, and innovative will and capacity to successfully implement the Third Offset Strategy. Tong Zeng of the (Chinese) Academy of Military Sciences has offered several reasons for this assessment. First, the United States is pursuing the Third Offset Strategy from a position of superiority compared to its opponents. Second, the US defense and civilian innovation systems have the technological expertise and innovative capacity to effectively implement the strategy (…) In assessing the implications of the Third Offset Strategy for China's defense … Zhang Xiaobin, a defense technology analyst at the State Administration for Science, Technology and Industry for National Defense, believes that there will be a significant detrimental impact. It will be far more difficult for China to successfully pursue leap-frog style developments in disruptive innovation, an important feature on Xi Jinping's innovation directed development strategy. This is because the US defense innovation system is far more capable of achieving technological surprises (…) China's efforts to develop core defense competencies in advanced areas could be undermined by being goaded into an arms race with the United States, forcing China to invest in R&D that it can ill-afford and in technologies in which it is

---

[46]Jesse Ellman, Lisa Samp and Gabriel Coll, Assessing the Third Offset Strategy, Center for Strategic & International Studies, CSIS, March 2017, https://csis-prod.s3.amazonaws.com/s3fs-public/publication/170302_Ellman_ThirdOffsetStrategySummary_Web.pdf. Accessed 17 June, 2019.

ill-equipped to compete over the long term. Zhang offers the example of the Reagan's 'Star Wars' during the 1980s…".[47]

U.S. MILITARY RUNNING OUT OF TIME

However, as it happened with so many other initiatives representing the Obama legacy, the Third Offset Strategy began fading into oblivion with Trump's arrival to the White House. As Paul McLeary wrote: "The Third Offset quickly became the new military buzzwords used to justify a variety of new programs and offices, including the Strategic Capabilities Office and the Defense Innovation Unit Experimental, which put a Pentagon office in the heart of Silicon Valley with a mandate to experiment with new technologies (…) But now the future of the two technology offices is unclear, and even the phrase 'Third Offset', so ubiquitous in the previous administration, has scarcely been mentioned since Donald Trump assumed office (…) Two defense officials told *Foreign Policy* that the language change comes with the change in priorities under the new administration (…) Under Mathis and the new Pentagon leadership, 'there's no vision for modernization', said technologist Peter Singer (…) Whether the Third Offset will be replaced by something new or simply fade into obscurity is yet to be seen".[48]

Writing for the military publication Military.com, Oriana Pawlyk quoted the information given by U.S. Air Force Lt. General Vera Linn Jamieson, Deputy Chief of Staff for Intelligence, Surveillance and Reconnaissance on the Air Staff at the Pentagon. According to

---

[47] Tai Ming Cheung, US-China Military Technological Competition and the Making of Chinese Weapons Development Strategies and Plans, Study of Innovation and Technology in China, University of California Institute on Global Conflict and Cooperation, January 2, 2017, https://escholarship.org/uc/item/43m5m3gp. Accessed June 20, 2019.

[48] Paul McLeary, The Pentagon's Third Offset May Be Dead, But Not One Knows What Comes Next, *Foreign Policy*, December 18, 2017, https://foreignpolicy.com/2017/12/18/the-pentagons-third-offset-may-be-dead-but-no-one-knows-what-comes-next/. Accessed September 30, 2019.

General Jamieson, in 2017, China's total spending on artificial intelligence systems with military applications reached US$12 billion; however, the USAF estimates that that amount will grow to at least US$70 billion by 2020. Meanwhile, Oriana Pawlyk stated that the Pentagon just spent around US$7.4 billion on emerging technologies in fiscal year 2017, of which AI represented 33%. If that is the case, the gap between China and the U.S. in emerging military technology expenditures in 2017 was simply overwhelming.[49]

The US$750 billion national defense budget unveiled on March 2019 provided a clearer guide as to the new direction that is being taken by the Pentagon. Good and bad news in relation to the modernization of the American armed forces were present there. On the positive side of it came the announcement that the military was shifting its emphasis from counterinsurgencies to competition with China and Russia; the Navy plans to retire one aircraft carrier and instead invest in drone ships, the Army to scale back legacy weapons and instead buy high-end ones, and the Air Force to dramatically increase investments in space. Conversely, the Department of Defense asked US$165 billion, a 139% increase, for its war-fighting account, which funds active conflicts in Iraq and Afghanistan; while talking about a large-scale recalibration of missile defenses, only US$9.43 billion was requested by the Missile Defense Agency; the Air Force requested a mix of older and newer fighter jets, including the first acquisition of F-15s since 2001, which skeptics characterized as "prioritizing the present over the future". Synthetizing all of this, Paul Sonne says: "Whether the changes go far enough to reshape the military for a new mission is a matter of debate".[50]

Fareed Zakaria, on his part, affirms: "The United defense budget is out-of-control, lacking strategic coherence, utterly mismanaged, ruinously, wasteful and yet eternally expanding (...) And the real

[49] Oriana Pawlyk, China Leaving US Behind on Artificial Intelligence: Air Force General, July 30, 2018, https://www.military.com/defensetech/2018/07/30/china-leaving-us-behind-artificial-intelligence-air-force-general.html. Accessed December 6, 2019.

[50] Paul Sonne, Pentagon takes aim at China in proposed $750 billion budget, *The Washington Post*, March 12, 2019.

threats of the future — cyberwar, space attacks — require different strategies and spending. Yet Washington keeps spending billions on aircraft carriers and tanks".[51]

It would thus seem that the modernization in process does not amount to a real offset in relation to the challenges posed by China. Given that in 2030 China is expected to surpass the U.S.' GDP in absolute terms, while in 2014 it did already surpass it in Parity Purchasing Power, time is not on Washington's side. China is increasingly on the winning side of the budgetary competition, which will consolidate after 2030. This should be a matter of much concern to the U.S., when considering Michael Pillsbury assertion: "By 2050, China's economy will be much larger than America's — perhaps three times larger, according to some projections (...) China will be able to outspend America militarily".[52] Moreover, once China attains such economic predominance, Pillsbury believes that "China's new status may have to be protected through military force".[53]

If that turns out to be the case, Washington will be faced with two unsavory options: Yield to China's conventional military supremacy and spaces of influence, or risk being pushed into bankruptcy, as the USSR did under America's pressure. As Paul McLeary writes: "Whatever policy is pursued, the Pentagon faces hard choices when it comes to future spending. 'I think there's widespread agreement in the building that our conventional overmatch is eroding', Work said. 'The only debate is how long we have'".[54]

U.S.–CHINA NUCLEAR CORRELATION

In terms of possession of nuclear weapons, comparative levels tell a different, although paradoxical, story. According to the Arms

[51] Fareed Zakaria, Defense spending is America's cancerous bipartisan consensus, *The Washington Post*, July 18, 2019.

[52] Michael Pillsbury, *The Hundred Year Marathon: China's Secret Strategy to Replace America as the Global Superpower*. New York, NY: Henry Holt and Company, 2015, locations 3363/7620, 3371/7620.

[53] *Ibid.*, location 590/7620.

[54] Paul McLeary, *op. cit.*

Control Association, the United States currently possesses 6,185 nuclear warheads versus the 290 in China's hands.[55] Two categories of nuclear weapons are herein involved: tactical and strategic. The first kind has a smaller explosive capacity and is designed to be used on a battlefield. The second type has a much larger explosive power and is designed to target an enemy away from the war front and within its own territory, essentially damaging the enemy's capability to wage war. The U.S.' superiority in tactical nuclear weapons is absolute, as China is not known to have any. However, as mentioned before, the long range, accuracy and extensive number of Chinese conventional ballistic missiles can cause great harm to U.S. targets without the need of going nuclear. As such, they can be a good match to America's tactical nuclear weapons.

As regards the strategic nuclear ones, America's superiority in numbers is overwhelming. As a result, China emphasizes a deterrent strategy, aimed at making the costs of America's first use of them prohibitory. By retaining the possibility of a retaliatory nuclear strike against U.S.' major cities, Beijing imposes upon Washington the need to restrain itself with regard to the use of its vastly superior nuclear arsenal. According to *The Economist*: "If America cannot hope to destroy most of China's missiles, then it cannot easily threaten China with a nuclear strike without putting its own cities at risk".[56] To such an end, China has developed new nuclear ballistic missiles, cruise missiles and sea-based nuclear delivery systems.

A good example of such armament is the DF-41 intercontinental ballistic missile, a solid-fueled road-mobile, which was exhibited during China's massive military commemoratory parade celebrating the 70th Anniversary of the People's Republic. This represents China's newest, most powerful and arguably more advanced nuclear weapons system capable of carrying 10 independent nuclear warheads

---

[55] Nuclear Weapons: Who Has What at a Glance, July 2019, https://www.armscontrol.org/factsheets/Nuclearweaponswhohaswhat. Accessed October 2, 2019.

[56] China's nuclear arsenal has been strikingly modest, but that is changing, November 20, 2019, https://www.economist.com/china/2019/11/20/chinas-nuclear-arsenal-has-been-strikingly-modest-but-that-is-changing. Accessed November 20, 2019.

with a range of 15,000 km.[57] Reference must be made, as well, to the JL-3 ballistic missile, also solid-fuel but launched from submarines, which plays a fundamental role in China's sea-based nuclear deterrence and whose full range is likely to exceed 9,000 km. To launch the JL-3 missiles, China uses four Jin-class nuclear submarines (an upgraded fifth is under construction) armed with up to 12 ballistic missiles each.[58]

Both road-mobile missiles, which are difficult for an adversary to find and destroy, and missiles based on submarines, also inherently mobile and difficult to discover, present a tremendous challenge for the United States. As such, they could deliver a second strike, thus dissuading its counterpart from a first strike. Moreover, China is also developing an air-launched nuclear ballistic missile and plans to build a long-range stealth bomber capable of carrying nuclear weapons. This would place China, together with the U.S. and Russia, within the nuclear field traid, capable of delivering nuclear weapons by air, sea and land. At the same time, China is fielding new technologies such as hypersonic glide vehicles designed to defeat the American defense systems.

If the U.S.' first use of its strategic nuclear arsenal is deterred, while China's conventional ballistic missiles as well as other weapons in its asymmetric arsenal are capable of matching the impact of America's tactical nuclear weapons, the superiority of the U.S. in this field can essentially be neutralized. It is quite possible, therefore, that even attaining the capability to outspend the United States at will, China will not try to match its overkill capability, considering it superfluous.

---

[57] Andrew S. Erickson, *op. cit.*; Cary Huang, China's show of military might risk backfiring, Inkstone, October 19, 2019, https://www.inkstonenews.com/opinion/chinas-show-military-might-risks-backfiring/article/3032979. Accessed October 19, 2019.

[58] Ankit Panda, China Conducts First Test of New JL-3 Submarine-Launched Ballistic Missile, *The Diplomat*, December 20, 2018, https://thediplomat.com/2018/12/china-conducts-first-test-of-new-jl-3-submarine-launched-ballistic-missile/. Accessed October 2, 2019; Greg Torode and David Lague, PLA's furtive underwater nukes test the Pentagon, *Reuters*, May 2, 2019. https://www.reuters.com/investigates/special-report/china-army-nuclear/. Accessed October 3, 2019.

Chapter Eight

THE ECONOMIC APTITUDE

Asia has become the new epicenter of economic growth. It is here where all the right opportunities are present: big funds, huge projects and a shared conviction on the merits of international trade by both governments and populations. It is there, too, where the emergence of a potent middle class opens the largest opportunities for such economic growth.

ASIA'S ECONOMIC MIGHT

It was in Asia where an impressive middle class became the main beneficiary of globalization, obtaining the lion's share of the economic growth that this process generated: 9 out of every 10 cases, as explained in Chapter Six. Moreover, according to the Organization for Economic Cooperation and Development (OECD), the world's middle class will increase from 3,300 million people in 2020 to 4,900 million in 2030. Of that amount, 80% of the increase will take place in Asia. As a result, an enourmous share of global consumption and investment will move to that continent.[1] Asia's middle class is, indeed, expected to reach 2.3 billion people, amounting to 65% of the world total, by 2030. China and India will experience the largest

[1] Homi Kharas, The Emerging Middle Class in Developing Countries, Working Paper N. 285, 2010, http://www.oecd.org/dev/44457738.pdf. Accessed June 12, 2018.

increase, but other countries of the region will the see their middle classes grow at a significant pace as well.[2]

Twenty-eight of the 44 free trade agreements proposed since 2013 are based in Asia, with almost 60% of their total trade being among themselves. Nine of the 10 busiest international flight connections in the world are between Asian cities. Asia now accounts for around one-third of global trade in goods, 40% of global airline travelers and 23% of the world's capital flows, while it is home to 21 of the planet's largest cities.[3]

Asia is now home to half of the 20 fastest growing economies of the world and generates two-thirds of global growth.[4] According to McKinsey Global Institute, in 2017, 42% of global GDP on purchasing power parity terms was in Asia, a percentage that is on course to represent 52% by 2040. In contrast, Europe's share in 2017 was 22% and North America's was 18%. In real GDP terms, Asia's share was 34% in 2017, and is expected to reach 46% by 2040. On the other hand, by 2040 Asia should be representing 39% of global consumption. Global cross-border flows are shifting towards Asia. Asia is not only diverse but also complementary, which makes the region more resilient in the face of any global volatility.[5]

The above trend is confirmed by the World Economic Forum, according to which by 2040 Asia could account for more than half of global GDP and about 40% of the global consumption. It comes as no surprise then, that PricewatherhouseCoopers estimates that in

[2] Evan S. Medeiros, The Changing Fundamentals of US-China Relations, *The Washington Quarterly*, Fall issue, 2019, p. 94.

[3] Parag Khanna, *op. cit.*, locations 2189/6214, 2206/6214, 2255/6214; Joanathan Woetzel and Jeonming Seong, The Asianized World Has Arrived, *Project Syndicate*, October 3, 2019, https://www.project-syndicate.org/commentary/asian-century-economic-rise-regional-integration-by-jonathan-woetzel-and-jeongmin-seong-2019-10. Accessed October 17, 2019.

[4] Evan S. Medeiros, *op. cit.*, p. 94.

[5] Oliver Tonby, Jonathan Woetzel, Wonsik Choi, Karel Eloot, Rajat Dhawan, Jeogmin Seong, and Patti Wang, The future of Asia: Asian flows and networks are defining the next phase of globalization. McKinsey Global Institute, September 2019, https://www.mckinsey.com/featured-insights/asia-pacific/the-future-of-asia-asian-flows-and-networks-are-defining-the-next-phase-of-globalization. Accessed September 19, 2019.

2050 the four largest economies in the world will be ranked in the following order: China, India, United States and Indonesia. In other words, three of the top four economies will be located in Asia.[6]

CHINA: ASIA'S ECONOMIC EPICENTER

At the epicenter of this amazing economic growth is China, which, as mentioned in Chapter Four, is not only the undisputed leader of globalization but also the fundamental promoter of Asia's economic integration. As McKinsey Global Institute points out, China "... acts as an anchor economy for the rest of the region and as a connectivity and innovation platform for neighboring countries".[7] Parag Khanna adds to this argument when saying: "China is not a giant island floating above Asia. Rather, with more neighbors than any other country, it is deeply embedded in the Asian economic system in mutually dependent and beneficial ways. The future is Asian — even for China".[8]

All around Asia, China is laying down fiberoptic cables and setting up 5G mobile phone operators for hundreds of millions of people, preparing the ground for major infrastructure construction and connectivity developments, strengthening coordination of economic policies, enhancing complementarity of development strategies, and so on. So far, the China Development Bank alone has earmarked US$890 billion for some 900 projects within the Belt and Road Initiative, most of which are in Asia.[9]

The Belt and Road Initiative "... could provide a big boost to China's economy and soft power image. China hopes to gain a

---

[6] David Law, Three scenarios for the future of geopolitics. World Economic Forum, June 21, 2018, https://www.weforum.org/agenda/2018/06/david-law-global-futures-3-scenarios/. Accessed June 29, 2018.

[7] Oliver Tonby *et al.*, *op. cit.*

[8] Parag Khanna, The Future is Asian: Global Order In The Twenty-First Century [Kindle Version] (London: Weidenfeld & Nicolson, 2019), retrieved from Amazon.com , location 2144/6214.

[9] Projects span rail, ports, industrial parks, *The Straits Times*, May 15, 2017.

better return on its foreign exchange reserves, create new overseas business opportunities for Chinese firms, create new markets for industries currently experiencing overcapacity, and stimulate economic development in poorer regions of China".[10] Although an intercontinental initiative, its main impact and benefits to China will derive from Asia itself, where, as mentioned above, more than half of the global GDP is expected to concentrate in about 20 years' time.

With this regional backdrop as a natural expansion ground for its technologies, services and excess inventories, China enjoys a very important comparative advantage for its exports. However, it is on the domestic front where the future of its economic growth lies.

CHINA'S ECONOMIC GROWTH

The year 2018 marked the 40th anniversary of China's economic reform and opening. In December 1978, China's "open door" policy put in motion a historic process that has lifted 800 million Chinese out of poverty. During those 40 years, China's GDP grew at an average rate of 10%, three times, that is, more than the United States during the same period. Although China's economy has matured, its GDP growth slowed from 14.2% in 2007 to 6.9% in 2017.[11] In 2019, and under the impact of the trade war with the U.S., the country grew 6.4% in the first quarter, 6.2% in the second quarter and 6% in the third quarter. However, Beijing has embraced this slower economic growth, labeling it as the "new normal", acknowledging the need for the country to rely less on fixed investments and exports.

---

[10] Congressional Research Service, China's Economic Rise: History, Trends, Challenges, Implications for the United States, June 25, 2019, https://fas.org/sgp/crs/row/RL33534.pdf. Accessed September 20, 2019.

[11] Peter Wong, China's four-decade route to the World's No. 1 economy, *South China MorningPost*, March 31, 2018, https://www.scmp.com/news/china/article/2139778/chinas-four-decade-route-worlds-no-1-economy. Accessed November 9, 2019; China's Economy Grows by 6.9% in 2017, *BBC News*, January 18, 2019.

As Frederic Neumann, co-head of Asian economic research at HSBC, pointed out: "It's not as if Chinese growth has completely fallen out of a cliff". On the contrary, it has been a relatively gradual slowdown. China's government has sought to support the economy through tax cuts and by taking measures to boost liquidity in the financial sector. Such measures, nonetheless, have been fairly restrained, as the country is also seeking to cool the rapid growth in recent years.[12]

However, China's slowdown has to be put into perspective. First, it has slowed down only in relation to its own historical growth path. Second, a 6.6% growth in relation to a US$12 trillion economy represented much more growth than, let us say, a 11.4% growth in relation to a US$2.286 trillion economy, which was the case of China in 2005. Third, in 2019 China grew 6.1%, which means that China added to its GDP the equivalent of the entire Australian economy, which is the world's 13th largest. Fourth, a magnitude of growth at around 6.5% should be sufficient to double China's GDP during the decade 2010–2020. Fifth, Japan and South Korea ended their period of high growth rates by plunging almost immediately to around 4%, and then even lower, which has not been the case in China. Sixth, slowing compared to whom? Between 2010 and 2016, the U.S. economy has averaged 2.1% growth annually, the European Union economies 1.3% and Japan 1.2%. Seventh, since the Great Recession, 40% of all the growth around the world has occurred in just one country: China.[13]

---

[12] Ana Nicolai da Costa, China's economic slowdown: How bad is it?, *BBC News*, September 27, 2019.

[13] John Wong, China's Economy 2018: Stabilising Slowdown to Gear up for a New Model of Growth, *East Asian Policy*, East Asian Institute, National University of Singapore, 2018, **10**(1), January/March 2018; Nick Leung, McKinsey & Company, China Brief: The State of the Economy, April 19, 2019, https://www.mckinsey.com/featured-insights/china/china-brief-the-state-of-the-economy. Accessed June 20, 2019; Investopedia.com, The 20 Economies in the World, June 7, 2019, https://www.investopedia.com/insights/worlds-top-economies/. Accessed October 7, 2019; Graham Allison, *op. cit.*, 'p. 12; Huileng Tang, "China's says its economy grew 6.1% in 2019, in line with expectations", CNBC, January 16, 2020, https://www.cnbc.com/2020/01/17/china-gdp-for-full-year-and-q4-2019.html.

The Chinese government pursues slower economic growth in order to avoid hitting the so-called "middle income trap": The moment when countries that have achieved a certain economic level begin to experience sharply diminishing economic growth rates, as they become unable to adopt new sources of economic growth. Consequently, emphasizing private consumption, services and innovation has become China's main priority. Growth now is dependent more on consumption than investment, and more on domestic demand than external demand. Domestic consumption will thus become the main driver of the economy, generating a more sustainable pattern of growth.

INNOVATION AS THE ENGINE DRIVER OF DEVELOPMENT

Higher quality growth has become more important than GDP increase. At the same time, innovation has become not only the number one engine driver of development but also the core of the overall national development process. The term innovation, it must be said, transcends technology and includes innovation in government administration and management as well. The most important meaning of the word, though, is raising the value chain in leading-edge industries.

According to a 2013 joint report by the World Bank and the Development Research Center of the State Council of the People's Republic of China, the country was well positioned to undertake the route towards a much more innovative economy. This process enjoyed advantages in eight different areas. First, spending on research and development (R&D), which followed a steep upward trend. Second, its manufacturing sector was not only large but also possessed wide-range capabilities. Third, its expanded educational system provided a rising quantitative and qualitative supply of science and engineering skills. Fourth, its elastic supply of long-term capital was being mobilized to support innovation and scale up production capacity. Fifth, its large and expanding middle-class consumer market provided stimulus for foreign and domestic innovative investments. Sixth, its pro-business and entrepreneurial culture, particularly represented in Guangdong's Pearl River Delta, Zhejiang and Fujian, supported the emergence of small firms and start-ups. Seventh, its relatively underdeveloped service sector allowed for considerable growth potential. Eight, its ambitious urbanization process and the realization of the merits of quality of life were transforming many of the cities into global centers capable of attracting and retaining global talent.[14]

Notwithstanding the important advantages just mentioned, the same joint report recognized significant innovation weaknesses. Among them were the following two points: One, the bulk of the R&D effort was being conducted by the State, with part of that effort seemingly divorced from the real needs of the economy. Two, although there had been a sharp rise in scientific patents and published papers, few had shown significant commercial relevance.[15]

The Chinese government's "Made in China 2025" initiative, launched in 2015, is modeled on Germany's "Industry 4.0 plan" and aims at upgrading and modernizing China's manufacturing in 10 key sectors. Within the plan, some of the weaknesses mentioned in the 2013 report seemed to be addressed, particularly by way of a clear connection between the State financing and coordinating R&D efforts and the real needs of the economy. By way of extensive government assistance, "Made in China 2025" wants to transform the country into a major global player in sectors such as new advanced information technology, automated machine tools and robotics, aerospace and aeronautical equipment, maritime equipment and high-tech shipping, modern rail transport, new energy vehicles and equipment, power equipment, agricultural equipment, new materials, and bio-pharma and advanced medical products. The 2025 Initiative also calls for greater emphasis on management capabilities.[16]

---

[14] *China 2030: Building a Modern, Harmonious, and Creative Society*, Washington D.C., 2013, p. 34, https://www.worldbank.org/content/dam/Worldbank/document/China-2030-complete.pdf. Accessed May 13, 2019.

[15] *Ibid.*, p. 35.

[16] Joseph Healy, *op. cit.*, p. 11.

China aims at becoming the world's leading manufacturer of telecommunications, railway and electrical power equipment by 2025, while its robotic, high-end automation and new energy vehicles industry should globally compete for the top position by 2025.[17]

Moving up on the technological ladder seems to be the obvious way to address many of the economic problems that China currently faces, reference to which was made in Chapter Three. Among these problems is the debt trap, the demographic or aging trap, the middle-income trap, the environmental challenge and the infrastructural misallocation of resources. Directly or indirectly, technology can help overcome those challenges.

To repay its debt, China will have to increase productivity, which can be attained by moving up the value chain into leading-edge industries. Increased productivity is also the best away to overcome the middle income trap. Robots and automated services can become the natural answer to the demographic trap, while electric cars and renewable energies are the best alternatives to combat environmental problems. Unnecessary infrastructural megaprojects might turn into useful tools of development, when increased productivity generates new infrastructural needs. If properly managed, many such problems can be solved within a modernizing, more productive and growing economy. The Belt and Road Initiative, for its part, would be able to absorb excess capacity resulting in overinvestment in many of its more traditional manufacturing plants, particularly steel.

CHANGING CHINA'S FACE

A September–November 2016 KPMG's survey of 841 high-tech executives from 15 countries concluded that "China is transforming itself from an investment-intensive, export-led model of growth to one driven by consumption and innovation. Through the use of disruptive technologies such as cloud computing, the Internet of Things, smart industrial robotics, Data & Analytics, and enhanced

---

[17] Congressional Research Service, *op. cit.*

automation, Chinese companies are capturing new business opportunities ... Chinese CEO's identified new product development, increasing data analysis capabilities, the Internet of Things, machine-to-machine technology, and the Industrial Internet as top focus areas for further investment in the next three years".[18] In other words, a virtuous circle of innovation-induced productivity is already in motion.

Joseph Healy makes reference to some of the privately owned companies that are changing the face of China through innovation: "Like Xiaomi, Haier, Huawei, JD.com., Tencent, Goodbaby, and Alibaba, are some of the new Chinese firms that may have the potential to be global disruptors, driving business model revolutions with unique disruptor strategies ... The Western world often seems preoccupied with Silicon Valley for technology-based innovation and risk overlooking what is happening in China and its so-called 'Silicon Dragons', with firms such as Internet giants Alibaba, Baidu and Tencent-owned WeChat, smartphone manufacturer Xiaomi, taxi-hailing firm Didi Kuaidi, peer-to-peer lending platform Lufax, and food delivery and movie ticket group Mituan-Dianping all growing into multi-billion valued enterprises".[19]

Although still very much centered in the gigantic Chinese consumer market, these are groundbreaking enterprises with huge global potential. According to *Forbes,* as China continues to rise, innovating faster through game-changing technologies and business models, it is now the West that is starting to copy China.[20] In the above-mentioned 2016 KPMG survey, a quarter of the 841 top high-tech respondents believed that, within the next four years, China held the greatest promise of creating disruptive technologies. An equal number of respondents, on the other hand, favored the

[18] Richard P. Appelbaum, Cong Cao, Xueying Han, Rachel Parker, Denis Simon, *op. cit.,* p. 13.

[19] Joseph Healy, *op. cit.,* pp. 11–12.

[20] Rebecca Fannin, Wake-Up Call: US-China Tech Race Could Only Be the Beginning, https://www.forbes.com/sites/rebeccafannin/2019/06/04/wake-up-call-us-china-tech-race-could-only-be-the-beginning/#154cbba231ff. Accessed October 4, 2019.

United States.[21] Being tied to the U.S. in innovation capability, in the expert's view, is definitely not a bad ranking. It does not come as a surprise, therefore, that according to the well-reputed U.S. business magazine *Fast Company*, the world's most innovative company in 2019 was the Chinese on-demand delivery service Meituan Dianping. This was the conclusion of their 2019 ranking of the 50 most innovative companies worldwide.[22]

Moreover, China is currently creating unicorns — startups valued at a billion dollars or more — at much the same pace as the United States. Chinese-led venture funding for start-ups in 2018 was about 15 times more than what is was in 2013, outpacing the United States' growth in this field. Significantly, in 2018, the U.S. venture funding had doubled in relation to 2013. This means that not even by doubling every five years can the U.S. maintain the level of growth evidenced by Chinese venture funding.[23]

State-owned enterprises (SOEs), for their part, are in many cases still a source of poor productivity and important costs for the economy. Despite official claims that this sector is to be reformed and that market discipline will play a greater role, evidence suggests that they are strengthening their grip on their respective sectors. Moreover, squashing suggestions of depoliticizing such enterprises, Xi Jinping lent his support to the principle of party control over them.

Innovation, though, is also called to play a role in the modernization of SOES. This includes, in some cases, partnering with high-tech private-owned companies. According to Parag Khanna: "The Chinese government has encouraged major companies such as Baidu and Alibaba to buy substantial stakes in China Unicom and other state-owned companies and bring in their technological know-how to retool them to be better performers".[24]

---

[21] Richard P. Appelbaum, Cong Cao, Xueying Han, Rachel Parker, Denis Simon, *op. cit.*, p. 13

[22] The World's 50 Most Innovative Companies 2019, *Fast Company*, https://www.fastcompany.com/most-innovative-companies/2019. Accessed September 15, 2019.

[23] Phred Dvorak and Yasufumi Saito, Silicon Valley Powered American Tech Dominance — Now It Has a Challenger, *The Wall Street Journal*, April 12, 2018.

[24] Parag Khanna, *op. cit.*, location 2499/6214.

Moreover, having turned many of those SOEs into so-called national champions, efforts, investments and synergies have been concentrated in upgrading their technology. The latter is done by frequently buying up foreign companies or divisions of companies that own the necessary technology, as was the case of the acquisition of GE Appliances by Haier. Besides Haier, Lenovo, Sunzone, Chery, Sinopec and China Telecom are good examples of national champions. Moreover, one could say that Huawei, one of the world's top high-tech companies, may be considered a SOE as well. Christopher Balding and Donal C. Clarke wrote a paper to explain how Huawei is in fact an SOE, given that is owned by a holding company, which is in turn approximately 1% owned by Huawei's founder Ren Zhenfgei and 99% by a trade union committee dependant of the State.[25] In fact, a great part of the nearly 100 Chinese corporations on the Fortune Global 500 list are SOEs.[26]

XI'S STAGES OF DEVELOPMENT

In the 19th Party Congress of the CCP, on October 14, 2017, Xi Jinping spelled out his long-term vision for the development of China's economy. This is marked by three distinctive stages. Stage 1 aims at becoming a moderately well-off society by 2020; Stage 2 strives to achieve a modern socialist economy by 2035; and Stage 3 looks at turning into a prosperous and strong society by 2050.[27]

Stage 1 coincides with the first centennial of the founding of the CCP and aims at an intermediate economic point in which the Chinese are "neither rich nor poor". However, it denotes a point in time when absolute poverty has been eliminated. By 2016, over 800 million people in China had been lifted out of poverty, and although urban poverty has basically been eradicated, rural areas still show extreme poverty. At the beginning of stage 1, the country's

[25] Who Owns Huwei?", SSRN, May 8, 2019, https://papers.ssrn.com/sol3/papers.cfm?abstract_id=3372669. Accessed October 23, 2019.

[26] Michael Pillsbury, *op. cit.*, location 3226/7620.

[27] John Wong, *op. cit.*, pp. 26–28.

GDP per capita will be about US$12,000, which implies being at the threshold of a developed economy status. By implication, this means that China will be about to escape the Middle-Income Trap. In total GDP terms, China will be an economy of US$15 trillion, a bit less than the US$19 trillion of today's United States. For China to attain that aim, it needed to have grown at a rate of 6.5% since 2017.

Stage 2 shall witness a modern socialist economy, not only a developed socialist economy but also the world's largest with a total GDP of US$30 trillion. With a GDP per capita of US$23,000, it will not be an affluent society like that of the United States, reaching but half of its GDP per capita, although it would reach the same level Taiwan is at today. In order to achieve that, it would have to grow at a rate of 5% on average between 2020 and 2035.

Stage 3, shortly after the first centennial of the People's Republic of China, would have made real and presented to the world the greatest achievement of them all: a prosperous and strong socialist society. High-quality and efficient economic growth would have been attained. Its total GDP would be a fantastic US$50 trillion, almost three times that of the United States today, while its GDP per capita would reach US$40,000, which is the equivalent of Germany currently. This would have implied having to grow at a rate of 3.5% on average from 2035 until 2050.

Undoubtedly, Xi's strong personality can translate into a steel-powered political leadership, capable of making the country embark in pursuit of such an economic agenda. "However his penchant for tighter political and ideological controls would also complicate state-market relations", adds John Wong.[28] While the former can help much, the latter can also greatly complicate China's economic success. Uncertainty hangs in the air. The main consideration involved, though, would be China's capability to maintain the kind of economic growth envisaged by Xi — 5% average growth between 2020 and 2035 and 3.5% average growth between 2035 and 2050.

In order to achieve this, China needs innovation and urbanization. Moving up the value chain into leading-edge industries is a

[28] *Ibid.*, p. 31.

must in order to improve productivity and growth, as seen before. We shall expand further on this subject in the following chapter.

Earlier this decade, Joseph Stiglitz proclaimed that the two significant forces that would shape global prosperity in the 21st century were to be U.S. technological innovation and urbanization in China. The latter process implies not only the moving of hundreds of millions of Chinese people from the countryside into developing urban areas but the vitality of such urban areas as well.

CITIES AND THE POPULATION FACTOR

James Kynge puts this in context when saying: "In China, urbanization is still an infant. There are approximately 400 million people living in big and small cities at this moment, but by 2050 it is expected this number to rise to 600 or 700 million to reach a billion or 1.1 billion people. The investment required to accommodate so many people in an urban environment is impossible to calculate precisely, but it is clear that the global demand of steel, aluminum, copper, nickel, iron, oil, gas, carbon and many other raw materials and resources will remain strong as long as urbanization in China reaches its limits."[29] According to the McKinsey Global Institute, it is expected that 100 new cities will emerge in China as a result of this urbanization process.[30]

As for the vitality of these urban areas, there has been a clear effort to improve the international competitiveness of Chinese cities. A raft of initiatives has focused on increasing the ease of doing business and attracting more global investments into them. China's big cities, indeed, have been overly successful in attracting multinationals. According to a 2018 report from AT Kearney consultants, China's cities are more competitive than those of any other region in the world. Moreover, the number of Chinese cities included in

[29] James Kynge, *China Shakes the World,* London: Phoenix, 2006, p. 29.

[30] Richard Dobbs *et al.*, Urban World: Mapping the Economic Power of Cities, 2011, http://www.mckinsey.com/insights/urbanization/urban_world_. Accessed March 12, 2018.

the 2018 Global Cities Index soared from 7 in 2008 to 27 ten years later. The index measures aspects like business activity, human capital, information exchange and cultural experience.[31]

On the other hand, Brookings' Global Metro Monitor draws on GDP and employment data from Oxford Economics to track the economic performance of the world's 300 largest metropolitan economies. In 2014, China accounted for fewer than 50 metropolitan areas within the top 300. In the 2018 monitor, measured using 2016 data, this number had increased to 103. This was more than what North America and Western Europe combined could exhibit. Moreover, again according to Brookings, in 2018, five Chinese cities were among the world's 10 best performing metropolitan economies.[32] Even if Chinese economy growth has slowed, its cities significantly outpaced the rest of the world.[33]

It is part of the plan to integrate several cities into a giant megalopolis. That is the case of the so-called Greater Bay Area in China's Pearl River Delta. The Greater Bay area encompasses Hong Kong and Macao along with the following nine cities in Guangdong province: Guangzhou, Shenzhen, Zhuhai, Zhongshan, Jiangmen, Zhaoqing, Foshan, Dongguan and Huizhou. Under an overall plan that looks as far ahead as 2035, the development of these 11 cities will be coordinated with the aim of fostering their complementarity and physical integration. Within them, four core hubs have been earmarked in order to promote the growth of particular industries. Within this scheme, Hong Kong will see its position as an international finance center enhanced, while its development will be

---

[31] Briony Harris, China's cities are rapidly becoming more competitive. Here's why, World Economic Forum, June 15, 2018, https://www.weforum.org/agenda/2018/06/china-cities-more-economically-competitive/. Accessed June 20, 2018.

[32] Max Bouchet and Joseph Padilla, The world's ten best performing metropolitan economies: 2018 edition, Brookings July 12, 2018, https://www.brookings.edu/blog/the-avenue/2018/07/11/the-worlds-ten-best-performing-metropolitan-economies-2018-edition/. Accessed July 17, 2018.

[33] Sifan Liu and Joseph Padilla, Meet the five urban China, Brookings, June 20, 2018, https://www.brookings.edu/blog/the-avenue/2018/06/19/meet-the-five-urban-chinas/? Accessed June 22, 2018.

focused on trade, navigation and finance as well. Macao will use its casinos, hotels and restaurants to develop into an international tourist destination. Shenzhen, home to high-tech giants, will build on its reputation as the most innovative city in China. Guangzhou, finally, will consolidate its position as an administrative hub. Billions of dollars have already been spent in boosting the physical infrastructural connectivity among these cities. This includes the world's longest sea bridge, linking Hong Kong, Zhuhai and Macao as well as a high-speed rail network. It is an ambitious project that aims at creating a world-class city cluster.[34]

And then, of course, we have to consider the population factor. Despite its fast growth in previous decades, Japan could have never expected to surpass the U.S. for the simple reason that its population is hardly 40% that of the United States. On the contrary, China only requires that its per capita income become a quarter of that of the United States in order to surpass America's GDP in size. This can be rephrased as follows. Japan's workforce is about one-third the size of America's, which means that the average Japanese worker would have needed to produce three time as much as their American counterpart for Japan to overtake U.S. output. That, of course, was impossible. Conversely, China's workforce is four times bigger than America's. Hence, China's output can easily overtake that of the United States when the average Chinese worker produces just one-quarter as much as the average American worker. Hereafter, China can guarantee itself several additional decades of sustained economic growth. In GDP per capita terms, China was in 2011 where Japan was in 1965, which means that there is still a lot of tissue to cut open.[35]

One might say, therefore, that the aims of sustaining a 5% average growth per annum between 2020 and 2035 (an amount in concordance with the estimates of the previously referred report by

---

[34] Alex Thornton, This is China's plan to eclipse Silicon Valley, World Economic Forum, February 22, 2019, https://www.weforum.org/agenda/2019/02/this-is-china-s-plan-to-eclipse-silicon-valley/. Accessed March 5, 2019.

[35] Hugh White, *op. cit.*, p. 28; Jacques Attali, Regional Outlook Forum, Institute of Southeast Asian Studies, Singapore, January 12, 2011.

The World Bank and the Development Research Center of the State Council of the People's Republic of China) and a 3.5% average growth between 2035 and 2050 are not unreasonable.

U.S.' LAGGING BEHIND

Conversely, since the early 1970s, the United States' growth slipped below 3% per annum, decelerating further to under 2% since 2000. Moreover, according to the Congressional Budget Office, by the mid-2020s, the U.S.' estimated annual growth in total GDP will just average 1.7% per year.[36] If so, and amid divergent growing curves, China should have become a much larger economy than the United States by mid-century. Based on several estimates, Robert Fogel mentions that in 2040 China's GDP could be almost three times as large as that of the U.S., with a 40% share of the global GDP versus 14% for the United States.[37] PricewatherhouseCoopers estimate is more cautious, although equally devastating for the United States: In 2050, China's GDP at Purchasing Power Parity will be US$58,499 trillion, whereas the United States' GDP at PPP will be US$34,102.[38]

One of the fundamental problems of the United States' economy today is its Public Debt. Two problems arise from this. First is its relation to the country's GDP. In December 2018, the debt represented 106.141% of the GDP. This makes it one of the largest in the world, ranking number 12 within an infamous list where it is only preceded by countries such as Japan, Greece, Sudan, Venezuela, Lebanon, Italy, Eritrea, Portugal and Mozambique, to name a few.[39]

[36] Jonathan Gruber and Simon Johnson, *Jump-Starting America: How Breakthrough Science Can Revive Economic Growth and the American Dream. New York, NY: Public Affairs,* 2019, p. 9.

[37] $123,000,000,000,000: China estimated economy by the year 2040. Be warned, *Foreign Policy*, 4 January, 2010.

[38] The Long View: How will the global economic order change by 2050?, February 2017, https://www.pwc.com/gx/en/world-2050/assets/pwc-world-in-2050-summary-report-feb-2017.pdf. Accessed September 23, 2019.

[39] Global Finance, Percentage of Public Debt to GDP Around the World 2018, https://www.gfmag.com/global-data/economic-data/public-debt-percentage-gdp.

Second, and this is a much more serious consideration, is the large amount of America's debt in foreign hands. Foreign countries hold US$6.433 trillion of a total public debt of US$16.17 trillion. Of this amount, China with US$1,113 trillion represents the number one foreign debt holder.[40] The simple fact that the U.S.' main strategic competitor is, at the same time, its largest international creditor makes Washington immensely vulnerable. Not surprisingly, manipulating such holding as a way of pressuring the United States was mentioned as one of China's possible retaliatory measures against Trump's trade war.

However, besides the obvious case just mentioned, there is another dimension of vulnerability. This is a consequence of the fact that, at a time in which the Asian appetite for U.S. Treasuries is waning, 55% of U.S. foreign debt is in Asian hands. Parag Khana explains the situation as follows: "Asian capital thus became a driver of the US dollar's stability and status as a global reserve currency. China and Japan remain the two largest foreign holders of US Treasuries, with more than $1 trillion each, and Hong Kong and Taiwan also rank in the top with nearly $200 billion each. All of these top ten foreign holders of US dollar reserves — including Saudi Arabia, South Korea, India and Singapore- are Asian economies, collectively holding more than 55 percent of US Treasuries (…) Yet a great diversion of capital is under way as Asians refocus on investing in Asia (and Europe) rather than in the United States (…) Instead of underwriting the US dollar, Asians are gaining confidence in investing in their own debt and capital markets (…) But the financial crisis laid bare how much US banks rely on financial engineering rather than underlying fundamentals to generate growth".[41]

Accessed September 23, 2019; World Population Review, Debt to GDP Ratio by Country 2019, http://worldpopulationreview.com/countries/countries-by-national-debt/. Accessed September 23, 2019.

[40] TreasuryDirect, Debt to the Penny, July 31, 2018, https://www.treasurydirect.gov/NP/debt/current. Accessed September 23, 2019; How Much, Understanding Money, The Biggest Foreign Holders of U.S. Debt in One Chart, https://howmuch.net/articles/foreign-holders-of-usa-debt. Accessed September 23, 2019.

[41] *Op. cit.*, locations 2736/6214, 2382/6214, 2388/6214, 2393/6214.

An important part of the problem behind the financial crisis that began in the U.S. in 2007 stemmed from the foreign holding of America's public debt. In C. Fred Bergsten words: "These huge inflows of foreign capital, however, turned out to be an important cause of the current economic crisis, because they contributed to the low interest rates, excessive liquidity, and loose monetary policies that brought the overleveraging and underpricing of risk..."[42] Many of the financial excesses committed in the United States were, indeed, helped by the underestimation of risk that came from easy money.

At present, the U.S. could face an opposite and even more worrisome problem. This derives from the drying up of the foreign inflows of capital that have accustomed Americans to live beyond their own means. Since private savings as a share of GDP has been declining for years, the large government deficits could not have been funded without borrowing from the rest of the world. As this borrowing capacity diminishes, America will be increasingly forced to live within its means. Amid other considerations, this could translate to defense budget limitations, as the U.S. would not be able to sustain the huge defense spending to which it had grown accustomed.

Much has been written about the Chinese public debt. However, this just represents 50.104% of the country's GDP (contrary to the 106.141% represented by the American one). Moreover, just about 2% of China's sovereign debt is owned by foreigners. With a public debt representing 238.225% of its GDP, Japan has been able to avoid much of the problems confronted by the so-called PIIGS countries in the Eurozone, precisely because its debt is an essentially domestic owned one. That gives an idea of the importance of not owing to foreign creditors. So relaxed is the situation of China in relation to its foreign debt that Beijing has indicated that it would be comfortable with augmenting it to 15% of the public one. Hence, it has given the green light to offshore the so-called renmimbi "panda bonds".[43]

---

[42] C. Fred Bergsten, The Dollar and the Deficits, *Foreign Affairs*, 2009, 88(November/December), p. 24.

[43] Parag Khanna, *op. cit.*, location 2406/6214; Global Finance, Percentage of Public Debt to GDP Around the World 2018, *op. cit.*

EMBRACING THE FOURTH INDUSTRIAL REVOLUTION

The pressure to compete in several fronts with an increasingly richer China, amid the drying out of foreign inflows of capital, will undoubtedly stress the American economy. Technology becomes the natural answer to this challenge. As Jonathan Gruber and Simon Johnson affirm: "Instead of sparring with China over trade, the United States should dramatically increase its own investment in research and development. Only by spurring domestic innovation can the United States counter China (…) The best way to counter China is to out-invest it".[44]

By embracing the Fourth Industrial Revolution, the United States would be able to keep its economy growing, while cushioning against the economic gap with China. Digital technology and robotics, additive manufacturing (3D printing), nanotechnology, bioengineering and genomics, the Internet of things and new energy technologies, among other technological leaps would lead the way.

However, while Beijing projects itself abroad through the Belt and Road Initiative and countless trade agreements and economic engagements, the United States may perhaps find a better alternative in the onshoring or reshoring of many previously offshored economic activities. And this, in addition to the technological substitution of many imported commodities.

Offshoring the manufacturing of goods to labor-intensive assembly lines can become obsolete if robotics and atomization are able to produce back home at lower costs. The competitive need of having factories at the other end of the world will tend to disappear, indeed, if American companies manage produce at a cheaper cost without leaving home.

---

[44]Jonathan Gruber and Simon Johnson, To Counter China, Out-Invent It: Trump's Trade War Ignores the Real Threat from Beijing, *Foreign Affairs*, 2019 (September/October), https://www.foreignaffairs.com/articles/china/2019-09-12/counter-china-out-invent-it. Accessed September 14, 2019.

This would imply, on the one hand, operating with the so-called "dark factories". In them, the assembly line runs for 24 hours a day, without direct human intervention, with low-level monitoring and maintenance and without need for light, heating or air conditioning. On the other hand, this would lead to operation with the so-called collaborative robots or "cobots", which emphasize their flexibility and capacity to work next to humans without putting them in danger. While "dark factories" are ideal for big companies, cobots, at an average cost of US$ 24,000, are particularly useful for small companies.[45] But besides being able to produce cheaper at home, American companies will have additional advantages through the onshoring or reshoring of their manufacturing activities. As explained by Martin Ford: "Factory reshoring dramatically decreases transportation costs and also provide many other advantages. Locating factories in close proximity to both consumer markets and product design centers allow companies to cut production lead times and be far more responsive to customers".[46]

The math was clear to Foxconn, a quintessential labor-intensive producer in China. This Taiwanese company decided to move a large part of its production to the United States, replacing one million Chinese workers with robots. If a Taiwanese company was willing to relocate close to its main consumer market, what argument would there be for American companies not doing the same? As a matter of fact, between 2010 and 2015, over 1,300 American companies either brought production back to the United States or chose to source from home suppliers instead of remaining overseas.[47] Within an extensive survey of U.S. companies, 71% believed

[45] T.X. Hammes, The end of globalization? The international security implications, War on the Rocks, 2 August, 2016, https://warontherocks.com/2016/08/the-end-of-globalization-the-international-security-implications/. Accessed February 13, 2017.

[46] *Op. cit.*, p. 9.

[47] Finbarr Livesey, *From Global to Local: The Making of Things and the End of Globalization*, New York: Pantheon Books, 2017, p. 125.

that advance manufacturing processes will improve the economy of localized production.[48]

Referring to producing in the United States, Jeffrey Immelt, then General Electric's CEO stated: "We can basically make every product GE makes and do it economically in the US today".[49] Just like GE, countless American companies could produce locally finished products or the parts thereof, thus avoiding the delay represented by long supply chains, import fees and trapped inventory.

3D PRINTING AND NANOTECHNOLOGY

Additive technology or 3D printing may also play a very important role in this onshoring process, thus eroding the dependence on labor-intensive assembly lines and supply chains that are at a distance. Intermediate trade of unfinished goods accounts for approximately 60% of current world trade.[50] Additive technology can be profoundly disruptive in this intermediate trade for two reasons. First, because it fosters local production of numerous parts. Second, because 3D printing makes possible the elimination of many previously needed parts and pieces in any given product.

But in addition to unfinished goods, 3D printing is evolving into the production of finished goods as well. This implies, of course, smaller volumes of production but, at the same time, a much more customized production. As a result, there would be a decentralization of the production process, with numerous 3D printing factories producing for localized markets. Companies could hence move towards having smaller production facilities, distributed along their different consumer markets. This, in turn, could help revitalize many decaying cities and regions.

---

[48] *Ibid.*, p. 124.

[49] Rick Smith and Mitch Free, *The Great Disruption: Competing and Surviving in the Second Wave of the Industrial Revolution*, New York: Thomas Dunne Books/St. Martin's Press, 2016, p. 145.

[50] Finbarr Livesey, *op. cit.*, p. 52.

A fundamental by-product of 3D printing factories near home will be speedy deliveries. This trend, introduced by Amazon Prime in 2005, allowed customers to pay US$79 for a two-day unlimited delivery. A Deloitte report asked over 4,000 U.S. costumers what they considered to be fast shipping, to which 90% replied in two days or less.[51] Americans are no longer willing to wait for their products. Local 3D printing will be the answer to this quest for immediacy, making supply chains and long delays even more outmoded, especially when each item can be customized and not be the product of mass standardization.

Traditional natural resources that foreign economies extract out of their grounds, till out of their fields or raise up in their farms might be targeted for substitution by local alternatives as well. Here, the onshoring process can take place just as well because technology may simply trump those gifts of nature. Molecular bonding between light atoms that result in new materials, cellular factories that replace the food dependency on living animals, controlled environment agriculture in reduced spaces, renewable energy are but a few examples of the way in which mass substitution of commodities could end up taking place in the United States.

The new materials resulting from nanotechnology are ideal for the construction of bridges and aircraft, but they are equally useful for many other applications. In K. Eric Drexler words: "In a wide range of products, performance depends of the strength and density of structural materials, and building with stronger, lighter materials can reduce product mass because structural materials make up almost all the mass of almost every industrial product".[52]

Being much lighter and stronger, these materials allow for the elimination of a substantial percentage of structural mass. Products less massive not only have a favorable impact on production costs but also, as in the case of aircrafts, considerably reduce the amount of fuel needed. And yet, it is not only in the area of aerospace where new

---

[51] *Ibid.*, p. 137.

[52] K. Eric Drexler, *Radical Abundance: How Revolution in Nanotechnology Will Change Civilization*, New York: Public Affairs, 2013, p. 162.

materials allow for energy saving. Carbon nanotubes can outperform and replace copper as an electrical conductor. Photovoltaic cells can improve significantly with nanotechnology materials, thus allowing for greater improvement in solar conversion efficiency. As such, they have the potential to alter the energy economy. Nanotechnology will also be able to replace steel, aluminum and plastic structures with stronger and more efficient materials, hence making these commodities increasingly redundant.

These new materials are potentially able to replace numerous commodities while, at the same time, saving energy by reducing mass or improving conductivity. In other words, steel, aluminum, copper, oil, gas, among many other commodities, are being targeted for profound disruption by nanotechnology. This implies not only the substitution of commodities in a mass scale but also the capacity for the United States to replace them locally.

TRANSFORMING A MULTI-MILLENNIAL RELATION WITH ANIMALS AND SOIL

This process of substitution does not stop at inanimate matter. If desired, it could include live creatures as well. This could lead to what Elsa Sortiaris calls "the post animal economy".[53]

Cellular agriculture, for instance, is a scientific field that uses genomics to replicate proteins and biomolecules produced by animals. These "cellular factories" can grow food and brew beverages locally and sustainable. Cow-free milk is an example of what can be produced. Within this post-animal feeding industry, we will find chicken-free chicken or beef-free beef. Cheap, scalable and locally produced meat only requires small biopsies from an animal to extract a group of cells to raise them up. This technology, which is already scientifically viable, will keep improving and eventually become commercially viable. It will require 95% less

---

[53] Elsa Sortiaris, 5 wild biotech products of the future, Singularity Hub, November 24, 2017, https://singularityhub.com/2017/11/24/5-wild-biotech-products-of-the-future/#sm.0001kyij62wlkw0ycu1io1plvs92. Accessed May 29, 2018.

water, 98% less land and 45% less energy, while generating 95% less greenhouse gases.[54]

Together with the above advancements, there would be many other leaps in sensors, production automation, robot farming or engineering, which will radically transform the multi-millennia relation between human beings and the soil. While those technologies materialize, indoor farms are beginning to take shape in the United States. These farms do not require herbicides or pesticides, use 97% less water and 40% less power, waste 50% less food and are not subject to weather irregularities. Moreover, depending on their production, indoor farms can have 11–15 crop cycles per year.[55]

One type of indoor farming is vertical farming. This method will be able to grow vegetables inside climate-controlled, light-controlled cylinders, located in towers. Instead of pesticides, herbicides or synthetic fertilizers, this method uses thousands of infrared cameras and collecting data sensors in order to optimize the growing of vegetables. One of its current developers, a Californian company call Plenty, claims that this technology can achieve yields up to 350 times greater than traditional agriculture while using 1% of the water and almost no land when compared to conventional methods.[56] As Peter Diamandis says: "Imagine ... growing all your food in a 50-story tall vertical farm in downtown LA or off-shore on the Great Lakes where the travel distance is no longer 1,500 miles but 50 miles. Delocalized

[54] Peter H. Diamandis, These 4 Tech Trends Are Driving US Toward Food Abundance, Singularity Hub, May 18, 2018, https://singularityhb.com/2018/05/18/these-4-trends-are-driving-us-toward-food-abundandance/#sm.0001kyij62wlkdw0ycu1io1plvs92. Accessed May 12, 2018; T. X. Hames, The end of globalization? The international security implications, August 2, 2016, https://warontherocks.com/2016/08/the-end-of-globalization-the-international-security-implications/. Accessed February 13, 2017.

[55] Michael Zappa,15 emerging agriculture technologies that will change the world, *Policy Horizons Canada,* May 6, 2015, http://www.businessinsider.sg/15-emerging-agriculture-technologies-2014-4/#18EzrTcMUDhrlBtw.97. Accessed September 5, 2016; Josie Garthwaite, Beyond GMOs: The rise of synthetic biology, *The Atlantic,* September 25, 2014; T. X. Hammes, *op. cit.*

[56] Ronald Holden, It's Called Vertical Farming, and it Could Be the Future of Agriculture, *Forbes Magazine,* 4 November, 2016.

farming will minimize travel costs at the same time that it maximizes freshness".[57]

CLEAN ENERGY

The energy sector also advances at amazing speed in the United States. In addition to technological advances in fracking and horizontal drilling, there have been impressive inovations in clean energies as well. According to a 2014 report by the International Renewable Energy Agency (IRENA), solar photovoltaic costs fell by two-third between the end of 2009 and 2013 — a speed of change comparable to that seen in the IT revolution. Indeed, in 2013, prices had fallen by 80% since 2008.[58] In addition, as expressed by a 2016 IRENA report: "Biomass for power, hydropower, geothermal and onshore wind can all now provide electricity competitively, compared to fossil fuel-power generation".[59] Further still, according to well-known futurologist Jeremy Rifkin, such technologies are moving towards the zero marginal costs stage where they will be able to run for free, once their development costs have been amortized.[60] Although electricity generated by wind, solar, geothermal and other renewable sources can be transmitted over long distances, it is mostly generated and consumed locally. Contrary to oil, gas and coal, it is not transported through extensive distances in tankers, ships or pipelines.

Within this new energy equation, electric cars are called to play a leading role. Lithium batteries, whose price has fallen radically

---

[57] Peter Diamandis, These 4 tech trends are driving us towards food abundance, *op. cit.*

[58] Edgar Meza, IRENA: PV prices have declined 80% since 2008, *PV Magazine*, September 11, 2014, https://www.pv-magazine.com/2014/09/11/irena-pv-prices-have-declined-80-since-2008_100016283/. Accessed February 29, 2018.

[59] International Renewable Energy Agency, The Power to Change: Solar and Wind Cost Reduction Potential to 2025, 2016, http://www.irena.org/DocumentDownloads/Publications/IRENA_Power_to_Change_2016.pdf. Accessed February 29, 2018.

[60] Jeremy Riffkin, *The Zero Marginal Cost Society: The Internet of Things, the Collaborative Commons, and the Eclipse of Capitalism*, New York: Palgrave, 2014.

since 2009 and whose storage capacity has augmented dramatically at the same time, are beginning to provide profitability to electric cars. Although still not competitive with vehicles powered by internal combustion energy in the small to mid-size cars, this should change in the next five to seven years as battery prices keep declining. Consumer preferences for electric vehicles in the United States are shifting, though, with up to 30% of consumers indicating their preference to consider them as their next purchase.[61] Meanwhile, synthetic-biological redesign of organisms could generate biofuel almost identical to gasoline. This would increase the life span of vehicles powered by internal combustion and with the use of a clean source of energy.[62]

BIG DATA AND THE AUTOMATION OF KNOWLEDGE

The service sector, for its part, is being transformed not only by robots and self-service technologies in menial jobs but also by "big data" and the automation of knowledge work in higher-skilled occupations. The volume of digitalized information today is so massive that it would fill five stacks of CD disks reaching as far as the moon. Big data allows all that universe of stored digital information to be instantaneously collated. As a result, we are leaving behind the realm of correlation.[63]

Martin Ford explains this in the following terms: "By one estimate, the total amount of data stored globally is now measured in thousands of exabytes (an exabyte is equal to a billion gigabytes),

---

[61]Yeon Baik, Russel Hensley, Patrick Hertzke and Stefan Knupfer, Making electric vehicles profitable, McKinsey & Company, March 2019, https://www.mckinsey.com/industries/automotive-and-assembly/our-insights/making-electric-vehicles-profitable. Accessed September 25, 2019.

[62]Josie Garthwaite, Beyond GMOs: The rise of synthetic biology, *The Atlantic*, September 25, 2014.

[63]Victor Mayer Schoenmberg and Kenneth Cukier, *Big Data: A Revolution That Will Transform How We Live, Work and Think*, London: John Murray, 2013.

and that figure is subject to its own Moore's Law — like acceleration, doubling roughly every three years. Nearly all that data is now stored in digital format and is therefore accessible to direct manipulation by computers (...) The vast majority of this data is what a computer scientist would call 'unstructured' (...) the ability to process a stream of unstructured information ... is, after all, one of the things for which humans are uniquely adapted. The difference, of course, is that in the realm of big data, computers are able to do this on a scale that for a person, would be impossible. Big data is having a revolutionary impact in a wide range of areas including business, politics, medicine, and nearly every field of natural and social science".[64]

Onshoring or reshoring also applies to foreign service providers and, therefore, also to the service sector. Searching for cheaper white-collar providers in distant places would no longer make sense when algorithms can provide the same kind of services locally, for even lower costs. Hence, aiming at the better qualified engineer, financial analyst or accountant at the lower available international costs may become unnecessary. India is a good case in point. Its lead in IT services, based on factors such as extensive experience at remote delivery of IT services to global clients, highly developed process rigor, in-depth knowledge of specific industries and fluency in the English language, is well known.

As Nida Najar explains: "India's information technology industry grew at a breakneck speed over the past two decades thanks to a trend commonly called offshoring ... But the global tech industry is increasingly relying on automation, robotics, big data analytics, machine learning and consulting — technologies that threaten to bypass and even replace Indian workers ... 'What we're seeing is an acceleration in shedding for jobs in India and an adding of jobs inshore', said Sandra Notardonato, and analyst and research vice president for Garter, a research and advisory company".[65]

---

[64] Martin Ford, *op. cit.*, pp. 85–87.

[65] Nida Najar, Indian Technology Workers Worry About a Job Threat: Technology, *The New York Times*, 25 January, 2017.

Even in America's heartland, technological onshoring is been seen as a way to boost its decaying economy. As argued in a Brookings Institution report: "Amid this rising inequality, the question of how to revive broad-base economic growth in the middle of the country has received substantial attention … These places — including large urban areas like Detroit, Pittsburg, and Cleveland, as well as smaller communities like Albany, Ga., Janesville, Wisc., ad Dubuque, Iowa- once formed the backbone of America's manufacturing economy, but have since struggled to transition to a more digital economy (…) The technologically advanced economy is a major driver of economic growth. And older industrial cities (OICs) are research powerhouses. These communities receive more grant dollars per capita from the National Institute of Health and National Science Foundation than their peers, and are home to many of the world-famous private research universities of the Northeast as well as the renowned land-grant colleges and universities of the Midwest. Notably, many of these research universities are located in down-town areas. Recent research from our Brooking colleagues suggests that this proximity to employers, entrepreneurs, capital, and other amenities that facilitate research commercialization positions these institutions well to serve as regional hubs of innovation and growth".[66]

Their reconversion into digital manufacturing centers is thus seen as a way out for these decaying older industrial cities. The comparative advantages that many of them enjoy, as research powerhouses, could indeed position them well for such an endeavor. Hence, they may become excellent places for the onshoring process that the Fourth Industrial Revolution could bring with it. And although new technologies are not conducive to job creation, they might energize decaying communities in many other ways. Therefore, as the Brooking's report remarks: "Local, regional and state leaders

[66] Cecile Murray and Alan Berube, The road to economic revival in the Heartland runs through older industrial cities, May 15, 2018, https://www.brookings.edu/blog/the-avenue/2018/05/15/the-road-to-economic-revival-in-the-heartland-runs-through-older-industrial-cities/. Accessed May 15, 2018.

are stepping up to retool these economies for growth and inclusion by supporting firm creation and expansion".[67]

Jonathan Gruber and Simon Johnson argue in the same direction. In their words: "In our book *Jump-Starting America,* we identify 102 urban communities that are plausible next-generation tech hubs. Spread across 36 states in all regions of the country, these cities and towns have large populations, highly educated workers, and a low cost of living. Examples include Rochester, New York; Baton Rouge, Louisiana; and Topeka, Kansas".[68]

A CATCH-22 SITUATION

Although the Fourth Industrial Revolution and the economic onshoring that comes with it are the best alternative to boost economic productivity and growth in the United States, this would hardly promote social inclusion as the lines above may lead to believe — much to the contrary! And even if many of the tasks that technology is called to take away were already lost to the American working population by way of blue-collar or white-collar offshoring, social problems and economic inequality will only exacerbate.

The missing middle, which was mentioned in Chapter Five when referring to the social polarization existing in the United States, will only grow in size. As Martin Ford explains: "The hollowed-out middle of the already polarized job market is likely to expand as robots and self-service technologies eat away at low-wage jobs, while increasingly intelligent algorithms threaten higher skill occupations. Indeed, a 2013 study by Carl Benedikt Ford and Michael A. Osborne at the University of Oxford concluded that occupations amounting to nearly half of US total employment may be vulnerable to automation within roughly the next two decades".[69]

The United States finds itself in a Catch-22 situation. In order to confront China's economic rise, the United States has to embrace

---

[67] Cecile Murray and Alan Berube, *op. cit.*

[68] *Op. cit.*

[69] *Op. cit.*, p. 59.

the Fourth Industrial Revolution to its full extent. The main reason for this is the decreasing levels of productivity that tend to follow from previous innovation breakthroughs. A couple of examples can attest to this. In 1965, Gordon Moore predicted that the number of transistors packed onto a computer would double every two years. Although he has been proven mostly right for more than 50 years, the number of researchers required to double chip density today is more than 18 times the number needed in the late 1970s. In other words, more and more money is needed to maintain the same rate of productivity growth over time. Something similar happens in agriculture. An increasing number of researchers work on improving agricultural crop yields. However, the rate of increase in yields slows over time. The productivity of research in this area declines by about 6% per year. This phenomenon is present in many other areas as well. The only way to counter it is by keeping the innovation spiral in continuous movement.[70] However, in doing so, the country's serious divide can only be aggravated, as the job disruption will keep its upwards trend.

In this respect, China finds itself in a more advantageous position. Even if China cannot disregard the disruptions brought about by automation and technology, they represent the obvious solution to one of its most serious problems: the demographic trap. George Magnus argues this well when saying: "In China, the coming dearth of younger people and glut of older aged workers with low skill levels are going to sit uncomfortably with ambitious economic plans, present a serious social welfare challenge, and validate concerns felt elsewhere about the major economic consequences triggered by ageing".[71] *The Economist*, for its part, says that "the connection between robots and ageing is a powerful one. Mr. Acemoglu reckons that ageing is the biggest single influence upon how many robots a country has".[72]

[70] Jonathan Gruber and Simon Johnson, *Jump-Starting America, op. cit.*, p. 109.

[71] George Magnus, *Red Flags: Why Xi's China is in Jeopardy*. New Haven, CT: Yale University Press, 2018, location 2232/6073.

[72] An ageing world needs more resourceful robots, *The* Economist, February 16, 2019.

With a rapidly aging population, as a result of the combination of low fertility rate and rising life expectancy, technology becomes a providential answer to the country's quest to attain its "rejuvenation" — a magical catchword that represents the glue that holds together the CCP and the Chinese population. Technology and rejuvenation thus become inseparable notions. Under those circumstances, the search for economic prosperity and nationalism, the two strongest legitimizing forces of the regime, blend in their support to technology.

The United States finds itself on a completely different playing field. According to the U.N. World Population Prospects, the U.S. population is estimated to increase from 328 million in 2018 to 370 million in 2050.[73] On the one hand, the U.S. has a high fertility rate by industrialized country standards, which is supported by a foreign-born population, which doubled from almost 20 million in 1990 to over 45 million in 2015. Between 2015 and 2065, future immigrants and their descendants are projected to account for 88% of the U.S. population increase, or 103 million people, as the nation grows to 441 million.[74] Although the country's racial profile is expected to be vastly different in 2050 (47% White, 29% Hispanic, 13% Black and 9% Asian), the United States will be able to count with a relay population.[75] This new America, as some analysts have described it, will be more racially and culturally diverse, younger, more secular, more immigrant and foreign born.

---

[73] Yi Fuxian, An aging China will never overtake the US economy, Inkstone, March 29, 2019, https://www.inkstonenews.com/opinion/yi-fuxian-china-will-never-catch-us-economy-thanks-population-aging/article/3003790. Accessed March 30, 2019.

[74] Pew Research Center, Modern Immigration Wave Brings 59 Million to U.S. Driving Population Growth and Change Through 2065, September 28, 2015, https://www.pewresearch.org/hispanic/2015/09/28/modern-immigration-wave-brings-59-million-to-u-s-driving-population-growth-and-change-through-2065/. Accessed September 25, 2019.

[75] Pew Research Center, U.S. Population Projections: 2005–2050, February 11, 2008, https://www.pewresearch.org/hispanic/2008/02/11/us-population-projections-2005-2050/. Accessed September 25, 2019.

A VOLATILE POLITICAL SYSTEM

On the other hand, contrary to China, the United States lacks unifying national banners. This is compounded by a highly volatile political system, which will tend to become even more volatile as the American divide increases as a result of the immense job disruption that technology will bring with it. While "Made in China 2025" set clear-cut strategic guidelines, in the search for that nation's "rejuvenation", the United States will keep zigzagging amid highly polarized visions of the country and its future. Trump and the populism that he embodies are good examples of how the U.S. can suddenly go back in time to the coal and the steel era of the 1950s as political priorities.

But populism is not Trump's monopoly. Preceded in recent times by the Tea Party and Occupy Wall Street, plus having had Bernie Sanders as a liberal counterpart during the 2016 presidential election process, Trump just represents one of America's several populist versions. As John B. Judis writes: "Trump and Sanders were continuing what Perot and Buchanan had started, but with a success that suggested the political consensus had become increasingly vulnerable".[76]

However, in all its different versions the populist credo maintains as a common denominator its proclaimed dichotomy between the "people", understood as the forgotten social majority, and the privileged few. Their grievance is directed against deaf, selfish, arrogant and corrupt political elites, which are complicit with the excesses and greediness of big corporations and a wealthy class. One way or another, extreme right and liberal populisms converge in undermining America's embrace of the Fourth Industrial Revolution — the former by regressing to bygone economic eras, the latter by scrutinizing, regulating, suing and dismembering high-tech giants, making them vulnerable to their Chinese counterparts.

According to a Pew Research Center poll, 81% of Trump supporters thought life for people like them had gotten worse over the

---

[76] John B. Judis, *The Populist Explosion: How the Great Recession Transformed American and European Politics,* New York: Columbia Global Reports, 2016, pp. 63–64.

previous 50 years, while only 11% thought it had gotten better. Moreover, Trump supporters were deeply pessimistic about the future, with 68% believing that the lives of the next generation would be even worse.[77] Not surprisingly, *The Economist* said: "Populism wave has yet to crest".[78]

Populism, indeed, will take time to crest, as the reasons that gave it rise are not bound to disappear any time soon. With robots and computers taking the relay from labor-intensive Chinese and Vietnamese workers in destroying American jobs (and with illegal immigration following its course, as wars and hunger abroad are a fact of life), populism is bound to become a normal feature within American politics.

Under those circumstances, China's strategic and straightforward path towards economic supremacy will most probably be met by acrimonious debate, instability and, of course, unsteadiness on the American side.

[77] Stephen D. King, *Grave New World: The End of Globalization, The Return of History*, New Haven: Yale University Press, 2017, p. 241.
[78] Left behind, *The Economist*, October 21, 2017

Chapter Nine

THE TECHNOLOGICAL APTITUDE

In his multi-volume *Science and Civilisation in China*, Cambridge University scholar Joseph Needham explained how the Chinese civilization, which between the first century BC and the 15th century AD was more efficient than the Western World in generating technological innovations, ceased to develop new techniques after the 16th century. He further refers about how when the Chinese inventions reached the West, they helped in transforming European Feudalism into Capitalism. The conclusion herein involved was that Europe ended up surpassing China in scientific innovations, using Chinese technologies.[1]

China's current march towards technological supremacy, having this narrative as background, would not only imply recuperating the technological primacy that it held during most of human history but also a historical payback time on what the West owes them. It seems obvious that Beijing aims not only at its "resurrection" as the world's technological leader but feels entitled to benefit itself, by whichever means available, from the West's technology.

---

[1]Robert Finlay, China, the West, and World History in Joseph Needham's Science and Civilisation in China, *Journal of World History*, 2000, **11**(2, Fall), pp. 265–303.

BUYING AND FUNDING FOREIGN TECHNOLOGY

China's dynamic growth in technology was initially fueled by foreign technology. This represented the policy of technological progress by way of the so-called "picking from the low-hanging trees". However, as that easy source has by now been exhausted, future productivity gains will have to come from its own R&D efforts, i.e., from indigenous innovation. Although official efforts in promoting the latter have been in place for many years, there is no way for China to circumvent this route now. The country, however, is more than prepared for this undertaking.

The policy of "picking from the low-hanging trees" nurtured itself from many sources, chief among them by buying technology, by financing the development of foreign technology, by forced technology transfer and by stealing technology.

Buying technology usually implies buying the Western companies that are producing it. This has gone from Volvo to MG, from IBM's Personal Computers Division to Thompson, from Motorola Mobility to Cirrus Wind Energy, from General Electric Appliance Business to Ingram Micro, from the Chicago Stock Exchange to Pirelli, and the list goes on, including numerous medium-sized Silicon Valley companies.

A variation in the format of buying the majority stockholding of foreign companies with desired technology has been the acquisition of significant stakes in them. This has been the case, for instance, in relation to firms such as the German Lilium, the U.S.' Xcerra or the U.K.'s Gilo Industries or Fine Organics. A study commissioned by the Asia Society in New York forecast, at the beginning of this decade, that over the next years China would invest as much as US$2 trillion to acquire overseas companies, plants or property.[2]

The closest thing to buying Western companies or parts thereof of its stockholding is funding companies that are developing useful technologies. China has acted as a powerful source of venture capital

---

[2]David Barboza, China's Growing Overseas Portfolio, *International Herald Tribune*, May 4, 2011.

both in the United States and Europe, aiming at technologies convergent with their own priorities. Silicon Valley has become one of its preferred destinations. A good example of such funding is illustrated by the case of Boston Power.

This company started in 2005 to work on improving lithium-ion technology. Although successful in rising funds during the initial stages of its work, it fell outside the purview of American venture investment when it wanted to go into large-scale manufacturing. It was also unable to secure a US$100 million federal government grant for which it had applied. Fortunately for the company, China was willing to step in, providing a US$300 million low-interest loan through its venture firm GSR. Moreover, additional grants and subsidies followed. The Chinese government has been willing to invest, as this case shows, where private U.S. venture capital has not.[3]

It has been estimated that Chinese entities have poured about US$14 billion into U.S. start-ups since 2000, with 80% of the deals occurring since 2014. However, a new American law, known as FIRRMA, expanded the powers of a previously obscure government agency called the Committee on Foreign Investments in the United States (CFIUS). Within its expanded authority, CFIUS will have to approve attempts by foreigners (meaning China), even to purchase minority stakes in U.S. start-ups.[4]

FROM FORCED TECHNOLOGY TRANSFER TO TECH THEFT

Next in line within the process of "picking from the low-hanging trees" is the forced technology transfer, as a precondition for doing business in China. This has been the case for countless foreign

[3]Jonathan Gruber and Simon Johnson, *Jump-Starting America: How Breakthrough Science Can Revive Economic Growth and the American Dream.* New York, NY: Public Affairs, 2019, pp. 102–103.

[4]Heather Somerville, Chinese investments in U.S. startups peaks but 'tremendous uncertainty' ahead, *Reuters,* May 8, 2019, https://www.businessinsider.com/chinese-investment-in-us-startups-peaks-but-tremendous-uncertainty-ahead-2019-5. Accessed October 8, 2019.

companies willing to access the gigantic Chinese market, which in 2018 exhibited a population of 1,393 billion people and a nominal GDP of US$14.2 trillion.[5] General Electric is a good example of such companies. In 2011, it handed over to China its most sophisticated aeronautical electronic technology, in order to benefit from this country's aeronautical market, which was expected to generate 400 billion dollars in sales during the next 20 years.[6]

According to the Peterson Institute for International Economics: "China has also adopted a set of policies deliberately designed to *force* foreign multinationals to transfer strategically sensitive technologies to indigenous Chinese firms. These policies are a key component of China's longstanding ambition to replace Western firms currently at the forefront of key technologies with Chinese national champions. In many cases, technology transfers are effectively required by China's foreign direct investment regime, which closes off important sectors of the economy to foreign firms unless they enter into joint ventures with Chinese entities they do not control. Examples of forced technology transfer abound in industries ranging from autos to information technology (IT)".[7] The Trump administration's trade confrontation is occurring on several fronts. The one against forced technological transfer is certainly the one that American companies are more likely to support.

The theft of Western technology is also on the list. Within a wider interpretation of this notion, forced transfer counts as technology stealing — in this case, of intellectual property rights. A more restricted interpretation of technology theft essentially would mean

---

[5] The World Bank, Population, total, data, worldbank.org, https://data.worldbank.org/indicator/SP.POP.TOTL. Accessed October 8, 2019; International Monetary Fund, World Economic Outlook Database, April 2019, https://www.imf.org/external/pubs/ft/weo/2019/01/weodata/index.aspx. Accessed October 8, 2019.

[6] Howard Schneider, GE 'all in' on aviation deal with China, *The Washington Post*, August 22, 2011.

[7] Lee G. Branstetter, China's Forced Technology Transfer Problem and What to Do About It, Peterson Institute for International Economics, June 2018, https://www.piie.com/publications/policy-briefs/chinas-forced-technology-transfer-problem-and-what-do-about-it. Accessed October 8, 2019.

industrial espionage. This is a subject that was partially covered in Chapter Seven, wherein we referred to military technology's cyber-theft by China. However, civilian technology has also been stolen on a grand scale by China's cyber-espionage. Many of the U.S.-targeted companies operated in sectors that Beijing considers important for their innovation purposes, such as aerospace, semiconductors and information technology. An independent commission estimated that the annual loss to the American economy from cyber-enabled theft of intellectual property surpasses US$300 billion. And up to 80% of that theft may originate in China.[8]

According to Graham Allison: "'The amount of theft that's going on is simply staggering', FBI director James Comey said in 2014. 'There's only two types of big corporations in America. Those who have been hacked by the Chinese, or those who don't yet know they've been hacked by the Chinese'".[9]

So politically sensitive is the subject that, in 2015, President Barack Obama struck a deal that few thought possible. According to this deal, President Xi Jinping agreed to put an end to his nation's old practice of breaking into the computer systems of U.S. companies, military contractors and government agencies to steal designs, technology and corporate secrets. Although for a while China's cyber-espionage almost disappeared, it picked up again in 2018. Cybersecurity firms have reported a new wave of hacking on U.S. companies. With the Trump administration restricting Chinese investments in high-technology sectors, blocking Chinese telecommunication companies from doing business in the U.S. and imposing tariffs on Chinese imports, Beijing may have reached the conclusion that it had little to gain by continuing to honor the 2015 agreement.[10]

---

[8] Lorand Laskai and Adam Segal, A New Old Threat: Countering the Return of Chinese Industrial Cyber Espionage, Council on Foreign Relations, December 6, 2018, https://www.cfr.org/report/threat-chinese-espionage. Accessed October 8, 2019.

[9] Graham Allison, *Destined for War: Can America and China Escape the Thucydides' Trap.* Boston, MA: Mariner Books, 2018, p. 17.

[10] David E. Sanger and Steven Lee Myers, After Hiatus, China Accelerates Cyberspying Efforts to Obtain U.S. Technology, *The New York Times,* November 29, 2018; Lorand Laskai and Adam Segal, *op. cit.*

SPYING: A CITIZENS' DUTY?

Direct espionage is another form of tech theft. In fact, spying for the State may have become a duty of Chinese citizens and corporations according China's 2017 National Intelligence Law. This demands that relevant Chinese bodies, organizations and citizens provide necessary support, assistance and cooperation to the State in national intelligence efforts. The law says that the State will grant "commendations and rewards to individuals and organizations that make major contributions to national intelligence efforts".[11]

As a result, according to Shen Lu and Robert Delaney: "In the past year, Trump administration officials — including FBI director Christopher Wray, senior White House figures and even the president himself — have portrayed Chinese studying in the US as threats to national security (...) But as the Trump administration has taken on a more antagonistic approach to China, Chinese students and scientist have been accused of spying on the US for Beijing".[12]

Moreover, Mark Magnier reported how while Indian workers are well accepted in Silicon Valley, China's tech workforce is being seen with mistrust. As he explains: "While Indian tech workers have flourished in the US, their Chinese counterparts have struggled to gain the same acceptance (...) Students, professor and researchers of Chinese descent face growing suspicion as potential spies (...) There's also a growing perception that Chinese workers more often violate non-compete clauses and divert crucial technology to Chinese state-linked ventures ...".[13]

Paranoia seems to have taken hold of the U.S. government and tech industries, affecting in the process not only the US$13 billion

---

[11] Yi-Zheng Lian, Where Spying is the Law, *The New York Times*, March 13, 2019.

[12] 'I am not a spy': Chinese students in US become 'cannon fodder' of politics", Inkstone, May 24, 2019, https://www.inkstonenews.com/politics/visa-processes-are-tightening-chinese-students-us/article/3011678. Accessed May 25, 2019.

[13] The India advantage: Why China's tech workforce can't gain traction in Silicon Valley, Inkstone, October 30, 2019, https://www.scmp.com/news/china/article/3035391/india-advantage-why-chinas-tech-workforce-cant-gain-traction-silicon. Accessed October 30, 2019.

yearly contribution that Chinese students represent to the American economy (as reported by Shen Lu and Robert Delaney) but also the much valued contribution of Chinese scientists to the American research and development (R&D) effort. However, China's 2017 National Intelligence Law leads to the unavoidable presumption that every Chinese citizen or company may become a tool for Beijing's intelligence gathering. Needles to say, in many situations this has indeed been the case, with U.S. technological know-how passing into Chinese hands.

CHINA AS AN INNOVATION SUPERPOWER

Notwithstanding the contribution that the policy "picking from the low-hanging trees" represented to China's technological advancement, at this point in time indigenous innovation firmly stands on its two feet. China is well on its way to becoming an innovation superpower. On the one hand, its industries are getting closer to the technological frontier in conventional areas such as high-speed railways, electronics, automobiles and aviation. On the other hand, the country is driving technological innovations in emerging areas such as artificial intelligence (AI), big data, robotics, renewable energy, e-commerce, space technology and next-generation communication technologies.

A 2014 article in *The Wall Street Journal*, citing technological executives from different parts of the world, already referred to the innovation process in China in the following terms: "China's technology sector is reaching a critical mass of expertise, talent and financial firepower that could realign the power structure of the global technology industry in the years ahead".[14] Many facts can prove this.

China already has 9 of the world's 20 biggest high-tech companies: Alibaba (number 5 with a market capitalization of US$407 billion), Tencent (number 7 with US$389 billion), Ant Financial (number 8 with US$150 billion), Bytendance (number 14 with US$75 billion),

[14]Juro Osawa and Paul Mozur, The Rise of China's Innovation Machine, *The Wall Street Journal*, January 6, 2014.

Baidu (number 15 with US$64 billion), Didi Chuxing (number 16 with US$41 billion), Xiaomi (number 17 with US$56 billion), Meituan Dianping (number 18 with US$38 billion) and JD.com (number 19 with US$31 billion). The remaining 11 companies are American ones, and no other country even makes it to the list.[15]

China is the second-largest spender on R&D after the United States, accounting for 21% of the world's total of nearly US$2 trillion in 2015. The country's spending on R&D grew by an average of 18% per year between 2010 and 2015, which is more than four times faster than U.S.' spending. Within the next 5–10 years, China's R&D spending is expected to surpass that of the United States. Venture capital investment in China, another fundamental piece to spur innovation, leapt from US$3 billion in 2013 to US$34 billion in 2016, increasing China's global share of venture capital funds to 27%. Although the U.S. still retains primacy in venture investment, China's share is rising several times faster: in 2018, it had outgrown its capacity by more than 15 times in relation to 2013.[16]

Since 2013, the world's fastest supercomputer has been located not in Silicon Valley but in China. Indeed, in the ranking of the world's fastest supercomputers, a list from which China was absent in 2001, it has now 167 — i.e., two more than the United States. Moreover, China's top supercomputer is five times faster than the closest American one on the list.[17]

According to *Science & Technology*, a publication by the U.S. National Science Foundation and the National Science Board: "China has become — or is on the verge of becoming — a scientific and technical superpower" in terms of R&D spending, technical papers and technical workforce. Measured by the number of scientific papers published in all journals indexed by the Science

---

[15] Mara Hvistendahl, Land of Giants, *MIT Technology Review* (The China issue: 120th Anniversary Issue), January/February 2019.

[16] Briony Harris, China is an innovation superpower. This is why, World Economic Forum, February 7, 2018, https://www.weforum.org/agenda/2018/02/these-charts-show-how-china-is-becoming-an-innovation-superpower/. Accessed November 10, 2018; Phred Dvorak and Yasufumi Saito, Silicon Valley Powered American Tech Dominance — Now It Has a Challenger", *The Wall Street Journal*, April 12, 2018.

[17] Graham Allison, *op. cit.*, p. 18.

Citation Index (SCI), China ranked second in the world in 2016, representing around 20% of the world's total. China's State Intellectual Property Office (CIPO) reported that in 2017 the number of patent applications increased 14.2% in relation to 2016, registering 1.38 million, of which 420,000 patents were granted.[18]

China plays a leading role in space exploration, being the only country that has articulated a long-term vision of space settlement and utilization. A good example of its prowess in this area was the unmanned Chang'e-4 probe, which touched down on the Moon's unexplored South Pole in 2019. It has been the sole country with the demonstrated capability to get to the lunar far side.[19]

China is also a world leader in AI, having filled 473 of the 608 AI patents lodged with the World Intellectual Property Organization (WIPO) in 2018. With 186 unicorn start-ups in 2018, China is home to a third of the world's unicorns. It is also the world's leader in renewable energy, having built more solar and wind electricity generating capacity than any other nation. Three of the world's five largest floating solar plants are in China, and it accounts for more than half of global electric car sales. At the same time, China makes more than half of the world's electric vehicle batteries and is also home to 99% of the world's electric bus fleet.[20]

CHINA'S TECHNOLOGICAL HUBS

China's innovation prowess is clustered in a series of world-class technological hubs, among which are Zhongguancun, Shenzhen, Hangzhou, Zhangjiang and Dalian.

---

[18] *Richard P. Appelbaum, Cong Cao,* Xuaeying Han, Rachel Parker, and Denis Simon, *Innovation in China.* Cambridge, MA: Polity Press, 2018, p. 68.

[19] Namrata Goaswani, China Had a Head Start in the New Space Race, *The Diplomat,* May 29, 2019, https://thediplomat.com/2019/05/china-has-a-head-start-in-the-new-space-race/. Accessed June 3, 2019.

[20] Douglas Broom, China by numbers: 10 facts to help you understand the superpower today, World Economic Forum, June 24, 2019, https://www.weforum.org/agenda/2019/06/china-by-numbers-10-facts-to-help-you-understand-the-superpower-today/. Accessed July 5, 2019.

Zhongguancun is a technology hub in the Haidan District of Beijing, which is home to a cluster of seven technological parks within a 488-square kilometer zone. It is home to more than 40 universities, including top Chinese ones like Peking and Tsinghua universities, plus several institutes of the Chinese Academy of Sciences. It also houses more than 200 research institutes and national-level laboratories, as well as to 9,000 high-tech firms including some of China's biggest internet firms such as Baidu and Sina Corp, while harboring half of China's 70 unicorns, among which are giants like Xianomi, Didi Chuxing and Meituan-Dianping. Moreover, Zhongguancun is the place wherein as many 80 tech starts-ups are conceived every day, thus being a leading incubator of tech innovation in China.[21]

Shenzhen has been China's fastest growing city and is about to become the heart of the Greater Bay Area — a "super economic zone", or a megapolis, of 70 million people in the Pearl Delta River. According to McKinsey, China's digital investors enjoy such notable advantages as close links with hardware manufacturers. If that is the case, Shenzhen is the place. In terms of software–hardware integration, the city is ahead of the curve. In sectors such as robotics, Internet of Things solutions, AI-integrated products, driverless cars, electric cars or smart machines, Shenzhen leads the game in China. It is home to companies such as Huawei, Tencent, DJI (the world's biggest maker of electric cars) and BGI (declared as a DNA superpower by the science journal *Nature*). It also hosts 15,000 logistics companies. Companies in Shenzhen file more international patents (which are mostly high quality) than those in France or Britain.[22]

According to *The Economist*: "Unlike Beijing, which has many top-flight universities, Shenzhen has only a handful of lackluster institutions of higher learning; but so many graduates from all over

[21] Meng Jing, Zhongguancun: Beijing's innovation hub is at the centre of China's aim to become a tech powerhouse, *South China Morning Post*, 13 November, 2018; Richard P. Appelbaum, Cong Cao, Xueying Han, Rachel Parker, Denis Simon, *op. cit.*, 124.

[22] Johan Nylander, *Shenzhen Superstars: How China's Smarter City is Challenging Silicon Valley*, Kenny Hodgart Editor, 2017.

China flock to the city that they make up a greater share of its population than do graduates in Beijing ... Shenzhen has done more than any place on the mainland to debunk the outdated myth of 'copycat China', becoming the global hub of innovation in hardware and manufacturing. Its entrepreneurs are coming up with entirely new industries".[23]

Hangzhou is a city that has become home to some of China's biggest technology companies, and to a growing number of Chinese overseas science graduates. This is becoming the place of choice for many of these graduates to develop their careers upon their return to China. Alibaba, Ant Financial and NetEase also have their headquarters there. The number of start-ups in the city surged 107% in the first half of 2014 after Alibaba went public. The city is also home to one of China's most prestigious academic institutions: Zhejiang University.[24]

Zhangjiang is a science and technology city located in the Pudong district of Shanghai. It aims essentially at R&D, rather than simply industrial production. In this context, it intends to become China's largest and most important science city on a site of about 84 square kilometers, an area exceeding that of Manhattan. Its designer adopted the strategy of creating a "living university" — a constellation of clusters around existing and future high-tech institutions (industries, universities and technology institutes). It is home to over 18,000 enterprises and 53 regional headquarters of multinational corporations. Its leading industries include integrated circuits, AI and biomedicine. Six of the top global chip design companies have set up regional headquarters and R&D centers there, and the top 10 Chinese chip design companies are located in this area as well. Multiple global organizations and local start-ups focusing on AI also have their presence there. It is home to more than

---

[23] Shenzhen is a hothouse of innovation, *The Economist,* April 6, 2017.

[24] Maggie Zhang and Hangzhou, *China's answer to 'Silicon Valley' is a hit with returning graduates,* study finds, July 2, 2018, https://www.scmp.com/business/companies/article/2152935/hangzhou-chinas-answer-silicon-valley-hit-returning-graduates. Accessed October 15, 2019; Zen Soo, After Beijing and Shenzhen, which are China's rising tech hubs?, *South China Morning Post,* August 12, 2017.

400 biomedical enterprises, over 20 large pharmaceutical manufacturers, 300 R&D-oriented enterprises and 100 purely R&D institutions for biomedicine or pharmaceuticals. Six of the top pharmaceutical companies in the world have set up regional headquarters in this area. The 2013-founded Shanghai Tech University aims at becoming the academic center of this science city, and Fudan University and Shanghai Jiao Tong University have established satellite campuses there as well.[25]

Dalian city hosts the hi-tech zone that bears its name. The latter comprises an area of 153 square kilometers, including a coastline of 41 km. It hosts 5000 registered enterprises, of which more than 900 are high-tech ones. It is also home to nearly 100 national or enterprise R&D centers. It has been awarded the title of "China's national software industry base", as 51% of its industrial structure is dedicated to Information Technology (IT). It is China's core area of software and service outsourcing industriy. Although over 100 of the Global 500 companies have presence there, it aims at enabling the development of Chinese start-ups with software and service outsourcing as their primary focus. This includes industrial design, technological finance, educational training, Internet of Things, cloud computing, etc.[26]

CHINA'S ADVANTAGEOUS FACTORS

Besides the unfair advantage obtained through the policy of "picking from the low-hanging trees", China's technological advancement has been mainly based on three other factors: The support given by the State, its sheer size and its educational effort. Later on, we shall refer to the first of these factors. We will now begin with the last two.

[25] Archello, Zhangjiang Science and Technology City as a 'Living University', https://archello.com/project/zhangjiang-science-and-technology-city-as-living-university. Accessed October 11, 2019; Pudong Government, About Zhangjiang Science City, October 4, 2019, http://english.pudong.gov.cn/2019-04/10/c_353887.htm. Accessed October 11, 2019.

[26] Dalian High-Tech Zone, https://www.dlhitech.gov.cn/english/introduction/intro/content.html. Accessed October 12, 2019.

Size matters, and China has as much of it as can be had. Size, indeed, is relevant on many accounts. First, given its status as the world's largest factory, the supply chains of numerous industries, which include thousands of component technology suppliers, are clustered in China. Hence, its R&D activities can be effective in identifying and creating new combinations that lead to incremental innovation. In other words, this allows for important improvements in the structure, design or methodology of working of existing technologies. Second, China's domestic market of close to 1.4 billion consumers, with a GDP per capita of US$15,000 in Price Purchasing Parity, promises sufficient return to cover the cost of ambitious technological undertakings. These include the cumulative learning process to catch up with frontier foreign technologies or the pursuing of development of expensive technologies. Third, in the same manner in which companies from around the world are attracted by the Chinese market returns, so are scientist from everywhere. In addition to all the local talent that China can muster, the country has also become a magnet for the best available international talent in science and technology.

The educational effort undertaken by China in the field of science and technology has been enormous. This is linked, as well, to the size of the country, as the magnitude of its population facilitates the gathering of human resources. However, China's tradition of emphasizing education is crucially important. The results of the last Program for International Evaluation Student Assessment (PISA) test, made public in December 2019, placed China as number one worldwide. In the three tested categories — mathematics, science and reading — Chinese students nabbed the first spot. The test, which originally evaluated 15-year-old students from the 35 OECD member countries, has been expanded to include students from 79 countries. Hence, China's students can be shown to have surpassed those of the most privileged economies, including small countries intensely focused on education such as Singapore and Finland.[27] Moreover,

[27] Moriah Balingit and Andrew Van Dam, U.S. students continue to lag behind peers in East Asia and Europe in reading, math and sciences, exams show, *The Washington Post*, December 3, 2019; Jenny Anderson and Amanda Shendruk,

from 1990 to 2010, Chinese enrollment in higher education rose eightfold, and the number of university graduates increased from 300,000 to nearly three million per year. In 2017, eight million students graduate from Chinese universities.[28]

While the government spends 20% of its budget on education, Chinese households also invest heavily in it, reaching levels equivalent to 50% of the government's education budget.[29] This covers students studying overseas or remaining at home. In relation to the former, China is the world's number one country in terms of the number of youngsters pursuing studies abroad. In 2016, 544,500 Chinese students were studying outside the country. For example, in the U.S. alone, Chinese students accounted for 16% of all doctoral degree recipients in science and technology in the 2015–2016 academic year. This is concomitant to an increasing ratio of graduate students returning home. As for those remaining home, eight million new university students graduated in 2017, as mentioned earlier. Of that amount, a large percentage are graduates in science and technology (S&T). Between 2000 and 2014, the annual number of graduates in S&T increased from 359,000 to 1.65 million. During the same period, the number of U.S. graduates in S&T went up from 483,000 to 742,000.[30]

But there has not only been an increase in the quantity but also in quality. This is particularly the case of its elite universities. Tsinghua University, China's MIT, awarded 1,385 S&T doctorates

---

QUARTZ, December 3, 2019, https://qz.com/1759506/pisa-2018-results-the-best-and-the-worst-students-in-the-world/?utm_source=email&utm_medium=daily-brief. Accessed December 4, 2019.

[28] Jonathan Gruber and Simon Johnson, To Counter China, Out-Invent It: Trump's Trade Wars Ignores the Real Threat from Beijing, *op. cit.*

[29] Yanfei Li, Understanding China's Technological Rise, *The Diplomat*, August 3, 2018, https://thediplomat.com/2018/08/understanding-chinas-technological-rise/. Accessed September 20, 2019.

[30] Briony Harris, *op. cit.*; Yanfei Li, *op. cit.*, John Wong, China's Economy 2018: Slowdown to Gear up for a New Model of Growth. East Asian Policy, 10(1). Singapore: East Asian Institute, National University of Singapore, 2018; Richard P. Appelbaum, Cong Cao, Xueying Han, Rachel Parker, Denis Simon, *op. cit.*, p. 23.

in 2017, compared with 645 conferred by MIT itself. Moreover, Tsinghua produced more of the top 1% most highly cited papers in mathematics and computing and more of the 10% of most highly cited papers in science, technology and engineering (STEM) than any other university in the world. Although MIT still retains the number one spot in STEM papers, Tsinghua is on track to becoming number one in five years or less. Moreover, China's share of STEM papers cited in Scopus, the world's biggest catalogue of abstracts and citations, rose from 4% in 2000 to 19% in 2016, more than America's contributions.[31]

WHERE DOES THE UNITED STATES STAND?

Where does the United States stand in relation to China's impressive advances? The answer leaves no room for doubts: As number one. As the technological superpower whose commanding status China wants to reach and eventually surpass. Three elements could attest to the above: first, the number of Nobel Prizes awarded to the United States; second, the commanding rank of its top universities; third, its clusters of innovation.

In relation to the first of those elements, the U.S. is the highest Nobel Prize–winning country, with a total of 375 winners till May 2019. The majority of these prizes have been in physics and physiology or medicine, but there have also been a substantial number of laureates in chemistry and in economics. Literature and peace are also on the list, but the bulk of the winners came from the scientific community, which confirms the top quality of U.S. researchers.[32] Conversely, there have been just 3 citizens of the People's Republic

---

[31] *The Economist*, Academic Research: Looking to beat the world, November 17, 2018.

[32] World Population Review, Nobel Prizes by Country 2019, http://worldpopulationreview.com/countries/nobel-prizes-by-country/. Accessed October 15, 2019; Ashley Kirk, Nobel Prize winners: Which country has the most Nobel laureates?, *The* Telegraph, October 12, 2015, https://www.telegraph.co.uk/news/worldnews/northamerica/usa/11926364/Nobel-Prize-winners-Which-country-has-the-most-Nobel-laureates.html. Accessed October 15, 2019.

of China who have become Nobel laureates. One for literature, one for peace and one for physiology or medicine. In other words, just one came from its R&D community — Tu Youyou, Nobel winner in Physiology and Medicine, for her research in combating malaria.[33]

The high quality of American universities is concomitant to the strength of its R&D community, which again is closely linked to the number of its Nobel laureates. According to the Times Higher Education rankings, of the ten universities producing the largest number of Nobel Prize winners since 2000, nine are located in the United States.[34] As for the ranking of American universities, they tend to be at the top among the different classes.

According to QS World University Rankings 2019, of the top 20, 11 come from the United States, including the first four. Of those 20, only one Chinese university is listed: Tsinghua University in the 17th position. The Times Higher Education World University Rankings 2019 places 15 American universities within the first 20, none of which are from China. The CWUR World University Rankings 2018–2019 has 16 American universities in the top 20 and not one Chinese university. The U.S. News & World Report Best Global Universities 2019 Rankings also has 16 U.S. universities within the first 20, without any reference to China within this group. Finally, the ARWU Academic Ranking of World Universities 2019 has 17 American universities within the top 20 pack. Again, none of them are Chinese. In other words, only the QS World University Ranking includes a Chinese university within its top 20 list.[35]

---

[33] The Nobel Prize, Tu Youyou: Nobel Prize in Physiology and Medicine in 2015, https://www.nobelprize.org/prizes/medicine/2015/tu/facts/. Accessed October 15, 2019.

[34] Ellie Bothwell, Top 10 universities for producing Nobel Prize winners 2017, The World University Rankings, October 13, 2017, https://www.timeshighereducation.com/news/top-10-universities-producing-nobel-prizewinners-2017. Accessed October 15, 2019.

[35] https://www.topuniversities.com/university-rankings/world-university-rankings/2019. Accessed October 15, 2019; https://www.timeshighereducation.com/world-university-rankings/2019/world-ranking#!/page/0/length/25/sort_by/rank/sort_order/asc/cols/stats. Accessed October 15, 2019; https://

Finally, among the reasons that define the U.S. commanding status in the technological arena, we find its clusters of innovation. These gather R&D laboratories from both corporations and universities, plus start-up capital funds. There would be no Silicon Valley without the R&D that takes place at Stanford University, nor the Boston–Cambridge technological miracle without MIT. Corporate laboratories, for their part, translate into commercially viable products and prototypes the more theoretical technological inputs coming from university labs. Amid this criss-crossing of talent, venture capital funds are ready to support start-ups representing fresh projects and new talent.

This clustering of innovation is highly concentrated along the Atlantic and the Pacific coasts. About a third of all R&D laboratories (1,035) are located in the Boston–New York–Washington, D.C. Corridor, while another quarter of them (645) are located in California. Patterns of concentrating clusters are notorious around Cambridge, Route 128 and major transportation hubs that reach down as far as Route 270 around Washington D.C. Alternatively in San Francisco's Bay Area, core clusters in Silicon Valley, stretching south from Stanford Research Park to San Jose, reproduce this pattern of innovation. But further south in California, the San Diego–Carlsbad and the Los Angeles–Long-Beach–Anaheim clusters continue on the same trend. But together with the above, there are scattered areas of innovation also present in Seattle, Detroit–Warren–Dearborn in Michigan, Durham–Chapel Hill, North Carolina, the Philadelphia–Camden–Wilmington in Pennsylvania, New Jersey, Delaware and Maryland, to mention but a few.[36]

---

cwur.org/2018-19.php. Accessed October 15, 2019. https://www.usnews.com/education/best-global-universities/rankings?int=a27a09. Accessed October 15, 2019; http://www.shanghairanking.com/Academic-Ranking-of-World-Universities-2019-Press-Release.html. Accessed October 15, 2019.

[36] Richard Florida, Where to Find Unsung Engines of Innovation and Economic Growth, Citylab, August 8, 2017, https://www.citylab.com/life/2017/08/the-clustering-of-rd-labs/531159/. Accessed October 15, 2019; Justin Song Up and Coming Tech Hubs in the US: 2019 Report, ValuePenguin, October 2, 2019, https://www.valuepenguin.com/identifying-tech-hubs. Accessed October 15, 2019.

The feedback and reinforcing dynamic which combines Nobel laureates, the world's leading universities and the main global hubs of innovation have turned the United States into a technological juggernaut. However, the simple fact that China has been able to challenge the *status quo* gives rise to a highly spirited situation. Today, the U.S. clearly leads, but one or two decades in the future the technological correlation between both countries may very well change in fundamental ways. This situation is being acknowledged by the U.S. high-tech establishment.

U.S.–CHINA TECHNOLOGICAL CORRELATION

An Independent American Task Force admitted the following: "China is investing significant resources in developing new technologies, and after 2030 it will likely be the world's largest spender on research and development ... China is closing the technological gap with the United States, and though it may not match U.S. capabilities across the board, it will soon be one of the leading powers in technologies such as artificial intelligence (AI), robotics, energy storage, fifth-generation cellular networks (5G), quantum information systems, and possibly biotechnology".[37]

According to the *Science and Engineering Indicators 2018* of the U.S.' National Science Foundation, although the United States is the global leader in science and technology, its global share of those activities is declining as other nations, and particularly that of China, continue to rise. An article in *ScienceDaily* noted: "The National Science Board (NSB) is the governing body of the National Science Foundation (NSF) and publishes the congressionally mandated report on the state of the U.S. science and engineering (S&E) enterprise every two years. The 2018 reports show the U.S. invests the most in research and development (R&D), attracts the most venture capital, awards the most advanced degrees, provides the most business, financial and information services, and is the largest producer

[37] James Manyika and William H. McRaven, Chairs and Adam Segal Project Director, *op. cit.*

in high-technology manufacturing sectors (...) 'This year's report shows a trend that the U.S. still leads by many S&T measures, but that our lead is decreasing in certain areas that are important to our country', said Maria Zuber, NSB Chair and Vice President for Research at the Massachusetts Institute of Technology. 'That trend raises concerns about the impacts on our economy and workforce, and has implications for our national security'".[38] The National Science Foundation's *Science and Engineering Indicators 2018*, as reported by ScienceDaily, compares the U.S. and China standing in several areas, and came up with the following results.

While the U.S. leads the world in R&D expenditures at US$496 billion (26% of the global total), China is in second place with US$408 billion (21%). However, since 2000 China's spending in R&D increased 18% annually, whereas the U.S. grew by only 4%.

Venture capital investment, which supports the commercialization of emerging technologies, totaled more than US$130 billion globally in 2016. While the U.S. was number one, attracting US$70 billion, slightly more than half of the global total, China was number two with US$34 billion, i.e., 27% of the total. However, venture capital in China rose from approximately US$3 billion in 2013 to US$34 billion in 2016, climbing from 5% to 27% of the total, the fastest increase seen in any economy.

Knowledge- and technology-intensive industries, in which science and technology are key inputs, are a major part of the global economy, comprising nearly one-third of the world's GDP. These industries are divided in two main sectors: business, financial and information services; and high-technology manufacturing. U.S. leads in business, financial and information sectors, representing 31% of the global share, while China represents 21% (although China experiences a 19% annual growth — the fastest growing rate). As for high-technology manufacturing, U.S. ranks number one with 31% of the global share, while China ranks second with

[38] Report shows United States leads in science and technology as China rapidly advances, *Science Daily*, January 24, 2018, https://www.sciencedaily.com/releases/2018/01/180124113951.htm. Accessed October 13, 2019.

24% (however, China has more than doubled its share over the last decade).

Higher education provides the advanced skills that are necessary in knowledge-intensive economies. In this area, the U.S. awarded 40,000 science and research (S&R) doctoral degrees — the highest number in the world — followed by China with 34,000. At the S&R bachelor's degree level, China led with 22% of the total versus 10% from the U.S. (since 2000, the number of S&R bachelor's degrees awarded in China grew by 300%). It must be noted, however, that of the U.S.' awarded degrees both at the doctoral and bachelor's levels, a significant share corresponded to foreign students, with Chinese students forming quite a relevant number of them.

Brookings defines the technological challenge represented by China in the following terms: "While competition between the United States and China is intensifying, these two powers are increasing their distance between themselves and every other country in the world in terms of economic size, pace of innovation, and overall national power. This separation of the United States and China from the rest of the pack is being fueled largely by both countries' technology sectors".

China and the U.S. are in direct competition in several key technological areas, with both parties enjoying particular advantages within this process. Although China cannot aspire as yet to overcome the U.S. technological superiority overall, the technologies in which they are competing have immense repercussion, as each of them has a multiplier effect over many other technologies. A few such areas include AI, fifth-generation cellular networks, superconductors, quantum information systems and space control.

ARTIFICIAL INTELLIGENCE

AI is an area where the U.S. currently leads but where China aims to become the world leader in 2030. AI could be defined as the ability of machines to use algorithms to learn from data and use what has been learnt to make decisions like humans would. Differently from humans, however, AI-powered machines can work 24 hours a day, seven days a week, and analyze massive volumes of information at once. Its ratio of errors is also significantly lower than that of human counterparts. For decades, the AI revolution seemed within reach, but failed to arrive. Thanks to the development, over the past few years, of deep learning (the process through which machines can learn by themselves), this revolution finally arrived.

As a consequence, AI is passing from the age of R&D into the age of implementation. This is the equivalent of Thomas Edison's harnessing of electricity, a technological breakthrough that allowed for the revolutionizing of dozens of different industries while lighting cities and homes. Once harnessed, AI can also be turned into real-world applications. Although the U.S. has a clear advantage in the area of R&D, being clearly ahead in the sphere of core research and benefiting of a larger talent pool, China exhibits several comparative advantages in this new implementation phase. For a start, it has a larger market scale, which translates into increased business opportunities; it has a much larger population, which means a greater data base to feed the machine learning process; it offers more dynamic and innovative opportunities for machines to learn (as exemplified by China's super-app, WeChat, which takes care of most of its users' daily needs); and it has legions of cut-throat profit-hungry entrepreneurs willing to exploit new practical applications.[39]

Both countries are thus being propelled forward in AI by unique attributes that no other country can replicate, and in the process keep distancing themselves from the rest. According to a widely cited study by PricewaterhouseCoopers, by 2030 the United States and China are set to capture 70% of the US$15.7 trillion windfall that AI is expected to generate.[40]

The different nature of their political systems also plays in China's favor, as it allows it to move faster in this area. The Chinese

[39] Kai-Fu Lee, *AI Superpowers: China, Silicon Valley and the New World Order*, New York: Houghton Mifflin Harcourt, 2018.

[40] Ryan Hass and Zach Balin, US-China relations in the age of Artificial Intelligence", Brookings, January 10, 2019, https://www.brookings.edu/research/us-china-relations-in-the-age-of-artificial-intelligence/.

government does not curtail the recollection of real data, being on the contrary a voracious consumer of it for political control purposes. This unparalleled amount of real-world data provides China with a major leg up in developing AI-driven services. As Yansheng Huang, a professor at MIT's Sloan School, explains: "In AI and big data, China is surging ahead, there's no doubt. These are areas compatible with the government's politics ... You just plunge ahead without privacy complaints, without safeguards, regulatory constraints. In a very crude sense, you can develop science very fast without constraints".[41]

The U.S. political system, on the contrary, is becoming highly sensitive in this matter. This hangs as a Damocles sword over the head of America's AI entrepreneurs, who are affected doubly. On the one hand, more data means faster machine learning process. This benefits their Chinese competitors, who can move without constraints. On the other hand, because any success that the U.S. companies may attain in obtaining data from their American customers will be turned against them for invading their privacy, greater success makes them more vulnerable *vis-à-vis* their own government.

According to Kai-Fu Lee, former president of Google China and successful venture capital entrepreneur: "I believe that China will soon match or overtake the United States in developing and deploying artificial intelligence. In my view, that lead in AI deployment will translate into productivity gains on a scale not seen since the Industrial Revolution. PricewaterhouseCoopers estimates AI deployment will add $15.7 trillion to global GDP by 2030. China is predicted to take home $7 trillion of that total, nearly double North America's $3.7 trillions in gains".[42]

5G TECHNOLOGY

The 5G technology represents a once-in-a-decade upgrade to the wireless systems. It is the fifth generation of cellular networks. Currently, wireless phone calls are routed through cell towers. With

[41] Yansheng Huang, China *vs.* the US: Who wins and who loses, *MIT Technology Review* (The China issue: 120th Anniversary Issue), *op. cit.*, p. 46.
[42] Kai-Fu Lee, *op. cit.*, p. 18.

5G, the link will be nearly direct cellphone to cellphone. This will enhance connectivity in remote locations, while allowing to connect sensors and robots. At the same time, it will enable vehicles, traffic control and factories to become more autonomous. As a consequence, it will fuel smart cities and digital economies, becoming the next key driver of the Fourth Industrial Revolution. Military equipment embedded with 5G communication devices will also become more autonomous and efficient.

It hardly comes as a surprise, therefore, the intense U.S.–China competition in this area, which is currently centered around Huawei. This Chinese company is in a prime position to snatch the lion's share of the 5G market, as it is well ahead of its competitors in this technology. Indeed, in May 2019, U.S. intelligence officials acknowledged that Huawei would be likely to control as much as 60% of the global 5G market.[43] As a result, it has become the target of repeated attacks by the U.S. government. Presently, the United States finds itself without a telecoms hardware champion that can compete with Huawei. This relates to its 1996 deregulation of this sector and its lack of national mobile standards, which allowed American carriers to choose among whatever mobile standards they preferred. Multiple standards, however, implied that economies of scale were difficult to attain.

As explained by Bengt Nordstrom, CEO of the Swedish consultancy firm Northstream: "In many aspects, the era from early 1990s to mid-2000s was lost time for the U.S. mobile industry". The fact is that Cisco System remains the only major American telecommunication firm. Its U.S. competitors, Lucent and Motorola, have been taken out of the equation by foreign acquisition, either of its stock or of its wireless network infrastructure assets. As it happens, though, Cisco System's sales in 2018 were valued at US$49.3 billion versus Huawei's US$100 billion. This means that Cisco has a difficult task ahead if it wants to become a true competitor to the Chinese firm.[44]

[43] Daniel W. Drezner, Economic Statecraft in the Age of Trump, *The Washington Quarterly*, Fall 2019, p. 13.

[44] Zen Soo, Why the US failed at 5G, Inkstone, April 3, 2019, https://www.inkstonenews.com/tech/why-has-us-failed-produce-5g-telecoms-leader-challenge-chinas-huawei/article/3004458. Accessed April 4, 2019.

Stalling Huawei's expansion into Western markets would thus give its American and Western competitors time to catch up, and so good reasons for Washington to keep putting obstacles on its way. However, legitimate national security concerns are also in line, especially so in view of the Chinese National Intelligence Law of June 27, 2017. This would compel Huawei to provide to the Chinese government accessed foreign information. Consequently, U.S. efforts in curtailing Huawei advancement are fed both by its desire to contain China's predominance in this area and by reasonable national security apprehensions.

So far, Washington has had only partial success in stalling Huawei's international positioning. Not even some of America's closest allies, indeed, seem ready to shut the door on Huawei. This company represents the standard bearer of a groundbreaking technology to which few seem willing to renounce. In Daniel W. Drezner words: "…the Trump administration months-long campaign to convince allies to block Huawei from participating in construction of their 5G networks failed. Only Australia has followed America's lead in effectively banning Huawei. NATO allies refused to do so, forcing the Trump administration to back down on its threats".[45]

In any case, Washington seemed to have been ready to deny Huawei access to U.S. products and technologies that were necessary for its operation. These included not only chips designed in America but also the Android mobile operating system. It seems, though, that the Trump Administration walked back from this decision after the Trump-Xi meeting at the 2019 G-20 summit, and after concluding that this would have only benefited America's European competitors. However, as we will see next in the case of the silicon chips, this highlights China's vulnerability in depending on foreign providers. Not surprisingly, Huawei announced that it would soon release its own mobile operating system to supplant America's Android.

THE CHIP

Superconductors represent another area of intense competition. While China is at the forefront of electronic products, it has been

[45] Daniel W. Drezner, Economic Statecraft in the Age of Trump, *op. cit.*, p. 13.

unable to master the production of integrated circuit microchips on which such products depend. The chip illustrates both the lingering limitation of China's capabilities and its vulnerability in relation to foreign producers of these silicon structures. In 2018, the U.S. government brought China's company ZTE to the brink of bankruptcy as a result of an export ban of American microchips to that company.

Although Washington later backtracked from this decision, the episode reminded China of why it needed to overcome its dependence on foreign technology, and particularly of the American one. Moreover, this case was highly relevant because more than the simple fate of ZTE, China's brilliant future in areas such as 5G technology, autonomous vehicles or quantum technology are closely linked to America's designed microchip. Consequently, China made the indigenous production of microchips a priority.

Fortunately for China, new types of chips are being invented to fully exploit the advances in AI. AI may, indeed, change the nature of the chip, allowing China to benefit from its strength in AI to leapfrog and even excel in the chip industry. Reporting about one of these new inventions, Shelley Fan said: "This week, a team from Pennsylvania State University designed a 2D device that operates like neurons. Rather than processing yes or no, the 'Gaussian synapse' thrives on probabilities. Similar to the brain, the analogue chip is far more energy-efficient and produces less heat than current silicon chips, making it an ideal candidate for scaling up systems".[46]

Chinese companies are deeply involved in this process as well, as Will Knight explains: "In July, search giant Baidu revealed that it is working on a chip called Kunlun for running deep-learning algorithms in its data centers. And in September, the e-commerce powerhouse Alibaba said it would spin out a new company dedicated to making AI chips ... The timing of AI boom is fortuitous for China's chipmakers. The deep-learning revolution was gaining speed just as

[46] Shelley Fan, Moore's Law is Dying. This Brain-Inspired Analogue Chip Is a Glimpse of What's Next, SingularityHub, September 29, 2019, https://singularityhub.com/2019/09/29/moores-law-is-dying-this-brain-inspired-analogue-chip-is-a-glimpse-of-whats-next/. Accessed October 1, 2019.

the government's latest chip push got under way".[47] In other words, China's advances in AI came handily when its government wanted to push forward the development of chips. This is a fortuitous situation that could turn out to be a very fortunate one for China.

In addition to this process of indigenous innovation, China was able to exploit a loophole in the U.S. legal and regulatory control to gain access to America's chip design technology. The recent acquisition by a Chinese firm of Advanced Micro Devices (AMD), a struggling company with unique chip design technology, now allows China to design and produce chips on its own, presenting an important challenge for American companies like Intel.[48]

QUANTUM TECHNOLOGY

Quantum information systems represent another area of intense competition. This is closely related to the fact that they have applications in multiple areas, including the military. In 2016, China evidenced a breakthrough in encrypted satellite quantum communication. This technology offers dual potential for whoever controls it: On the one hand, it will lead to development of new forms of secure and unbreakable communications; on the other, it will make it easy to break the encryption used by others to protect financial data and military secrets. China, which is racing ahead in this field, has the ambition to create a globe-spanning constellation of satellites, representing a super-secure quantum internet.[49]

Meanwhile, the United States is ahead in building powerful quantum computers. Quantum computers will be able process vast numbers of calculations simultaneously. Moreover, they would boost machine learning and solve special sets of problems many magnitudes of order faster than traditional computers. Google,

---

[47] Will Knight, The chip leap forward, *MIT Technology Review* (The China issue: 120th Anniversary Issue), *op. cit.*, p. 32.

[48] Evan S. Medeiros, The Changing Fundamentals of US-China Relations. *The Washington Quarterly*, Fall issue, 2019, p. 101.

[49] Amit Natwala, Why China's perfectly placed to be quantum computing's superpower, Wired, November 14, 2018, https://www.wired.co.uk/article/quantum-computing-china-us. Accessed April 5, 2019.

IBM and Intel have been investing considerable funds into quantum computing for several years. In addition to that, venture capital funds have also been investing heavily in this area.

At the beginning of 2019, America's IBM Q unveiled System One, which opens the door as the first integrated universal quantum computing system. In October of the same year, Google announced that it had achieved quantum supremacy. The term refers to the point at which a quantum computer can perform calculations "beyond the most powerful classical computer imaginable". Google's contention, though, was not accepted by its domestic competitor IBM. While controversy emerged between the two big firms, Harvard University announced at the end of October that its scientists had already attained quantum supremacy.[50]

While both countries wrestle for the control of quantum information systems, each still retains comparative advantages in specific sectors. China dominates in secure quantum communications, while the United States prevails in quantum computing. However, both are trying hard to catch up with each other and surpass the other's strengths where possible.

SPACE COMPETITION

A space control competition is also in motion between the two countries. The U.S. has spent considerable time trying to hinder the progress of Chinese space plans. In 2011, a U.S. law prohibited bilateral contacts between NASA and Chinese scientists, while Washington foreclosed China's participation in the U.S.–Russia International Space Station (ISS). However, this has not stopped

[50] Edd Gent, Investment in Quantum Computing Is Booming — But Will a Quantun Winter Follow?, SingularityHub, October 14, 2019, https://singularityhub.com/2019/10/14/investment-in-quantum-computing-is-booming-but-will-a-quantum-winter-follow/. Accessed October 17, 2019; Tom Simonite, IBM says Google's Quantum Leap Was Quantum Flop, Wired, October 21, 2019, https://www.wired.com/story/ibm-googles-quantum-leap-quantum-flop/. Accessed October 22, 2019; Alvin Powell, Riding the quantum computing 'wave', *The Harvard Gazette*, October 29, 2019, https://news.harvard.edu/gazette/story/2019/10/harvard-weighs-in-on-googles-quantum-supremacy/. Accessed October 30, 2019.

China. While ISS' future is in doubt and will most probably not survive beyond 2024 according to experts, China steadily advances towards the completion of its own space station in 2022.

At the same time, China is developing a space telescope that will have the same resolution than America's potent Hubble, while China's Long March 9 rocket scheduled for 2028 compares to America's Saturn V, still the most powerful rocket ever built. Moreover, Long March 9 will far exceed NASA's Space Launch System, also scheduled for 2028. The Long March 9 would be capable of landing a man on the moon and launching a Mars sample-return mission. Meanwhile, last December, China landed a robotic rover on the far side of the moon, being the first spacecraft to do so. It is important, nonetheless, to point out a difference between both the countries' peaceful space programs. While NASA's plans have shifted with each new administration and struggled to find support in Congress, the China Academy of Launch Vehicle Technology, CALT (NASA's Chinese counterpart), has had steady mandate and funding from the Chinese government.[51]

However, together with space's technology for peaceful purposes, there is a military side to it as well. It is the dual civilian–military nature of this technology that makes this competition particularly sensible. China's advances in the military aspects have been very relevant, as briefly explained when referring to its asymmetric weapons in Chapter Seven. To respond to China's advances in this area, President Trump issued, at the beginning of 2019, Space Policy Directive-4, which formally established the United States Space Force as a new branch of the U.S. military. In other words, together with the Army, the Navy and the Air Force, there is now this new branch. This implies that its budgetary needs will be cover by the National Defense Budget.[52]

[51] Joan Jonhson-Freese, The rockets' red glare, *MIT Technology Review* (The China issue: 120th Anniversary Issue), pp. 52–55.

[52] Peter Juul, Trump's Space Force Gets the Final Frontier All Wrong, *Foreign Policy*, March 20, 2019, https://foreignpolicy.com/2019/03/20/trumps-space-force-gets-the-final-frontier-all-wrong/. Accessed October 30, 2019.

Another aspect of the U.S.–China space competition is provided by the private companies of both countries involved in this area. In 2014, the Chinese government allowed private investment in space-related industries. Amid Chinese private start-ups, we find Landscape, LinkSpace, iSapace or OneSpace. LinkSpace is planning to launch a vertical takeoff, vertical landing rocket in 2020. These "launch rocket" companies are operating hand in hand with a group of privately funded companies that are focused on performing specific tasks "in" space, rather than getting there. The U.S., on its part, has had private investment in the space sector for a long time. However, Elon Musk's SpaceX has changed the face of the American aerospace industry. After decades of domination of this sector by old-line companies, SpaceX has become the most significant member of a new generation of companies that is dramatically lowering launch costs while seeking to revolutionize both human space travel and satellite launching. In 2015, SpaceX's Falcon 9 made the first ever vertical landing of a rocket, a technology in which China's LinkSpace is also competing.[53]

TWO MODELS

At the end of the day, this struggle for technological supremacy in certain key areas is dependent on the efficiency of two very different technological development models: The state-guided and funded one, and the market oriented one. While China follows the first, the U.S. follows the second.

China has focused state-led efforts on ensuring that science, technology and innovation propel the country as a fundamental growth engine. China's R&D as a percentage of GDP went up from 0.9% in 2000 to 2.1% in 2016. At the same time, the country has set ambitious targets in technological capacity-building in a range of specific sectors. Just between 2001 and 2011, the overall growth rate of its R&D surpassed the 20% mark annually. However, China has

[53]Joan Jonhson-Freese, *op. cit.*, pp. 52–55.

continued to increase its R&D spending with the aim of overtaking both the European Union and the United States and becoming the world's top R&D spender in 2019.[54]

At the same time, it has stimulated private sector and venture capital efforts in this area, guiding them toward a set of strategic goals. As a result, China has not only some of the world's largest private high-tech companies but has also become the second largest world market for venture capital investment. More than that, from the public to the private, from the national level to the state and municipal ones, all the forces of the country converge in funding and supporting the targeted technological priorities. A tremendous multiplier effect thus converges in a group of key technologies. Meanwhile, the State directs a large percentage of its annual budgets towards education, with science and technology as it main priority.

The combination of State financial support for R&D, its sustained attention to science policy (including continued reform efforts), its support and guidance of the private sector's efforts towards strategic targets, and the sheer size of the science and technology talent pool resulting from the official efforts in education have led to an explosive growth in scientific output.

The United States, as yet the leading technological superpower, has a market-oriented approach to technology. The private sector, in whose hands technology generation relies, focuses solely on assessing if the returns of any of the investments is high enough to justify the risks. This is the case of both high-tech companies when assessing new development projects and of venture capitalists when judging the merits of investing in a start-up. Moreover, private R&D has increasingly turned away from basic scientific research and focused on the applied sector. This means emphasizing commercially oriented product developments at the expense of capital-intensive long-run research projects. As Victor Bulmer-Thomas states: "There is nothing wrong with applied research, but it is unlikely to have the same transformative effects on the whole economy as basic

[54] Richard P. Appelbaum, Cong Cao, Xueying Han, Rachel Parker and Denis Simon, *op. cit.*, pp. 13–14.

research".[55] Until 1987, one-third of private R&D was still directed to basic research, an amount which has fallen today to one-fifth. Innovation, as a consequence, is becoming more incremental and less able to produce technological breakthroughs.[56]

CONS AND PROS OF BOTH MODELS

Both the Chinese State-led model and the American market-oriented one have demonstrable cons and pros. China has evidenced an important misallocation of resources: "The central government still controls a significant share of the R&D funding, which is often distributed without necessary regard to merit or transparency; and its use has all too often been ineffective, wasted and abused".[57] In addition to that, State interference and the Chinese National Intelligence Law of June 27, 2017, which forces Chinese companies to become informants of the State, depict a serious flaw in the model. The latter generates a high and well-deserved degree of mistrusts against Chinese high-tech companies and scientists all around the world. This can hardly work to their advantage, imposing upon them a huge burden. Having said that, however, it is obvious that China would not have achieved its current global status in science, technology and innovation had it not been for the State-led model. The synergy resulting from the combined effort of all the forces of the nation in pursuit of common goals has been simply overwhelming.

Clearly, within the U.S.' market-oriented model, the kind of misallocation of resources seen in China is out of the picture. However, as the Edward Snowden revelations showed, electronic communications passing through the U.S. by way of Microsoft, Google and the

[55] Victor Bulmer-Thomas, *Empire in Retreat: The Past, Present, and Future of the United States* [Kindle version], New Haven: Yale University Press, 2018, retrieved from Amazon.com, pp. 295–296.

[56] Jonathan Gruber and Simon Johnson, *Jump-Starting America, op. cit.*, p.107.

[57] Richard P. Appelbaum, Cong Cao, Xueying Han, Rachel Parker and Denis Simon, *op cit.*, p. 49.

like, had to be turned over to the United States National Security Agency (NSA) when they matched court-approved search terms. Although not as intrusive as the 2017 Chinese National Intelligence Law, these revelations showed that the U.S. government's prying on information obtained by private companies was not out of the picture. The American model, though, has other serious flaws directly related to their market-oriented nature.

As mentioned, private companies are unwilling to invest if they do not foresee clear and full returns from their investments. Hence, their scope is limited and mainly centered on product development. Meanwhile, financiers who support start-ups prefer those that yield fast results, five years at the most, than those with potentially distant payoffs, i.e., projects where the commercial viability is established quickly and where returns can be obtained equally quickly. As a consequence, capital-intensive long-run research projects, where major technological breakthroughs usually take place, are not the aim of either of them.

Alzheimer disease research is a good example of the former. According to James Hendrix, director of global sciences initiatives at the Alzheimer's Association: "The way our patent laws are set up doesn't work for the protracted studies into Alzheimer's treatment. Trials often take between five and ten years, sometimes more, before it can be determined if a drug or intervention is working. Patent protection and market exclusivity will likely be expired or nearly expired by that time. The loss of exclusivity makes it difficult for drug companies to justify the cost of the study".[58] Not surprisingly, little has been attained in this area, which represents a major global health problem.

As stated by Jonathan Gruber and Simon Johnson: "Private companies do not have an incentive to do the path-breaking research that moves the frontier forward for others. Private financiers are not structured to provide the large financial commitments to innovate in rapid-intensive areas".[59]

---

[58] Jonathan Gruber and Simon Johnson, *Jump-Starting America*, op. cit., pp. 97–98.
[59] *Ibid.*, p. 114.

WHEN THE FEDERAL GOVERNMENT USED TO RUN THE SHOW

Curiously enough, the U.S. technological system would not be what it is today had the State not acted as a catalyst for development. This was the model that prevailed until a few decades ago, a period when breakthrough inventions paved the ground for what Silicon Valley and its other high-tech American counterparts are today. From the development of integrated circuits and the associated miniaturization of computer hardware to the Internet, from the GPS to magnetic core memory (a major breakthrough in the storage and access of data), from semiconductors to the satellite industry, the examples are countless. All of these inventions — the gigantic shoulders on which America's high-tech stands today — would have not been possible without capital-intensive basic research and long-run projects. And this could not have been attained without a State-guided and -funded model.

The innovation that led to the U.S.' rapid growth after World War II was the direct result of a fruitful partnership among the private sector, universities and the federal government, where the last played the leading role. An essential part of this process was the meteoric transformation of higher education in America, including a massive expansion in the number of university-educated engineers and scientists. Another essential part was the massive funding provided by the federal government to R&D: From 1940 to 1964, such funding increased 20-fold. At its peak in the mid-1960s, this spending represented around 2% of the annual gross domestic product.[60]

This process was the natural continuation to the State-led effort to win WWII, with the invaluable support of the private sector and the scientific establishment. However, after the so-called Sputnik moment (the American shock resulting from the Soviet's launching of the first ever satellite to orbit Earth), such processes received a new boost. In the decade that followed Sputnik, federal funding for

---

[60] *Ibid.*, p. 6.

research at universities increased by more than four times in inflation-adjusted terms. Funding for science education, including classrooms and laboratories, also increased dramatically. The most significant post-Sputnik development, though, was the Apollo program, which at its peak comprised 2.2% of all federal spending. According to NASA's count, at least 2000 products or services were helped into development and commercialization as a result of the scientific research that took place during those years.[61]

From mid-1960s onwards, a divergence of positions between the federal government and the scientific community began to take shape. Vietnam, no doubt, had much to do with it. Moreover, the budgetary pressures arising from the Vietnam War and the Great Society program set new priorities. The election of Ronald Reagan in 1980, who had run on a powerful anti-tax platform, put in motion a retreat from federally funded activities. The combination of these different elements translated into a progressive but drastic withdrawal of the federal government not only from R&D funding but also as the driving force in scientific and technological innovation. Federal spending on research and development fell from 2% of economic output in 1964 to around 0.7% today. In Jonathan Gruber and Simon Johnson's words: "Converted to the same fraction of GDP today, that decline represents roughly US$240 billion per year".[62]

THE WITHDRAWAL OF THE FEDERAL GOVERNMENT

Even so, this dramatically reduced funding percentage can still be sufficient to fulfill path-breaking research, when federal leadership is available. That was the case of the Human Genome Program. After the scientific community convinced the U.S. federal government to make this a priority, Congress agreed to fund the National

[61] *Ibid.*, pp. 45–46
[62] *Ibid.*, p. 8.

Institutes of Health (NIH) for research on the human genome. At the beginning, in 1988, this undertaking took off, and the National Center for Human Research (NCHGR) was created to coordinate the collective efforts of NIH, the Department of Energy, public research institutes and private companies. Economic activity associated with human genome sequencing between 1988 and 2012 amounted, directly or indirectly, to US$965 billion. However, the NIH estimates that the Human Genome Program results have produced so far nearly US$1 trillion in economic growth. In addition to the medical sector, this has benefited pharmaceuticals, agriculture, biotechnology, biofuels and food processing, among many other industries. The breakthrough represented by the human genome decoding might have never been attained without the federal government leading the way.

Unfortunately, the above example represents the exception, not the rule. The withdrawal of the federal government has had catastrophic results in education, an area which it had championed in the past. In just one generation, the United States fell from the number 1 position to number 12 in the world's proportion of its young people with graduate degrees. In Arianna Huffington words: "Our high schools have become dropout factories. We have one of the lowest graduation rates in the industrialized world: Over 30% of American high school students fail to leave with a diploma. And even those who graduate are often unprepared for College. The American testing Program, which develops the ACT college admission test, say that fewer than one in four of those taking the test met its college readiness benchmark: English, reading, math and science (…) Even the top 10% of American students, our best and brightest, ranked only twenty-four in the world in math-literacy".[63]

In the 2015 Program for International Evaluation Student Assessment (PISA), the U.S. score was significantly below the OECD average, while in the 2017 survey of 35 OECD countries the U.S. ranked 31 in mathematics, 19 in science and 20 in reading. Not

[63] Arianna Huffington, *Third World America*, New York: Crown Publishers, 2010, pp. 114–115.

surprisingly, the most recent Stanford University comparison of students entering college in the fields of engineering and computer sciences found that Chinese students who arrive have a three-year advantage over their American counterparts.[64]

Moreover, while the GI Bill unleashed the force of university education in the U.S. by providing tuition and financial support to WWII veterans wanting to go to college, 44 million Americans currently hold around US$1.5 trillion in student debt.[65] Nearly three-quarters of a million veterans followed scientific education as a result of the GI bill, which democratized college studies in America.[66] Nowadays, by contrast, high costs have become an important deterrent to university education in the United States.

President Obama was able to capture the seriousness of the situation. In its 2011 Discourse of the Union, he made reference to the need for a new Sputnik moment. Moreover, during his period in office he also presented two insightful initiatives: Its "Winning the Future" agenda and its "Race to the Top" educational program. None of it, though translated into concrete results. The truth may be that a Sputnik-type reaction to the current challenges is no longer attainable.

The conditions have substantially changed since President Eisenhower, later followed by President Kennedy, assumed the challenge of not falling behind the Soviets in the space conquest. They were, indeed, able to count on the extraordinary capacity to build domestic political consensus that characterized their time. Building consensus around big national objectives is something that has become unattainable nowadays, amid an utterly and bitterly polarized Congress and society. Moreover, with a public debt that is now

---

[64] Graham Allison, *op. cit.*, p. 16; Victor Bulmer-Thomas, *op. cit.*, p. 294; U.S. students continue to lag behind peers in East Asia and Europe in reading, math and sciences, exams show, *The Washington Post*, December 3, 2019.

[65] Abigail Hess, Here's how much the average student loan borrower owes when they graduate, CNBC, February 15, 2018, https://www.cnbc.com/2018/02/15/heres-how-much-the-average-student-loan-borrower-owes-when-they-graduate.html. Accessed November 23, 2019.

[66] Jonathan Gruber and Simon Johnson, *Jump-Starting America, Ibid.*, p. 36.

more than US$22 trillion, massive federal expending of the kind undertaken by China is not politically feasible in the United States.

The private sector has virtually become the sole force in guarding the U.S.' high-tech fortress against China's formidable challenge. However, it is very much on its own within an inquisitive and regulatory ambience. While the threat of dismemberment hangs in the air for the most successful of them, the government has been unhelpful in providing them access to the foreign talent that they might lack at home. Who knows if a Werner von Braun — the German scientist who headed the American Space project — would have been allowed to work in the United States nowadays due to H1B visa restrictions. According to New York's former mayor Michael Bloomberg, co-founder of "Partnership for a New American Economy", even though immigrants play a relevant role in three out of four patents at America's top universities, foreign-born innovators today face "daunting or insurmountable immigration hurdles that force them to leave and bring their talents elsewhere.[67]

At the end of the day, the Chinese have become the best pupils in following the textbook of America's innovation success story in the decades that followed WWII. Although hampered by nationalistic overtones, their route map in science, technology and innovation looks much more coherent and holistic than the one been followed in the United States. In Graham Allison words: "Each of these achievements demonstrates China's ability to undertake costly, long-term, path breaking projects and see them through successful completion — a capability that has atrophied in the US".[68] Although the U.S. still commands technological heights, trends seem to be pointing toward China's overall performance and its emergence in a group of fundamental technologies.

[67] Andrew Martin, Immigrants are crucial to innovation, study says, *The New York Times*, June 25, 2012.

[68] Graham Allison, *op. cit.*, p. 18.

CONCLUSION

Did China challenge the United States too hard and too soon and, by doing so, seriously affect the chance to attain its objectives? Can Washington still contain China's ascendancy and retain its current leading status?

There seems to be no doubt that the Chinese have made their aims more difficult to achieve by speeding times, heralding their ambitions and boasting about their capabilities, while at the same time hardening their geopolitical and military stances. They have created for themselves many unnecessary problems and instead of sailing with the winds, as used to be the case, they are now sailing against them. But again, did this come too early for the Chinese, or is it already too late for the Americans to reverse the Chinese ascendancy?

In order to provide an answer, this book proceeded to survey their comprehensive national power by way of comparing six different aptitude categories: those of convergence, mistake avoidance, universality, military, economic and technological.

After comparing those six aptitudes, it is possible to have a better understanding of the power correlation between both countries and be, as a result, in a better position to assess what follows. China stands better in relation to the convergence aptitude and the mistakes avoidance aptitude. Conversely, the United States is much better placed in relation to the universality aptitude.

Although, the United States still prevails in the military, economic and technological aptitudes, reverse trends in motion favor China in the three categories. Economically, China's ascendancy and its surpassing of the United States seems almost inevitable. Militarily, China's asymmetric power has the capacity to neutralize much of the United States current superiority, while the inversely evolving budgetary capability of both countries will clearly play in favor of China. Moreover, the U.S.' superiority in nuclear weapons may prove to be more theoretical than effective if China's overwhelming advantage in conventional ballistic missiles can match the U.S.' tactical nuclear capability, while its second-strike capacity can deter a U.S.' first strike. Finally, although the United States possesses overall technological superiority, China will be able to match it or surpass it in a group of key technologies. Also, its emphasis on strategically oriented basic research outweighs America's market-oriented applied research.

All of the above leads one to conclude that although China may have brought unto itself many unnecessary problems by challenging the United States too openly, it did not act prematurely. In other words, at this point in time the United States does not seem to have the capability to revert China's ascendancy in any meaningful way. Moreover, by openly challenging the United States, China strengthens the nationalistic resolve of its population. This helps to shield the CCP against the unpleasant side effects resulting from its economic and technological strategies. At the same time, it provides a boost and a clear sense of direction for the attainment of those strategies. It is thus possible that, after assessing costs and benefits, the CCP may have concluded that the benefits of acting openly and decisively outweighed the costs of overtly challenging the United States.

The Middle Kingdom and the exceptional nation seem particularly ill prepared to accept the second rank in this power contest. Endowed with a profound sense of entitlement, neither of them seems prepare to yield easily to the other. The outcome of this serious, multilayered and far-reaching state of affairs may thus evolve into different options.

The first of those possible options would be a long-term containment policy of China by the United States. This follows the main lines of the one that the United States put in motion in relation to the Soviet Union between 1947 and 1989. George Kennan in his famous "Long Telegram" of 1946 initially conceptualized such a policy. According to him, the Soviet Union was "to be contained by the adroit and vigilant application of counterforce at a series of shifting geographical and political points".[1] Given the final success of this policy in relation to the USSR, this is obviously Washington's preferred option in relation to China as well. Since the "pivot to Asia", and with shifting priorities, this has been the policy followed by the United States.

One main difference comes to mind when comparing the case of China with that of the Soviet Union, though. During the Cold War, neither the Americans nor the Soviets challenged each other's main spheres of influence, limiting their confrontation to client states in peripheral zones. The contrast of this with the current situation is notorious. The United States' containment of China not only includes Taiwan — which China considers to be an integral part of its territory — but takes place in an area that for millennia was a tributary dependent region of the latter. It is difficult to assume that China might be restrained in relation to its aspirations to incorporate Taiwan to the People's Republic or will be willing to accept an indefinite subsidiary role in its own backyard. What is involved is not only China's "Great Unification" of its territory but also the restoration of its glorious past.

Conversely, the United States might not easily yield presence from an area where it has been a major power since 1854 and the first one to be a focus of its international attention after its own hemisphere — an area where it has fought three major wars and where it has five formal treaty allies. Moreover, this is a region where the U.S. currently deploys 60% of its fleet — 350,000 troops of its

[1] George B. Nash, Containment Defined. In George B. Nash and Julie Roy Jeffrey, Editors, *The American People Creating a Nation*, New York: Pearson Education, 2008, p. 825.

Indo-Pacific Command based in Hawaii, 50,000 troops in Japan and around 24,000 in South Korea.[2]

For both China and the United States, the stakes are exceedingly high. If the CCP yields, it will be devoured by the tiger of domestic nationalism. If the U.S. yields, it will immediately loose its superpower status. However, while the U.S. may wish to keep containing China's ascendancy indefinitely, this policy remains clearly unsustainable in the long run.

The second option that might ensue from the serious impasse between China and the United States would be a power sharing agreement. It is the case that among mainstream U.S. strategists there is currently a debate about whether the country should continue to pursue hegemony and primacy in Asia or switch to a strategy based on the premise of strategic balance amid major powers (essentially the U.S. and China).[3]

In these last few years, Henry Kissinger and Paul Kennedy have been advocating for a compromise between the two countries. In March 2017, Kissinger wrote an essay in *Foreign Affairs* whose title said it all: "The Future of U.S.-Chinese Relations: Conflict is a Choice not a Necessity". In his words: "A major war between developed nuclear countries must bring casualties and upheavals impossible to relate to calculable objectives". According to him, to avoid such an outcome both countries must be willing to compromise to create a new regional order.[4]

The former would lead to the U.S. remaining as a major power in Asia under a power-sharing structure with China. In Hugh White's words, that would imply for America "to try to find a way to share power with China in Asia. That would mean negotiating a new distribution of political authority and influence to more closely match the new distribution of power (...) To have any chance of success,

[2]Evan S. Medeiros, The Changing Fundamentals of US-China Relations. *The Washington Quarterly*, Fall issue, 2019, p. 95.

[3]*Ibid.*

[4]Hugh White, *The China Choice: Why We Should Share Power* [Kindle version], Oxford: Oxford University Press, 2012, retrieved from Amazon.com, p. 8.

the United States would have to be prepared to treat China as an equal".[5]

But would China be willing to accept a power-sharing structure in its historical sphere of influence? As seen, China's objective is to expand its area of control up to the Second Island Chain. The Chinese vision of power sharing, hence, seems to be none other than for them to control the Eastern Pacific while the United States controls the Western Pacific. Conversely, Hugh White describes how the United States visualizes itself in relation to other powers, and in this case with China: "As the primary power, America might consult other countries, but it does not negotiate with them as an equal. It sees itself as the only great power in the system".[6] Finding a mutually agreeable solution, thus, does not look like an easy task.

The third possible option that might emerge would actually be war. Incapable of reconciling their differences, an armed conflict might ensue. Two options could therein be plausible. A Thucydides' Trap situation or a Power Transition Theory type of conflict.

If the former ensues, the leading power triggers war before the emerging one becomes too powerful: "Thucydides repeats, 'the growth of the power of Athens, and the alarm which this inspired in Sparta, made war inevitable' (…) The distinction clarifies what Thucydides keeps trying to tell us: that *fear* inspired by the *growth* of Athenian power caused the Peloponnesian War".[7] Under this perspective, the United States might precipitate a war before it is too late for winning it. Martin Jacques believes that an increasingly insecure United States indeed becomes a matter of serious concern: "The greatest danger is not the rise of China but how the United States will react to China's rise and its own consequent loss of primacy".[8] He further insists: "As the world once more enters

[5] *Ibid.*, pp. 103–104.

[6] *Ibid.*, p. 7.

[7] John Lewis Gaddis, *On Grand Strategy*. London, UK: Penguin Books, 2019, pp. 59 and 66.

[8] Can the West's democracy survive China's rise to dominance?, *The Economist*, June 14, 2018.

dangerous waters, in my view our concern should not so much be China but the United States".[9]

The Power Transition Theory — a theory about the nature of war developed by A.F.K. Organsky at the University of Michigan and later expanded by other authors such as Douglas Lemke — seeks to explain trends between warring states in the past 500 years. According to this theory, it is the weaker rather than stronger power that is more likely to become the aggressor. Dissatisfied emergent powers are the ones that most likely initiate a conflict.[10] Under this perspective, China might be the most probable candidate to begin hostilities. This coincides with China's military doctrine, which believes in the advantages of a surprise attack when the factors materialize in the right configuration.

Whichever the way in which an armed conflict is triggered, what really matters is the way in which it develops. War development could be categorized by its width and length, i.e. how many participants might be involved in it and how long would the conflict take.

The best-case scenario for such a war would be just two participants: China and the United States. Alliances tend to complicate things, introducing additional agendas and grievances, which in turn generate complex dynamics. The worst-case scenario, under this last perspective, would be an alliance between China and Russia. This is for three reasons: First, Russia's nuclear superpower status might increase the risk of escalation into that threshold. Second, because of Russia's long list of grievances against the West since the collapse of the Soviet Union, and its desire to provide itself with a sphere of influence that shields the country from further Western encroachments in its background. Third, because Russia's involvement in the conflict under such circumstances

[9]Martin Jacques, When China and the US Collide: The End of Stability and the Birth of a New Cold War. JPI Peace Net, 24 June, 2019, http://www.martinjacques.com/articles/when-china-and-the-us-collide-the-end-of-stability-and-the-birth-of-a-new-cold-war/. Accessed December 9, 2019.

[10]A.F.K. Organsky, *World Politics*, New York: Random House, 1968; Douglas Lemke, *Regions of War and Peace*, Cambridge: Cambridge University Press, 2002.

would trigger NATO's response. A Beijing–Moscow axis would immensely complicate any potential war, giving it a global dimension while increasing the risk of nuclear escalation.

The length of a war could vary as well. The best-case scenario would be a short one, followed by a peace treaty that clearly defines mutually accepted rules. The worst-case scenario would be a prolonged state of war or a long belligerence that triggers periodical armed conflicts. According to the Power Transition Theory, hegemonic periods last approximately 60–90 years, while conflicts leading to a new power distribution last approximately 20 years.[11] The two chapters on the long war that took place between 1914 and 1945, during which Germany aimed unsuccessfully at positioning itself as the leading European power, exemplify this kind of conflict. If the worst-case scenario prevails, a long war might ensue between China and the United States.

The fourth possible option that might emerge from this state of affairs would be America's withdrawal. In Chapter Four, reference was made to a group of authors who believed that an isolationist process was already in motion as a result of Trump's actions. Richard Hass, Daniel Quinn Mills, Steven Rosefielde and Robert Kagan all believed that such was the case. Victor Bulmer-Thomas also subscribes the thesis of America entering into an isolationist period.[12]

It is difficult to reconcile this thesis, however, with the pugnacity shown by Trump on almost every international front. Isolationists, by definition, seek a low international profile. Perhaps the most plausible explanation of events is the one given by Mark Leonard, also mentioned in Chapter Four. According to him, Trump follows a process of creative destruction that aims at undermining existing international institutions. However, his purpose is not withdrawal but the imposition of generalized bilateral renegotiations on terms more favorable to Washington, i.e., defining a new playing field in which his country's superior power, unconstrained by multilateral

---

[11] Eugene R. Wittkopf, *World Politics: Trends and Transformation*, New York: St. Martin's Press, 1997.

[12] *Op. cit.*

limitations, can prevail more easily.[13] Presented in those terms, Trump's purpose would appear to be much closer to George W. Bush's blatant unilateralism than to isolationism.

But Trump's actions do not preclude the fact that an important part of America's society might indeed welcome an introspective process. The simple reason that authors, like the ones mentioned before, believed that both Trump and his electorate are embarked on an isolationist process says much about this. The countless American jobs lost to globalization and the trauma resulting from 18 years of continuous wars in the Middle East, which have dilapidated gigantic economic resources needed to solve grave domestic problems, have become fertile grounds for isolationism. These sentiments are clearly visible both at the right and left of the political spectrum. Two elements must be factored in to this situation.

On the one hand, it must not be forgotten that the United States' foreign policy has been shown to possess its very particular *yin* and *yang* qualities — seemingly opposing forces that actually belong to the same Oneness. The Oneness, in this case, being America's self-perceived moral superiority and the *yin* and *yang* representing the shifting periods of international missionary impulses and isolationism. As such, the high moral ground that Americans have always claimed and reclaimed for themselves can relate to both: either by proselytizing its beliefs or by putting barriers to alien models or events. The period between the first and the second world wars was clearly isolationist in nature, as Americans did not want to be contaminated by European events. The succeeding one was marked by the missionary impulse expressed in the foreign policy consensus of liberal hegemony. Thus, a shift is always an open possibility.

On the other hand, China is trying to alter the regional *status quo* by entrenching itself in the ground while increasing its asymmetric superpower status. The aim of this is none other than to increase America's costs in defying its actions and, by extension, induce its retreat. In Howard W. French's words: "Military power, though, is an essential strategy in this effort; indeed, the overwhelming

[13] Britain's lonely future in the age of clashing empires, *op. cit.*

preponderance of strength it is building towards constitutes the very foundation of this strategy".[14] This follows the presumption that a society weary of war and foreign military engagements becomes prone to yield if sufficient deterrence is applied. As a matter of fact, the U.S. is already recognizing the possibility of being defeated by China. According to former U.S. Deputy Defense Secretary Robert O. Work and Greg Grant, "the US Joint Force could face defeat in the hands of the Chinese military in plausible scenarios".[15]

The impressive display of military might that characterized the 70th Anniversary parade of the People's Republic followed the same logic. Some Chinese military analysts have even suggested that a show of force, like the sinking of an American aircraft, would increase the perception of China's indeclinable determination, thus fostering the notion that withdrawal is preferable to a highly costly confrontation with uncertain results. However, this is a risky line of thought. From Pearl Harbor to 9/11, the United States has always reacted in might when provoked. Moreover, overplaying the card of military strength and determination might end up generating exactly the opposite result that China seeks. There is, indeed, a weak line of separation between inducing retreat and inviting a Thucydides Trap's–triggered war.

The fifth possible option that might emerge would be the collapse of the CCP. Several articles that predicted the demise of the party were published on the occasion of the 70th Anniversary of the People's Republic. Two of those articles gave overwhelming importance to the "longevity frontier".

Minxin Pei said that the CCP is approaching the longevity frontier for one-party regimes. In his words: "Mexico's Institutional Revolutionary Party retained power for 71 years (1929–2000); the Communist Party of the Soviet Union ruled for 74 years (1917–1991); and Taiwan's Kuomintang held on for 73 years (from 1927 to

[14] Howard W. French, *Everything Under Heaven: How the Past Helps Shape China's Push for Global Power* [Kindle version], New York: Alfred A. Knopf, 2017, retrieved from Amazon.com, p. 66

[15] Evan S. Medeiros, *op. cit.*, p. 96.

1949 on the mainland and from 1949 to 2000 in Taiwan). The North Korean regime, a Stalinist family dynasty that ruled for 71 years, is China's only contemporary competition".[16]

Larry Diamond also alluded to the longevity factor. Referring to Marilyn Monroe's "The Seven Year Itch" film, that depicts the average time in which serious marital problems arise, he wrote: "There is an interesting parallel in politics; specifically, the life span of one-party regimes, though in this case we might call it the '70-year itch'. The U.S.R.R. is a prime example ... When the Soviet Union collapsed in 1991, the Communist Party had been in power for little more than 70 years".[17]

There is no scientific basis for this time-length assertion, whose only support is in a few scattered examples. In as long as CCP enjoys the modern equivalent to the "Mandate of the Heavens", providing internal order, economic growth and social stability, while standing tall to foreign powers and giving their citizens a sense of pride in their country, the rule of the communist regime does not seem to be, in any way, endangered.

An article by Ian Buruma captures this point: "But there is a deeper historical reason for the success of the Communist Party in China ... And yet, Mao's feat of unifying the country and restoring national pride is still a reason for many people in China to respect his legacy, and for the Chinese Communist Party (C.C.P.) to justify its continued monopoly in power. The fear of violent disorder runs deep and is consistently drummed into Chinese of all ages. Party propagandists insist that China without Communism rule would descend once more into chaos and fall prey to hostile foreign powers. There are, however, other reasons the C.C.P. is still in power in China, even after Communist rule has collapsed almost everywhere

[16]Minxin Pei, The Coming Crisis of China's One-Party Regime, Project Syndicate, September 20, 2019, https://www.project-syndicate.org/commentary/crisis-of-chinese-communist-party-by-minxin-pei-2019-09. Accessed September 25, 2019.

[17]Larry Diamond, Chinese Communism and the 70-Year Itch, *The Atlantic*, October 29, 2013, https://www.theatlantic.com/china/archive/2013/10/chinese-communism-and-the-70-year-itch/280960/. Accessed November 19, 2019.

else. The party adapted extremely well to capitalism … The C.C.P. will continue to justify its rule by standing for order, national greatness and something call 'Socialism with Chinese Characteristics' while (some people) continue to get rich".[18]

Were that to be the case, the communist regime's hold on power might be put in jeopardy only if the mandate of the heavens (i.e., economic growth, domestic order or peace) derailed, or if the nationalist sense of pride in the achievements and greatness of the country were betrayed. Hence, the CCP might collapse as a result of either option or by a combination of the two. The impossibility of overcoming the economic and social challenges currently faced by the country, with significant internal disruption and violent disorders ensuing as a result, might give shape to the first option. Not standing tall to foreign powers, not responding firmly enough to an international challenge able to generate national humiliation or failing to maintain or materialize China's "Great Unification" (the highest ethic of Ancient China and the source of legitimacy of all dynasties and republican governments) might lead to the second option. A lost war might trigger a combination of both.

Maintaining economic growth, social stability, internal order and peace, while simultaneously riding the tiger of nationalism, is not an easy task to accomplish. As yet, China has managed to do so. How much longer will it be able to keep doing so is a different consideration. But certainly not one mechanically linked to a "70-year itch".

"May you live in interesting times" is an English expression that purports to be a translation of a Chinese curse. Definitely, the years to come are going to be anything but boring and uninteresting, although we might certainly wish that they were.

---

[18] Ian Buruma, The Tenacity of Chinese Communism, *The New York Times*, September 28, 2019.

BIBLIOGRAPHY

Allison, G. (2018). *Destined for War: Can America and China Escape the Thucydides' Trap*. Boston, MA: Mariner Books.

Allison, G., Blackwill, R.D. and Wyne, A. (2013). *Lee Kuan Yew: The Grand Master's Insights on China, the United States and the World*. Cambridge, MA: MIT Press.

Appelbaum, R.P., Cao, C., Han, X., Parker, R. and Denis, S. (2018). *Innovation in China*. Cambridge, MA: Polity Press.

Arciniegas, G. (2001). *Cuando América Completó la Tierra*. Bogotá, Colombia: Villegas Editores.

Baik, Y., Hensley, R., Hertzke, P. and Knupfer, S. (2019). Making electric vehicles profitable. McKinsey & Company, March 2019.

Bajoria, J. (2008). *Nationalism in China*. New York, NY: Council on Foreign Relations, April 22.

Berglof, E. (2015). Will China change the world's financial institutions? World Economic Forum, November 25.

Bergsten, C.F. (2009). The dollar and the deficits. *Foreign Affairs*, (November/December).

Bernstein, T.P. (). Muted Differences: The Negotiations to Normalize U.S.-Chinese Relations. Washington, DC: Institute for the Study of Diplomacy, Case Study Program, Edmund A. Walsh School of Foreign Policy, Georgetown University, Case 140.

Blackwill, R. and Harris, J. (2016). *War by Other Means: Geoeconomics and Statecraft*. Cambridge, MA: Harvard University Press.

Branstetter, L.G. (2018). China's Forced Technology Transfer Problem and What to Do About It. Washington, DC: Peterson Institute for International Economics. June 2018.

Brown, G. (2010). *Beyond the Crash: Overcoming the First Crisis of Globalisation.* London, UK: Simon & Schuster.

Brown, S.R. (2009). *Merchant Kings.* New York, NY: Thomas Dunne Books.

Brzezinski, Z. (2007). *Second Chance: The Presidents and the Crisis of American Superpower.* New York, NY: Basic Books.

Bulmer-Thomas, V. (2018). *Empire in Retreat: The Past, Present and Future of the United States.* New Haven, CT: Yale University Press.

Clinton, H. (2011). America's Pacific Century. *Foreign Policy,* October 11.

Congressional Research Service (2019). China's Economic Rise: History, Trends, Challenges, Implications for the United States. Washington, DC: June 25.

Cooper Ramo, J. (2004). *The Beijing Consensus.* London, UK: The Foreign Policy Centre.

Cooper Ramo, J. (2007). *Brand China.* London, UK: The Foreign Policy Centre.

Drezner, D.W. (2019). Economic Statecraft in the Age of Trump. *The Washington Quarterly,* Fall issue.

Drexler, K.E. (2013). *Radical Abundance: How Revolution in Nanotechnology Will Change Civilization.* New York, NY: Public Affairs.

Ellman, J., Samp, L. and Coll, G. (2017). Assessing the Third Offset Strategy. Washington, DC: Center for Strategic & International Studies, CSIS.

Fabey, M. (2018). *Crashback: The Power Clash Between the U.S. and China in the Pacific.* New York, NY: Scribner.

Ferguson, N. (2004). *Colossus: The Rise and Fall of the American Empire.* New York, NY: Penguin Books.

Ferguson, N. (2011). Civilization: *The West and the Rest.* London, NY: Penguin Books.

Finlay, R. (2000). China, the West, and World History in Joseph Needham's Science and Civilisation in China. *Journal of World History,* **11** (2, Fall).

Fogacs, D. (2001). *Antonio Gramsci Reader.* London, UK: Lawrence & Wishart.

Ford, M. (2015). *The Rise of Robots: Technology and the Threat of a Jobless Future.* New York, NY: Basic Books.

French, H.W. (2017). *Everything Under Heaven: How the Past Helps Shape China's Push for Global Power.* New York, NY: Alfred A. Knopf.

Friedman, T.L. (2005). *The World is Flat: A History of the Twenty-first Century.* New York, NY: Farrar, Strauss and Giroux.

Fukuyama, F. (1989). The End of History? *The National Interest,* Summer issue.

Gallager, K.P. and Roberto, P. (2010). *The Dragon in the Room.* Stanford, CA: Stanford University Press.

Glaser, J., Preble, C.A. and Trevor, T.A. (2019). *Fuel to the Fire: How Trump Made America's Foreign Policy Even Worse (and How We Can We Recover).* Washington, DC: Cato Institute.

Green, M. (2019). China's Debt Diplomacy. *Foreign Policy,* April 25.

Gruber, J. and Johnson, S. (2019). *Jump-Starting America: How Breakthrough Science Can Revive Economic Growth and the American Dream.* New York, NY: Public Affairs.

Gruber, J. and Johnson, S. (2019). To Counter China, Out-Invent It: Trump's Trade War Ignores the Real Threat from Beijing. *Foreign Affairs,* September/October.

Gunder Frank, A. (1994). The World Economic System in Asia before European Hegemony. *The Historian,* **56**(December 2).

Harrison, L.E. (2013). *Jews, Confucians and Protestants.* Plymouth, UK: Rowman & Littlefield Publisher, Inc.

Hass, R. (2005). The Politics of Power. *Harvard International Review,* Summer issue.

Hawthorn, G. (2014). *Thucydides on Politics: Back to the Present.* Cambridge, UK: Cambridge University Press.

Hendrix, J. (2017). Leveraging History: What Britain's Decline and America's Rise Can Tell Us about China's Future. Washington, DC: Center for a New American Security, April 7.

Hendrix, J. (2018). Filling the Seams in U.S. Long-Range Penetrating Strike. Washington, DC: Center for a New American Security, September 10.

Huffington, A. (2010). *Third World America.* New York, NY: Crown Publishers.

Hughes, C.R. (2009). Globalisation and nationalism: squaring the circle in Chinese international relations theory. The London School of Economics and Political Sciences, LSE Research Online, March.

Huntington, S.P. (2004). *¿Quiénes Somos? Los Desafíos de la Identidad Estadounidense.* Barcelona, Spain: Paidós.

Ignatieff, M. (2015). *Fire and Ashes: Success and Failure in Politics.* Toronto, ON: Vintage Canada.

Inter-American Development Bank (2005). *The Emergence of China: Opportunities and Challenges for Latin America and the Caribbean.* Washington, DC: March.

International Renewable Energy Agency (2016). The Power to Change: Solar and Wind Cost Reduction Potential to 2025. Abu Dhabi.

Jacques, M. (2009). *When China Rules the World: The Rise of the Middle Kingdom and the End of the Western World'.* London, UK: Allen Lane.

Jones, B. (2019). The era of U.S.–China cooperation is drawing to a close — What comes next? Washington, DC: Brookings, January 7.

Jones, S.G., Newlee, D., Harrington, N. and Bermudez Jr., J.S. (2019). Iran's Threat to Saudi Critical Infrastructure. Washington, DC: CSIS, Center for Strategic and International Studies, August 8.

Judis, J.B. (2016). *The Populist Explosion: How the Great Recession Transformed America and European Politics* New York, NY: Columbia Global Reports.

Kagan, R. (2018). *The Jungle Growths Back: America and Our Imperiled World.* New York, NY: Knopf Publishing Group.

Kagan, R. (2019). The New German Question. *Foreign Affairs*, May/June.

Kaplan, R.D. (2014). *Asia's Cauldron: The South China Sea and the End of a Stable Pacific.* New York, NY: Random House.

Karabell, Z. (2009). *Superfusion: How China and America Became One Economy and Why the World's Economy Depends on It.* New York, NY: Simon & Schuster.

Khanna, P. (2019). *The Future is Asian: Global Order in the Twenty-First Century.* London, UK: Weindefeld & Nicolson.

Kharas, H. (2010). The Emerging Middle Class in Developing Countries. Paris: OECD, Working Paper N. 285.

Ki, M. (2015). The Motives of China's 'New Model of Major Country Relations'. *Journal of International Relations and Foreign Policy*, **3**(1).

Kindelberger, C.P. (1973). *The World in Depression, 1929–1939.* Berkeley, CA: Berkeley University Press.

King, S.D. (2017). *Grave New World: The End of Globalization, The Return of History.* New Haven, CT: Yale University Press.

Kirchick, J. (2018). Europeans want to break with America: They'd do so at their peril. Washington, DC: Brookings, May 25.

Kissinger, H. (1994). *Diplomacy.* New York, NY: Simon & Schuster.

Kissinger, H. (2012). *On China.* New York, NY: Penguin Books.

Kosiak, S.M. (2017). Is the U.S. Military Getting Smaller and Older: And How Much Should We Care? Washington, DC: Center for a New American Security, March 14.

Krejsa, H. and Suh, H. (2017). Phishing in Troubled Waters. Washington, DC: Center for a New American Security, April 10.

Kissinger, H. (2001). *Does America Need a Foreign Policy?* New York, NY: Simon & Schuster.

Kynge, J. (2006). *China Shakes the World.* London, UK: Phoenix.

Laski, L. and Segal, A. (2018). A New Old Threat: Countering the Return of Chinese Industrial Cyber Espionage. New York, NY: Council on Foreign Relations.

Le Baron, M. and Cooker, J. (2000). Why the 'Foreign' Matters in Foreign Affairs. *Harvard International Review,* Autumn.

Lee, Kai-Fu. (2018). *AI Superpowers: China, Silicon Valley and the New World Order.* New York, NY: Houghton Mifflin Harcourt.

Lemke, D. (2002). *Regions of War and Peace.* Cambridge, UK: Cambridge University Press.

Leonard, M. (2008). *What Does China Think.* New York, NY: HarperCollins.

Lewis Gaddis, J. (2019). *On Grand Strategy.* London, UK: Penguin Books.

Lewis, J.A. (2018). Technological Competition and China. Washington, D.C.: CSIS, Center for Strategic and International Studies, November.

Livesey, F. (2017). *From Global to Local: The Making of Things and the End of Globalization.* New York, NY: Pantheon Books.

Luce, E. (2017). *The Retreat of Western Liberalism.* London, UK: Little, Brown.

Madison, A. (2003). *The World Economy: Historical Statistics.* Paris, France: OECD.

Magnus, G. (2018). *Red Flags: Why Xi's China is in Jeopardy.* New Haven, CT: Yale University Press.

Mahbubani, K. (2008). *The New Asian Hemisphere: The Irresistible Shift of Global Power to the East.* New York, NY: Public Affairs.

Mahbubani, K. (2019a). *Has the West Lost It? A Provocation.* London, UK: Penguin Books.

Mahbubani, K. (2019b). What China Threat? How the United States and China can avoid War. *Harper's Magazine,* February.

Manyika, J. and McRaven, W.H. (2019). Innovation and National Security: Keeping our Edge, Independent Task Force Report No. 77. New York, NY: Council on Foreign Relations.

Marshall, T. (2015). *Prisoners of Geography: The Maps that Tell You Everything You Need to Know About Global Politics.* London, UK: Elliot and Thompson Limited.

Maurois, A. (1972). *Historia de los Estados Unidos.* Barcelona, Spain: Círculo de Lectores.

Mearsheimer, J. (2014). *The Great Tragedy of Great Power Politic.* New York, NY: W.W. Norton.

Mearsheimer, J. (2019). Bound to Fail: The Rise and Fall of the Liberal International Order. *International Security*, **43**(April 4).

Medeiros, E.S. (2019). The Changing Fundamentals of US–China Relations. *The Washington Quarterly*, Fall issue.

Menzies, G. (2003). *1421: The Year China Discovered America.* London, UK: Bantam Books.

Milanovic, B. (2016). *Global Inequality: A New Approach for the Age of Globalization.* Cambridge, MA: The Belknap Press of Harvard University Press.

Muro, M. and Whiton, J. (2019). America has two economies — and they are diverging fast. Washington, D.C.: Brookings, September 19.

Naisbitt, J. and Naisbitt, D. (2010). *China's Megatrends.* New York, NY: Harper Business.

Nash, G.B. and Roy Jeffrey, J. (Editors). (2008). The *American People Creating a Nation.* New York, NY: Pearson Education.

Nasr, V. (2006). *The Shia Revival: How Conflicts Within Islam Will Shape the Future.* New York, NY: Norton.

Nathan, A.J. (2019). How China Sees the Hong Kong Crisis: The Real Reasons Behind Beijing's Restraint. *Foreign Affairs*, November/December.

Nazemroaya, M.D. (2012). *The Globalization of NATO.* Atlanta, GA: Clarity Press.

Nye, J.S. (2002). *The Paradox of American Power.* Oxford, UK: Oxford University Press.

Nylander, J. (2017). Shenzhen Superstars: How China's Smarter City is Challenging Silicon Valley. Kenny Hodgart (Editor).

Office of the Secretary of Defense (2018). Annual Report to Congress: Military and Security Developments Involving the People's Republic of China 2018. Washington, D.C.: Defense Department.

Organsky, A.F.K. (1968). *World Politics.* New York, NY: Random House.

Pillsbury, M. (2015). *The Hundred Year Marathon: China's Secret Strategy to Replace America as the Global Superpower.* New York, NY: Henry Holt and Company.

Perkovich, G., Hibbs, M., Acton, J.M. and Dalton, T. (2015). Parsing the Iran Deal. Washington, D.C.: Carnegie Endowment for International Peace.

Pietri, P., Plummer, M.G., Shujiro, U. and Zhai, F. (2017). Going It lone in the Asia-Pacific: Regional Trade Agreements Without the United States. Washington, D.C.: Peterson Institute for International Economics.

Powell, A. (2016). The cost of inequality: When a fair shake isn't. *The Harvard Gazette*, February 1.

Prestowitz, C. (2003). *Rogue Nation: American Unilateralism and the Failure of Good Intentions.* New York, NY: Basic Books.

PricewatherhouseCoopers. (2017). The Long View: How will the global economic order change by 2050?.

Quinn Mills, D. and Rosefielde, S. (2016). *The Trump Phenomenon and The Future of US Foreign Policy.* New Jersey, NJ: World Scientific.

Riffkin, J. (2014). *The Zero Marginal Cost Society: The Internet of Things, The Collaborative Commons, and the Eclipse of Capitalism.* New York, NY: Palgrave.

Ríos, X. (2008). *China de la A a la Z.* Madrid, Spain: Editorial Popular.

Ríos, X. (2010). *China en 88 Preguntas.* Madrid, Spain: La Catarata.

Ríos, X. (2016). *China Moderna.* Barcelona, Spain: Tibidabo.

Roett, R. and Guadalupe, P. (2016). *Latin America and Asian Giants: Evolving Ties with China and India.* Washington, D.C.: Brookings Institution Press.

Ropp, P.S. (2010). *China in World History.* Oxford, UK: Oxford University Press.

Rozman, G. (2014). *The Sino-Russian Challenge to the World Order: National Identities, Bilateral Relations and East versus West.* Washington, D.C.: Woodrow Wilson Center Press.

Sanders, B. (2017). *Our Revolution: A Future to Believe in.* London, UK: Profile Books, 2017.

Schoenmberg, V.M. and Cukier, K. (2013). *Big Data: A revolution That Will Transform How We Live, Work and Think.* London, UK: John Murray.

Shell Group of Companies. (2002). *Peoples and Connections: Global Scenarios for 2020.* London: Shell.

Simpfendofer, B. (2011). *The New Silk Road.* New York, NY: Palgrave Macmillan.

Singer, P.W. and Cole, A. (2016). *Ghost Fleet: A Novel of the Next World War.* Boston, MA: An Eamon Dolan Book.

Smith, R. and Free, M. (2016). *The Great Disruption: Competing and Surviving the Second Wave of the Industrial Revolution.* New York, NY: Thomas Dune Books/St. Martin Press.

The State Council Information Office of the People's Republic of China (2019). China's National Defense in the New Era. Beijing, China: State Council Information Office.

Tonby, O., Woetzel, J., Choi, W., Eloot, K., Dhawan, R., Seong, J. and Wang, P. (2019). The future of Asia: Asian flows and networks are defining the next phase of globalization. McKinsey Global Institute, September.

Toro Hardy, A. (2007). *Hegemonía e Imperio.* Bogotá, Colombia: Villegas Editores.

Toro Hardy, A. (2013). *The World Turned Upside Down: The Complex Partnership Between China and Latin America.* New Jersey, NJ: World Scientific.

Toro Hardy, A. (2017). *Understanding Latin America: A Decoding Guide.* New Jersey, NJ: World Scientific.

Toro Hardy, A. (2018). *The Crossroads of Globalization: A Latin American View.* New Jersey, NJ: World Scientific.

Walt, S. (2005). *Taming American Power.* New York, NY: W.W. Norton and Company.

Ward, J.D.T. (2019). *China's Vision of Victory and Why America Must Win.* Washington, D.C.: The Atlas Publishing and Media Company.

White, H. (2012). *The China Choice: Why We Should Share Power.* Oxford, UK: Oxford University Press.

Wittkopf, E.R. (1997). *World Politics: Trends and Transformation.* New York, NY: St. Martin's Press.

Wong, J. (2018). China's Economy 2018: Slowdown to Gear up for a New Model of Growth. *East Asian Policy*, **10**(1). Singapore: East Asian Institute, National University of Singapore.

Woodward, J. (2017). *The US vs China: Asia's New Cold War.* Manchester, UK: Manchester University Press.

Work, R.O. and Grant, G. (2019). Beating the Americans at Their Own Game. Washington, D.C.: Center for a New American Security.

World Bank. (2011). *Latin America and the Caribbean's Long Term Growth: Made in China?* Washington, D.C.: World Bank.

World Bank. (2013). *China 2030: Building a Modern, Harmonious, and Creative Society.* Washington, D.C.: World Bank.

Xi Jinping. (2017). Secure a Decisive Victory in Building a Moderately Prosperous Society in All Respects and Strive for a Great Success of Socialism with Chinese Characteristics for a New Era. Presented at the 19th National Congress of the Communist Party of China, Beijing, China. October 18.

Zakaria, F. (2019a). *The Post-American World and the Rise of the Rest.* London, UK: Penguin Books.

Zakaria, F. (2020). The Self Destruction of American Power: Washington Squandered the Unipolar Moment. *Foreign Affairs* (July/August).

Zakaria, F. (2020). The New China Scare: Why America Shouldn't Panic About Its Latest Challenger. *Foreign Affairs* (January/February).

INDEX

CPSIA information can be obtained
at www.ICGtesting.com
Printed in the USA
BVHW061923170720
583885BV00008B/24

9 789811 218514